SAFEGUARD:

WHY THE ABM MAKES SENSE

SAFEGUARD:
WHY THE ABM MAKES SENSE

Edited by William R. Kintner

HAWTHORN BOOKS, INC.   PUBLISHERS   NEW YORK
W. Clement Stone, President

Contents

APPENDICES

Editor's Foreword

On March 14, 1969, after an extensive review of the United States defense posture and the strategic offensive capabilities of other nations, President Nixon announced his decision to begin the operational development of the Safeguard ballistic missile defense system. This decision was immediately both warmly received and strongly attacked. Rarely in American history has a decision affecting the future of so many people been so thoroughly debated. Although the issues involved in the Safeguard decision are complex, they are not beyond the grasp of the average educated citizen.

There is no more urgent public business than limiting the stakes in the U.S., Soviet, and Chinese nuclear confrontation in which all of us are hostages to the judgment of the leaders of Washington, Moscow, and Peking. We know from long experience that it takes two to reach agreement on arms limitation and that the process of achieving agreement is long, difficult, and uncertain. Until verifiable arms control agreements permit the mutual de-escalation of the arms race, we must maintain our defenses. In reaching a decision on the building of antiballistic missiles, we must look at (1) the adequacy of our defensive posture, (2) the magnitude of the threats that now confront us and might be reasonably expected to confront us in the future, (3) the lead-time required to meet future threats, (4) the effect of our decision on arms talks and the prospects for their success, (5) the bargaining posture of the two superpowers, and (6) the impact of missile defenses on the negotiating strategies and the objectives of the two parties.

This book has been gathered in the interest of further illuminating the central problems of this debate. Some essays have been written expressly for this volume; others have been published elsewhere or have been presented to various committees in Congress.

President Nixon's speech announcing his Safeguard decision stands on its own, of course. Richard J. Whalen's article, "The Shifting Equation of Missile Defense," appeared in *Fortune* Magazine in June 1967. This prescient piece set forth both the developing Soviet threat and the need for some kind of hard-point defense for our own Minuteman ICBMs. My article, "The Prudent Case for Safeguard," provides an overview of the political, technical, military and arms control problems implicit in the Safeguard decision.

Because of its candidness, Secretary of Defense Melvin R. Laird's statement to the Military Subcommittee of the House Committee on Appropriations, May 22, 1969, is almost without precedent. As originally presented to the Committee, it was classified Top Secret.

Dr. John S. Foster's article, "The Safeguard Decision Before Congress," examines the technical feasibility of the Safeguard system and the necessity for modest funding, during the session of Congress, of the program so that it could be carried forward without highly deleterious interruption.

x

Senator Henry M. Jackson's piece on "Negotiating the Future," deals with Soviet strategic doctrine and with the likely bearing of the Safeguard decision upon future arms control agreements with the Soviet Union.

William T. Lee, in "Rationale Underlying Soviet Strategic Forces," relates the Soviet force position to the rationale that lies behind the Soviet effort to achieve superiority in most forms of strategic weaponry.

The article by Dr. Harry G. Gelber, "The Impact of Chinese ICBMs on Strategic Deterrence," explains why the Chinese Communist nuclear and missile capability constitutes a uniquely complicating factor in the deterrent equations of both the United States and the Soviet Union.

D. G. Brennan, in his article "The Case for Population Defense," also deals with aspects of Soviet strategy and the role of a city ballistic missile defense (BMD) system with respect to possible arms control agreements. The contribution of BMD to strategic stability is set forth in Richard B. Foster's article, "Safeguard BMD Proposal and Arms Control Prospects for the 1970s."

Senator Howard H. Baker, Jr.'s article discusses the persuasive reasoning behind President Nixon's Safeguard decision.

The last chapter offers views and statements of experts that will contribute to the reader's understanding of the issues.

Finally, there are two appendices, one containing official Soviet views, the other questions and answers which should enable the reader to obtain at a glance authoritative opinion regarding the questions raised by the President's Safeguard decision.

WILLIAM R. KINTNER
Philadelphia
June 19, 1969

Introduction

Senator Gale McGee

The decision by Congress on the Safeguard ABM may hold in balance more answers to the mystery of the future than any of us would like to believe. For this reason, making the "right" decision becomes a more awesome responsibility than any one mortal could possibly prefer in his own time. The course of current events is not likely to bypass its need. So, therefore, someone is going to have to make some kind of decision somewhere along the line.

Until recently, much overstatement and misstatement has characterized the public dialogue on the ABM. Wishful thinking and emotional "druthers" have often swept the debaters beyond the normal rules of reason. And most serious of all, the longer the debate has gone on, the more intransigent have the proponents and opponents become.

A major casualty of the ABM dispute has been the open mind or the flexible judgment. The temptation to freeze one's opinion—to lock-in one's case—and then to assemble as much evidence as possible to prove it seems to dominate the nation's forensics on the question.

For this reason, there ought to be a greater understanding of the importance of protecting the President's options—of allowing the President the opportunity to hedge his bets in order to keep open the choice of correcting or adjusting the national course as we learn more and as the known factors permit a more sophisticated judgment. As the country in general and the Senate of the United States in particular face the decision-making demands of the ABM, I believe it important to keep uppermost in our minds the requisite of Presidential responsibility in arriving at that decision.

This particular volume underscores this consideration from many directions. The book attacks no one. It does not appeal to emotions or fears. The monographs, with few exceptions, are timely and informative. They embrace a broad spectrum of intelligence and philosophy, stemming as they do from the efforts of writers, professors, Cabinet officers, Senators, and a former Secretary of State. Among them are liberals as well as conservatives, Democrats and Republicans. Together they make a case that deserves the attention of each of us who is concerned about the survival of man and the chances for peace throughout the world.

The writers themselves would be the first to deny that they have supplied the last word on the ABM. Likewise, they would be the last to assert that they are sure they are absolutely right. But all who may sample of this collection of judgments will emerge, as I did, with a deeper sense of perspective about the substance and the implications of the ABM issue and, hopefully, a keener sense of appreciation of the President's lonely responsibility.

The well-being of the human race as well as the national interest of the United States demand "absolute" judgments to the following questions on the ABM: Is it necessary? Can it work? Will it trigger an even greater arms race? What are the other options?

As imperative as is the need for certainty in responding to those questions, the current status of data, facts, information, and the interminable unknown have surfaced only one firm conclusion: No one knows for sure. This becomes the burden of the hours and hours of hearings and the pages and pages of testimony. What it comes down to is the need to weigh the implications of one's "druthers" when set alongside one's responsibilities.

This Senator, as an individual human being, for example, is plainly structured constitutionally in opposition to military might; he is philosophically fearful of unrestrained arms races. His personal "druthers" would be to oppose the ABM. As a Senator, however, one has to isolate in his own conscience that public sense of responsibility particularly as it devolves upon the shoulders of the President of the United States. This becomes the key to one's gropings for the necessary answer regarding the deployment of the ABM. And it is precisely at that point that, as a Senator, I will support the President's decision for limited deployment.

The President of the United States—any President, not just this one—I presume, must start from his own assumption that his decision may be wrong. Only in this way can he then measure the consequences of human error for the people of his country. Should he decide to deploy the ABM system and this turns out to be a wrong decision, would the consequences be irretrievable? Or, on the other hand, should he decide to veto the system and this turned out to be a wrong decision, what would it mean? It boils down to the President's having to "back into" the lesser of two evils. While a Senator on either side of the argument can still afford to be wrong with less disastrous consequences for the country or for the world, the President cannot.

SAFEGUARD:

WHY THE ABM MAKES SENSE

President Richard M. Nixon's Announcement of the Safeguard Decision, March 14, 1969

THE WHITE HOUSE

STATEMENT OF THE PRESIDENT

Immediately after assuming office, I requested the Secretary of Defense to review the program initiated by the last administration to deploy the Sentinel Ballistic Missile Defense System.

The Department of Defense presented a full statement of the alternatives at the last two meetings of the National Security Council. These alternatives were reviewed there in the light of the security requirements of the United States, and of their probable impact on East-West relations, with particular reference to the prospects for strategic arms negotiations.

After carefully considering the alternatives, I have reached the following conclusions: (1) the concept on which the Sentinel program of the previous administration was based should be substantially modified, (2) the safety of our country requires that we should proceed now with the development and construction of the new system in a carefully phased program, (3) this program will be reviewed annually from the point of view of (a) technical developments, (b) the threat, (c) the diplomatic context including any talks on arms limitation.

The modified system has been designed so that its defensive intent is unmistakable. It will be implemented not according to some fixed, theoretical schedule, but in a manner clearly related to our periodic analysis of the threat. The first deployment covers two missile sites; the first of these will not be completed before 1973. Any further delay would set this date back by at least two additional years. The program for Fiscal Year 1970 is the minimum necessary to maintain the security of our Nation.

This measured deployment is designed to fulfill three objectives:

1. Protection of our land-based retaliatory forces against a direct attack by the Soviet Union;
2. Defense of the American people against the kind of nuclear attack which Communist China is likely to be able to mount within the decade;
3. Protection against the possibility of accidental attacks from any source.

In the review leading up to this decision, we considered three possible options in addition to this program: A deployment which would attempt to defend U.S. cities against an attack by the Soviet Union; a continuation of the Sentinel program approved by the previous administration; and indefinite postponement of deployment while continuing Research and Development.

I rejected these options for the following reasons:

Although every instinct motivates me to provide the American people with complete protection against a major nuclear attack, it is not now within our power to do so. The heaviest defense system we considered, one designed to protect our major cities, still could not prevent a catastrophic level of U.S. fatalities from a deliberate all-out Soviet attack. And it might look to an opponent like the prelude to an offensive strategy threatening the Soviet deterrent.

The Sentinel system approved by the previous administration provided more capabilities for the defense of cities than the program I am recommending, but it did not provide protection against some threats to our retaliatory forces which have developed subsequently. Also, the Sentinel system had the disadvantage that it could be misinterpreted as the first step toward the construction of a heavy system.

Giving up all construction of missile defense poses too many risks. Research and Development does not supply the answer to many technical issues that only operational experience can provide. The Soviet Union has engaged in a build-up of its strategic forces larger than was envisaged in 1967 when the decision to deploy Sentinel was made. The following is illustrative of recent Soviet activity:

1. The Soviets have already deployed an ABM system which protects to some degree a wide area centered around Moscow. We will not have a comparable capability for over four years. We believe the Soviet Union is continuing their ABM development, directed either toward improving this initial system, or more likely, making substantially better second-generation ABM components.
2. The Soviet Union is continuing the deployment of very large missiles with warheads capable of destroying our hardened Minuteman forces.
3. The Soviet Union has also been substantially increasing the size of their submarine-launched ballistic missile force.

3

4. The Soviets appear to be developing a semi-orbital nuclear weapon system.

In addition to these developments, the Chinese threat against our population, as well as the danger of an accidental attack, cannot be ignored. By approving this system, it is possible to reduce U.S. fatalities to a minimal level in the event of a Chinese nuclear attack in the 1970s, or in an accidental attack from any source. No President with the responsibility for the lives and security for the American people could fail to provide this protection.

The gravest responsibility which I bear as President of the United States is for the security of the Nation. Our nuclear forces defend not only ourselves but our Allies as well. The imperative that our nuclear deterrent remain secure beyond any possible doubt requires that the U.S. must take steps now to insure that our strategic retaliatory forces will not become vulnerable to a Soviet attack.

Modern technology provides several choices in seeking to insure the survival of our retaliatory forces. First, we could increase the number of sea- and land-based missiles and bombers. I have ruled out this course because it provides only marginal improvement of our deterrent, while it could be misinterpreted by the Soviets as an attempt to threaten their deterrent. It would therefore stimulate an arms race.

A second option is to harden further our ballistic missile forces by putting them in more strongly reinforced underground silos. But our studies show that hardening by itself is not adequate protection against foreseeable advances in the accuracy of Soviet offensive forces.

The third option was to begin a measured construction on an active defense of our retaliatory forces.

I have chosen the third option.

The system will use components previously developed for the Sentinel system. However, the deployment will be changed to reflect the new concept. We will provide for local defense of selected Minuteman missile sites and an area defense designed to protect our bomber bases and our command and control authorities. In addition, this new system will provide a defense of the continental United States against an accidental attack and will provide substantial protection against the kind of attack which the Chinese Communists may be capable of launching throughout the 1970s. This deployment will not require us to place missile and radar sites close to our major cities.

The present estimate is that the total cost of installing this system will be $6–$7 billion. However, because of the deliberate pace of the deployment, budgetary requests for the coming year can be substantially less—by about one half—than those asked for by the previous administration for the Sentinel system.

In making this decision, I have been mindful of my pledge to make every effort to move from an era of confrontation to an era of negotiation. The program I am recommending is based on a careful assessment of the developing Soviet and Chinese threats. I have directed the President's Foreign Intelligence Advisory Board—a nonpartisan group of distinguished private citizens—to make a yearly assessment of the threat which will supplement our regular intelligence assessment. Each phase of the deployment will be reviewed to insure that we are doing as much as necessary but no more than that required by the threat existing at that time. Moreover, we will take maximum advantage of the information gathered from the initial deployment in designing the later phases of the program.

Since our deployment is to be closely related to the threat, it is subject to modification as the threat changes, either through negotiations or through unilateral actions by the Soviet Union or Communist China.

The program is not provocative. The Soviet retaliatory capability is not affected by our decision. The capability for surprise attack against our strategic forces is reduced. In other words, our program provides an incentive for a responsible Soviet weapons policy and for the avoidance of spiraling United States and Soviet strategic arms budgets.

I have taken cognizance of the view that beginning construction of a U.S. ballistic missile defense would complicate an agreement on strategic arms with the Soviet Union.

I do not believe that the evidence of the recent past bears out this contention. The Soviet interest in strategic talks was not deterred by the decision of the previous administration to deploy the Sentinel ABM system—in fact, it was formally announced shortly afterwards. I believe that the modifications we have made in the previous program will give the Soviet Union even less reason to view our defense effort as an obstacle to talks. Moreover, I wish to emphasize that in any arms limitation talks with the Soviet Union, the United States will be fully prepared to discuss limitations on defensive as well as offensive weapons systems.

The question of ABM involves a complex combination of many factors:

- numerous, highly technical, often conflicting judgments;
- the costs;
- the relationship to prospects for reaching an agreement on limiting nuclear arms;
- the moral implications the deployment of a ballistic missile defense system has for many Americans;
- the impact of the decision on the security of the United States in this perilous age of nuclear arms.

I have weighed all these factors. I am deeply sympathetic to the concerns of private citizens and Members of Congress that we do only that which is necessary for national security. This is why I am recommending a minimum program essential for our security. It is my duty as President to make certain that we do no less.

CHAPTER 1

The Shifting Equation
of Nuclear Defense*

Richard J. Whalen

Although published two years ago, this article remarkably anticipated the surging development of Soviet strategic nuclear forces.

The author, a former member of FORTUNE's Board of Editors, is currently writer-in-residence at the Georgetown University Center for Strategic Studies. While at the Georgetown Center, Mr. Whalen participated in a study of The Soviet Military Technological Challenge *(1968), and* Nato After Czechoslovakia *(1969). He served as a national security advisor to Mr. Nixon in the 1968 presidential campaign and currently is writing a book on American politics during the decade of the 1960's.*

THE UNEASY ENVIRONMENT OF SURPRISE

The experts who read the intelligence reports on Soviet activity are aware, as the public is not, that the enormous U.S.

---

* This article, which was originally published in the June 1, 1967, issue of *Fortune,* is reprinted with the permission of *Fortune.*

advantage in weaponry and technology of the 1950s and early 1960s is steadily being narrowed. Not only has the Soviet Union run harder; the United States, wishing to avoid leading an arms race, has also deliberately limited production and deferred deployment of major new offensive and defensive weapon systems. The Russians, in effect, have been told: "We won't build it if you won't." The appealing notion has prevailed that weapon technology stands on a "plateau." As former White House scientific adviser Jerome B. Wiesner declared in 1963, the "scientific military revolution" has "stabilized."

The limited nuclear Test Ban Treaty, which ushered in the present period of search for a détente, has been widely interpreted as a joint U.S.-Soviet admission that further arms competition was pointless. A "stalemate psychology" has spread, which takes for granted and even discounts the military superiority the United States has enjoyed throughout the trials of the cold war. Reductions have been made in "soft" first-strike weapons such as bombers, and the U.S. missile deterrent force, after rising rapidly throughout the early sixties, is now leveling off. It consists of 1,000 Minutemen, 54 Titan IIs (to be phased out in 1970), 656 missiles aboard 41 Polaris submarines (about half of which are on station at any given moment), and 680 strategic bombers, which will be cut back to 465 in 1972. From a peak of $11.2 billion in fiscal 1962, U.S. outlays for strategic forces declined to a low of $6.8 billion in fiscal 1966 and stood at $7.1 billion in fiscal 1967.

The relatively stable level of R & D spending over this period conceals a significant shift in emphasis, away from innovation and toward refinement of existing weapon systems. The United States has chosen not to maintain the initiative, while the U.S.S.R. has visibly bent every effort toward seizing it.

Now a new era is opening in which the United States and the U.S.S.R. can be expected to possess increasingly comparable military technology. Far from being an omen of "stability,"

9

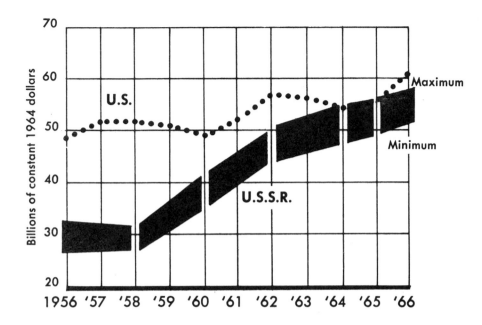

The expenditure record shows clearly that the U.S.S.R. has, for all practical purposes, overtaken the U.S. in defense and space spending. U.S. figures are actual expenditures as published in the national income and product accounts; Soviet figures are estimated within the range indicated by the wide line by Stanford Research Institute on the basis of published budget data and production statistics. Practically all the Soviet increase since 1958 is believed to be in the area of space and strategic weapons—perhaps as much as $25 billion. This is almost double comparable U.S. spending. Even with the inclusion of the space budget in U.S. strategic expenditures, these have been declining (in constant dollars) while Soviet expenditures have been increasing.

that elusive nirvana of the thermonuclear age, the environment of near parity promises to be extremely unpredictable and therefore marked by much apprehension. The United States, to be sure, has carefully hedged against foreseeable Soviet capabilities; over the past few years, for example, more than $1 billion has been spent to prepare advanced warheads and sophisticated penetration aids to defeat the newly installed Soviet ABM defenses. However, this kind of hedging leaves the United States vulnerable to surprise in the form of an unforeseen or successfully concealed weapon advance on the Soviet side.

In a congressional hearing more than a year ago, General John P. McConnell, Air Force Chief of Staff, warned: "We know . . . the Soviets today are engaged in a massive program of research and development in military weapons systems of all types. In a program of such great scope, the possibility of technological surprises or dramatic breakthroughs cannot be overlooked, particularly when such surprises could erase the margin of strategic superiority which we currently enjoy." In spite of improved U.S. satellite surveillance, the Russians have simultaneously improved their skill in the art of concealment, and they are now capable of deploying weapons that the West has never seen tested.

Close observers of the unfolding Soviet R & D enterprise worry because the adversary has a dynamic view of military capability and strategy, as contrasted with the static conception of technology and strategy implicit in the U.S. posture. Deterrence depends not only on existing forces; it also depends on the adversary's state of mind. The very rationality of Soviet leaders, which the United States relies upon to restrain attack, could find in advancing technology the incentive to consider the gamble of a first strike. A veteran analyst of the nuclear balance observes: "Never has fundamental strategy been so sensitive to a few—a *very* few—technical parameters."

11

The intentions of the uncommunicative Soviet leaders are a mystery, perhaps even to themselves, but it requires a minimum of theorizing to grasp the point of what they are currently doing. They are altering the existing balance of strategic forces that favors the United States, and they are doing it at a pace that startles the most knowledgeable American students of Soviet military capability. Just two years ago McNamara said the Soviet leaders "have decided that they have lost the quantitative race, and they are not seeking to engage us in that contest." Now Pentagon authorities are no longer sure. In contrast to the earlier false alarms of the bomber and missile "gaps," based on projections of potential that went unfulfilled, the present rate of confirmed Soviet hardware deployment is forcing upward revisions of Russia's potential.

"NOW WE SEE THE THREAT"

Soviet production of intercontinental missiles has surged ahead, from an annual rate of 30 to 40 in 1962 to 110 to 120 last year, and this rate appears to be accelerating. Since Khrushchev backed down in the missile confrontation of the fall of 1962—and the date is relevant because of the long lead-times involved—the operational Soviet ICBM force based on land and sea has grown from fewer than 75 to an officially estimated 470 (as of October 1966) and a likely current figure of close to 600. By mid-1968, according to informed estimates, land- and sea-based Soviet ICBMs could leap to between 800 and 900, or more than half the U.S. force. And there is no reason to assume the Soviets will halt there.

The rapid growth in numbers, however, is less significant than the *qualitative* improvements, apparent and suspected, between the first and second generation of Soviet ICBMs. Two new missiles—the SS-9 and the SS-11—have been identified as

12

entering the operational inventory in dispersed and hardened silos. The SS-9 is a large three-stage missile propelled by storable liquid fuel, which is not necessarily a sign of inferiority when compared to solid-fuel U.S. missiles. Storable liquid and semiliquid fuels provide greater thrust than solids. The SS-9 is roughly comparable in size to the U.S. solid-fuel Titan II, but it carries a warhead twice as heavy, estimated at over twenty megatons. The SS-11 is a small single-stage missile, propelled by either solid or storable liquid fuel. It resembles the early Minuteman in range and ability to carry a similar one-megaton warhead.

The Russians, well ahead of the build-up schedule assumed until recently by American defense planners, are fast approaching a critical point in the development of their ICBM force. If their missiles are equipped with the advanced warheads and the more accurate guidance systems known to be within their technical ability, their force could quickly become a real threat to the hardened Minuteman missiles that are the backbone of the U.S. deterrent. In designing the U.S. deterrent forces, Pentagon planners have weighed the alternatives open to an aggressor: a strike against our cities; a "counterforce" strike against our retaliatory missile sites; or a combination strike aimed at some key population centers and some portion of the land-based ICBMs. The United States has sought to deny an aggressor the "counterforce" option by building and deploying a thousand Minutemen, presumably a large enough number of targets to be safely beyond the productive and economic capacity of the Russians. This estimate of their capabilities has now been rudely shaken.

"As recently as a year ago," says a high-ranking officer in the Pentagon, "we didn't think the Soviets could get a counterforce capability. Now we see the threat." It could materialize by the mid-1970s.

13

THE "NEW MATH" OF MIRV

The United States itself has discovered how to use a single ICBM launcher to carry several individually propelled warheads, which can be guided accurately to different targets hundreds of miles apart. The multiple, individually guided reentry vehicle, known as MIRV, could revolutionize nuclear strategy if the Soviet capability should match our own.

The strong side of Secretary McNamara's philosophy of deterrence is apparent in the improvement of U.S. striking power. The entire front end of new missiles is being redesigned. The land-based Minuteman III, scheduled to replace the Minuteman I, and the submarine-launched Poseidon, the successor of the Polaris A-3, will be equipped with MIRV, decoys, and penetration aids. When they are in place within the next three years, McNamara declares that these formidable missiles will surely be capable of penetrating the Soviet antimissile defenses currently being deployed. And so they doubtless will—*if* they are ever fired in anger.

By preparing to meet a changing offensive threat *and* defensive capability with an improved offense only, however, McNamara displays the weak side of his strategic philosophy. The development of MIRV in missiles means that a new way of calculating striking power is needed, and therefore a new way of appraising the U.S. deterrent. The long-vaunted U.S. lead in ICBM boosters, currently estimated at three to one, no longer provides the reassurance it once did, and Pentagon officials now quietly downgrade such rough numerical comparisons. As McNamara himself said in his posture statement, "It is not the number of missiles which is important, but rather the character of the payloads they carry; the missile is simply the delivery vehicle."

He did *not* add that with all the additional payload weight

14

resulting from multiple warheads and penetration aids, the thrust of the delivery vehicle also becomes a critical factor— and in the case of the United States at the present, a sharply limiting factor. Except for the relative handful of Titan IIs, which are scheduled to be phased out, the lift capacity of U.S. missiles averages about one megaton for each booster. Soviet boosters, in contrast, can carry an average warhead load of more than seven megatons. If these missiles are, in addition, capable of being fitted with multiple warheads, the U.S. booster advantage of three to one over the Russians could quickly become a fiction. The new SS-9 could be fitted, at least in theory, with ten or more individually guided warheads. In one fashion or another, MIRV introduces a new kind of missile math—a relatively inexpensive means for the U.S.S.R. swiftly to achieve parity or better with the United States in terms of deliverable megatonnage. They are known to have *tested* the components of a multiple-warhead system. Therefore, U.S. watchers on the outside, peering through the cracks in a closed society, are anxiously anticipating an operational capability because of the short lead-time involved. As little as eighteen months could separate our discovery of a MIRV development program and the operational deployment of Soviet missiles carrying multiple warheads. Those who would know whether such a development program has been detected are quite properly silent.

THE IMPLICIT AND EXPLICIT THREAT

The memory of the nonexistent ICBM "gap" debated during the 1960 presidential campaign may prompt a certain skepticism toward the potential new danger implicit in a Soviet resort to multiple warheads. This time, however, the Soviet missiles that might be fitted with such warheads *already* exist; the numbers

15

are growing rapidly; and the new missile math suggests the advantages of their going the route of MIRV if they can. The kind of targeting problem that the United States poses for Soviet war planners provides the logic for traveling that route. The major U.S. cities, in which population and industry are concentrated, have long been the presumed targets of a relatively few Soviet ICBMs fitted with high-yield warheads. So long as an ICBM could deliver only one warhead to one target, the small Soviet missile force was believed to be checkmated by the sheer number of U.S. Minuteman and Titan missiles in their dispersed and hardened silos. But the problem of multiple targets could be brought temptingly near "solution," however Soviet planners may define it, through the use of multiple warheads on their growing missile force.

Until last year MIRV was considered so secret that even members of the congressional defense committees had not heard about it in executive session. Reports of multiple-warhead contracts were published in the technical press late last year, and discussion began in earnest last November when McNamara announced the accelerated program to produce and deploy the Poseidon in the Polaris fleet. Oddly enough, within four months after MIRV came into public view, it was abruptly covered up again by the Secretary's order. No longer a secret, it has become an un-word scarcely ever uttered in the Pentagon. "It's ridiculous, this trying to stuff the genie back in the bottle," comments a dissenting official. "Apparently we're concerned that the Soviets might be alerted to their own capability. It's part of trying not to be provocative."

THE MOVE TO ABM

The mounting uncertainties facing decision-makers in the White House and the Pentagon center on the Soviet construction of extensive new ABM defenses. Reconnaissance satellites and monitoring radars alerted the Joint Chiefs of Staff to this activity in 1965. In January 1966 McNamara secretly briefed the members of the congressional defense committees, and last November he publicly disclosed that the United States had "considerable evidence" of the Soviet ABM deployments without being specific about their nature and location. However, he declared: "I think it is important that we assume [the Soviet ABM system] is effective, and, of course, that will be the assumption on which we base the development and deployment of our own ICBM's." This prudent assumption leaves unanswered the urgent question: *How* effective are the Soviet defenses?

The United States possesses a good deal of intelligence data, but it does not support definitive judgments. If experience counts for anything, as it surely does in this esoteric realm of weaponry, the U.S.S.R.'s capabilities should be taken very seriously. It is known that the Russians, heeding their doctrinal imperative of balance between offensive and defensive military forces, began concurrent development of missiles and antimissiles as early as 1948. By the early 1960s they had built what was apparently the prototype of a defense system aimed against medium- and intermediate-range missiles, and they deployed it at Leningrad. U.S. intelligence rated this system capable of handling as many as five targets simultaneously, but it was regarded as ineffective against ICBMs. In a rare secret session of the Senate in April 1963 Senator Strom Thurmond, of South Carolina, a member of the Armed Services Committee, warned that Russia had an operational ABM system, and he urged that the United States proceed at once with the Nike-Zeus, then ready to go into production. Soon afterward, the United States turned to the improved Nike-X system (see "Countdown for Nike-X," *Fortune*, November 1965).

The Zeus ABM system, which grew out of the Nike-Hercules

17

antiaircraft defenses deployed in 1958, had a limited range and "kill radius," and its effectiveness against a large-scale attack was doubtful. The successor Nike-X (the X stood for "unknown") exploited major breakthroughs in radar technology, which greatly increased the number of targets the system could handle; and it also supplemented the Zeus missile with a new high-acceleration interceptor, Sprint, which was designed to provide last-ditch defense against ICBMs that got past Zeus. Even with the improvements, however, the Nike-X remained a "point" defense intended to protect a single target by engaging incoming ICBMs in a "bullet-to-bullet" duel in the atmosphere. An "area defense," which would protect several targets at once, would be much more effective, but this kind of ABM requires a long-range missile equipped with a large warhead that can intercept ICBMs above the atmosphere. In 1965 the United States began development of such a missile, named the Spartan, which will replace Zeus in the Nike-X system. But by this time the Russians had abandoned the Leningrad ABM and were well along in the development of more advanced concepts.

Incomplete and often contradictory information currently available on the Soviet antiballistic missile defenses has caused some divergence of opinion within the U.S. intelligence community. There is no question that an "area defense" system has been deployed in the vicinity of Moscow. The command center, containing radar scanners and computers, is a multilevel structure built entirely underground. A large phased-array radar is located northwest of the city, and it is integrated with small tracking radars at several points.

THE TALLINN ABM SYSTEM

A quite different type of installation has appeared in an arc extending several hundred miles along the northwestern border of the country, and this is the focus of disagreement within the

United States. Known as the "Tallinn line" after the Estonian city where one of the defensive sites has been detected, this deployment has been subject to various interpretations: as an advanced antiaircraft system, another type of ABM, or perhaps a combination of both. Existing Soviet SAM-2s and SAM-3s would seem to provide ample defense against aircraft, particularly in view of the declining U.S. reliance on bombers. Moreover, the line sits athwart the principal "threat corridor" of land-based missiles launched over the North Pole from the United States. It is the unanimous judgment of the Joint Chiefs of Staff that the Tallinn line is an antimissile system, but McNamara so far remains publicly unpersuaded.

In addition to the Moscow and Tallinn deployments, informed sources report a great deal of activity elsewhere in the Soviet Union at existing antiaircraft installations and new sites as well. Some of these sites are in the south and may represent the early stages of defenses directed against Polaris missiles launched from U.S. submarines on station in the Mediterranean. Other sites spotted east of the Ural Mountains face Red China. The small tracking radars along the Tallinn line are apparently tied together with the phased-array radar at Moscow. As evidence of such links accumulates, the likely scope of Soviet ABM plans expands, confirming McNamara's statement to Congress last January: ". . . we must, for the time being, plan our forces on the assumption that they will have deployed some sort of an ABM system around their major cities by the early 1970s." Not only the cities, of course, would be defended, but also military installations, particularly hardened offensive missile silos within a vast territory.

MEETING MIRV IN MIDCOURSE

Debate continues inside the Pentagon concerning the characteristics of the antiballistic missile (or missiles) that the

Russians are deploying. In November 1963 a missile was shown in a Moscow parade for which the Russians claimed an ABM capability. Western officials, who code-named the missile Griffon, were skeptical, and inclined toward the belief that it was primarily intended for interception of supersonic aircraft and their air-to-surface missiles; but they did not rule out the possibility that it had been developed originally to counter the medium-range Thor, Jupiter, and Polaris A-1. Griffon was not credited with an exoatmospheric (above the atmosphere) range, though some observers, reflecting now on the pace of subsequent Soviet advances, believe it should have been. An advanced model of Griffon, in fact, may be deployed on the Tallinn line; or the ABM missile there may be one the West has never seen.

The missile used in the Moscow ABM system was first shown a year later than Griffon, in 1964, when tractors dragged it through Red Square coyly concealed in its protective canister. Given the unglamorous code name Galosh, it is believed to be a solid-fuel, long-range interceptor carrying a high-yield warhead. Estimates of Galosh's range cluster around a few hundred miles, comparable to the Spartan missile the U.S. is now developing. But a minority opinion maintains it could have a much longer range, perhaps as much as two thousand miles.

This minority view begins with the fact that the best anti-ballistic missile system the United States has been able to devise uses *two* missiles and several types of radar. It is suggested that Galosh, the only missile deployed at Moscow, may combine the long range of Spartan with the high acceleration of Sprint, the companion short-range interceptor of the Nike-X system. If this is the case, or if the missile used in the Tallinn line has such such a performance capability, the Soviet Union could engage incoming ICBMs far away from their territory and above the atmosphere where fallout would not be a problem—in midcourse of the missiles' trajectory, before multiple warheads and

20

penetration aids could separate. An effective midcourse ABM would provide a formidable defense against multiple warheads. An experienced defense scientist cautions against overdrawing Soviet capabilities from scant information ("generalizing from the heel of the dinosaur"), but he adds: "If you're honest, you can't say flatly that the Soviets *can't* do what some people say they are doing. We just don't know."

WEAPONRY IN THE VOID

Easily the most important area of uncertain knowledge, and one where secrets and doubts are kept most carefully guarded, concerns the effects of high-yield nuclear explosions in the thin upper atmosphere and above. This is the environment in which our own and Soviet ABM missiles would function. Questions about the precise "kill mechanism" of an ABM have aroused intense speculation and prompted official reassurance, with the result that the known facts often get lost in a welter of alarming or comforting words. Much of the confusion is penetrated by a scholarly, relentlessly factual new book, *The Test Ban Treaty: Military, Technological, and Political Implications*, by James H. McBride (Regnery), which draws together the highlights of eighteen months of hearings conducted by two Senate committees on the treaty that attempted to curb the fearful competition in nuclear weapons technology.

"All witnesses agreed," McBride writes, "that at the current state of the art in nuclear technology the greatest need for nuclear testing is in the area of weapons effects. . . ." Again and again in the quoted testimony, the word "void" crops up, as when Dr. John S. Foster, Jr., then director of the Lawrence Radiation Laboratory and now director of Defense Research and Engineering, told the Foreign Relations Committee: "The most serious void has to do with the effect that nuclear explo-

21

sions have on the operation of the system, whether it is an offensive or defensive explosion or an offensive or defense system." This point is absolutely critical because the United States has adopted a second-strike posture, which means its weapons must survive the effects of a first strike and then penetrate enemy defenses to destroy their assigned targets.

The effects of nuclear weapons vary principally with their design and yield and the altitude at which they are exploded. (Other factors, including the time of day a weapon is exploded, also play a significant role.) The predominant effects of weapons designed to be detonated *in* the atmosphere are blast and heat; weapons for use *above* the atmosphere are designed to maximize the release of energy in the form of radiation, the most useful effect in this environment. Witnesses who testified during the test-ban hearings generally assumed that the United States held a marked lead in the technology of smaller-yield (one megaton and below) weapons while the Russians were well ahead in the very high yield (twenty megaton and above) range.

The advantage in the intermediate range (one to twenty megatons) was open to debate, but there was no arguing the fact that the Russians, during their massive 1961–62 test series that broke the *de facto* moratorium, had exploded many more weapons than the United States in this intermediate range both in the atmosphere and above, providing them with the opportunity to learn more and apply their knowledge. The Soviet tests had clearly been planned years in advance. Among their seventy-one shots were proof tests, weapon-system tests, effects tests, and tests with missiles and radar. The Russians, obviously extending their ABM technology, on two occasions during the tests launched an ICBM, intercepted it with a nuclear blast, and then fired a *second* missile, presumably to determine whether its warhead was affected by the radiation resulting from the prior explosion. They also studied the blackout effects of the blasts on their radar.

THOUGHTS ABOUT AN UMBRELLA

Such sophisticated Soviet tests could not have been matched at the time by the United States. In the summer of 1958 the United States had detonated its first-altitude explosions, code-named Teak and Orange. These megaton-range explosions produced astonishing results that clearly heralded the dawn of a new era in weapon effects. Communication links in the Central Pacific were blacked out for several hours, and satellites detected charged particles trapped in the earth's magnetic field. In the Argus series that quickly followed, the United States exploded three kiloton bursts, which disrupted shortwave radio and radar and again produced man-made belts of charged particles. The creation of these belts suggested, at least in theory, the possibility of a transient "shield" or "umbrella" ABM defense, provided the particles could be created in sufficient density. However, U.S. scientists concluded that the belts formed by the Argus shots were too weak to injure a warhead passing through them at five miles per second. Even so, the United States at least discovered that the obvious ABM problems of early warning, discrimination, and precision tracking could be greatly compounded by the mysterious effects of high-altitude nuclear explosions.

Following the Soviet tests, the U.S. staged a hastily prepared and politically restricted series in 1962–63, which provided valuable data but also disclosed great gaps in our scientific knowledge. Dr. Edward Teller, testifying on the test-ban treaty, revealed that the United States had not even completed theoretical studies of some of the high-yield effects the Russians had actually tested. Impressed by recurrent descriptions of the

23

"void" in U.S. nuclear technology, the Senate Preparedness Subcommittee concluded that the treaty "will affect adversely the future quality of this nation's arms, and . . . will result in serious, and perhaps formidable, military and technical disadvantages."

With the signing of the treaty banning atmospheric testing, the United States put its ingenuity to work underground and discovered that more could be learned there than its experts had believed. Under a top-priority program, the Atomic Energy Commission has been staging low-yield, directional explosions in deep, instrument-crammed tunnels from which the air has been pumped to simulate as nearly as possible the vacuum of space. But the apprehensions brought to light almost four years ago in the test-ban hearings have scarcely been buried. At bottom, the present controversy over the Soviet ABM capability revolves around whether these half-forgotten fears of technological surprise are now being realized.

Recent uninformed speculation has suggested the possibility that the Russians, by exploding very high yield weapons above the atmosphere at the proper altitude and latitude, might be able to create dense belts of charged particles and so establish a "shield" type of ABM defense. U.S. scientists, extrapolating from data provided by tests of much smaller yield explosions, are reported to have erred by a factor of 1,000 in estimating the number of such particles that would be caused by a 100-megaton blast. The AEC isn't saying what its latest calculations have disclosed, but a high-ranking AEC official emphatically declares: "Right now, we don't see how the effects of any radiation belt could be made to persist." An impressive body of scientific opinion, within and outside the government, says there is no technical foundation for theorizing about what a Pentagon R & D official calls the "ping," or residual umbrella defense. Before the man-made radiation belts could achieve a particle density lethal to warheads the earth's magnetic field would prove too weak to support them, and the umbrella would "leak."

THE ANTIMISSILE THAT GOES "ZAPP!"

The improbability of a "shield" form of defense does not rule out other possible defenses using radiation effects. Quite the contrary; the United States intends to use such effects in the improved Nike-X system now under development. The Spartan missile carrying a warhead of more than one megaton will rely upon what is believed to be the most efficient anti-missile defense above the atmosphere—the so-called zapp effect, that is, the tremendous surge of thermal or "hot" X rays produced by a high-yield explosion. As Dr. Foster has explained to the Senate Armed Services Committee: "Nuclear explosives have a very small surface area to them. . . . When they release [their] energy, they get very, very hot. A small surface that has to release enormous energies in a very short time cannot do so without getting so hot that it radiates its energy away. This radiation [is] . . . of such a temperature that it is in the X-ray region."

As much as 75 percent of the total energy of the detonated ABM warhead would escape in the form of such X rays and flash over thousands of miles in the near-vacuum of space. Within the much smaller "kill radius," which would vary with the yield and design of the warhead and the altitude at which it was exploded, the thermal X rays would deposit their immense energy within any unshielded object, such as a missile warhead, causing its components to explode internally. An ABM system using the X-ray effect can provide an "area defense" covering thousands of square miles with relatively few installations. Moreover, the requirements for guidance accuracy are greatly

25

reduced, a factor worth bearing in mind when the Soviet radars are described as somewhat "crude."

The United States takes the X-ray threat from Soviet ABM defenses seriously enough to be engaged in costly modification of missiles whose components are vulnerable. For example, the fine gold wires (which readily absorb X rays) are being replaced in the guidance computer circuitry of the Minuteman II, and the change is being incorporated into the design of Poseidon and Minuteman III. Because reflective coatings used to protect a missile nose cone from the heat of reentry are ineffective against thermal X rays, new hardening techniques and shielding materials are being sought. The test ban makes it impossible to expose such materials to actual thermal X rays, and underground explosions are no substitute, so experimenters are using newly created electron beams of comparable energy—beams capable of depositing energies inside a test material a thousand times greater than the pulse from the most powerful production laser.

U.S. missiles have been modified more than once to counteract an unforeseen or newly arising hazard. During the test-ban hearings, many military officers, nuclear scientists, and informed senators dared not give publicly a major reason for their opposition to the treaty. They feared that the Russians, through their high-yield testing, had discovered a kind of "ultimate ABM," and might be able to use nuclear weapons effects to turn much of the U.S. missile force into a Maginot Line. An offensive first strike would simultaneously achieve a defensive objective, not only destroying American cities with blast and heat, but also creating electromagnetic pulse (EMP) effects extending well beyond the radius of destruction that might deactivate the electronic systems of missiles in their silos. The United States has since revised the electrical circuits in the Minuteman silos, and has modified and shielded missiles, warheads, computers, and guidance systems to protect them against electromagnetic pulse. These countermeasures, of course, can be only as effective as our grasp of such phenomena.

GROWING DOUBTS, BRAVE CERTAINTIES

Last fall, an extraordinary study known as Strat-X (for "Strategic Exercise") was launched by Secretary McNamara's order to lay out the full range of alternatives for improving the posture of U.S. offensive forces through the mid-1970s. Strat-X will evaluate offensive missile and warhead designs in terms of different sea- and land-basing options, and it will weigh the resulting force "mixes" against various levels of threat from the Soviet Union and Red China. In this study the Nike-X is being considered only for the defense of U.S. offensive missile forces —not cities. This shift of emphasis is striking because up to this point the whole debate about Nike-X has concentrated on its use in city defense. This new turn in the thinking of key officials is a clear indication of the changing Soviet threat. A preliminary report will go to the Secretary in a few weeks and a final report is due in September. Little has been said about this highly secret study, and an official in the Office of Defense Research and Engineering tersely summarizes the objective of Strat-X: "more survivable payload." Another high defense official, concerned about appearances, confides: "From the outside, it may look as though we're not sure of the deterrent. That's not so. We *are* sure."

The determined air of confidence in the upper reaches of the Pentagon does credit to earnest men performing difficult tasks. What worries informed observers on the outside is the apparent assumption that the United States can safely confine itself to reacting within familiar parameters to a changing threat. The perils of losing the initiative are coming plainly into view. In

27

a recent speech Dr. Harold Agnew, the forty-six-year-old head of·the weapon division at the AEC's Los Alamos Scientific Laboratory, said the "apparent drift in national policy on the concept of balance of power and stability is resulting in a stifling of innovation." Because U.S. scientists are authorized to build or consider only those systems that respond to a clearly defined threat, "We are continually in danger of coming up with answers to threats which have changed." The prevailing official attitude of certainty may not take account of a steadily widening range of uncertainty.

THE ULTIMATE UNBALANCING FACTOR

It is Secretary McNamara's firmly held conviction that the possession of secure "second-strike" (retaliatory) missile forces by both the United States and the Soviet Union creates a stable condition of mutual deterrence. As he told a British television interviewer earlier this year, ". . . technically it's a relationship that's very difficult for either of us to move out of unless the other simply fails to act in a rational fashion." By deploying antiballistic missile defenses, the Russians, according to McNamara's logic, are behaving irrationally. The United States has reacted by making preparations to upgrade its offensive missile forces to the point where the effect of the Soviet defenses will be negated and the prospect of assured destruction by a U.S. second strike will be maintained. However, the hoped-for maintenance of stability depends not only on the U.S. estimate of the situation, but also on the Soviet Union's, and the Russians are clearly moved by their own judgments and not McNamara's. Their belief that they have upset the U.S. deterrent would be, as McNamara himself has declared, "the ultimate unbalancing factor."

In the radically altered strategic circumstances that may lie

28

just ahead, the Russians could begin to doubt U.S. capacity and willingness to inflict unacceptable damage upon them. As General Earle G. Wheeler, Chairman of the Joint Chiefs of Staff, testified earlier this year: "Should the Soviets come to believe that their ballistic-missile defense, coupled with a nuclear attack on the United States, would limit damage to the Soviet Union to a level acceptable to them, *whatever that level is* [italics *Fortune*'s], our forces would no longer deter, and the first principle of our security policy is gone."

It should always be remembered that the vast U.S. deterrent force exists solely to influence Soviet behavior. If it ever must be used, deterrence has failed and catastrophe looms. The threat of its use was a rational instrument of national policy during the days of overwhelming U.S. preponderance under Eisenhower and Dulles, and even as recently as the Kennedy administration's eyeball-to-eyeball confrontation with Khrushchev. Now, however, such a U.S. threat made in the face of the Soviet offensive build-up would amount to an irrational summons to mutual suicide. The Russians soon may be able to use *their* deterrent to inhibit the United States and gain for themselves greater freedom of maneuver. Short of an all-out Soviet attack, it is difficult to imagine a provocation sufficiently extreme to warrant U.S. resort to the means of assured self-destruction.

Though the emerging second-strike capability on both sides may satisfy the definition of "stability" favored by McNamara and the Pentagon's defense intellectuals, this symmetry of opposing offensive forces is upset by the Soviet commitment to ABM defenses. Add to this the possible first-strike, counterforce use of the proliferating Soviet ICBMs and "stability" vanishes. Though offensive capabilities may match up neatly, intentions and therefore uncertainties do not. The deterrent equation is in danger of becoming unbalanced by the one-sided shift of uncertainty to the U.S. side.

U.S. behavior is already being influenced by the Soviet deterrent. The likely failure of the diplomatic attempt to talk the Russians out of their "worthless" ABM defenses has forced the United States into offsetting offensive steps involving major spending—*e.g.*, the $3.3-billion accelerated development and deployment of Poseidon. And the anticipated Soviet counterforce capability is shifting all serious discussion of deploying Nike-X —at least within McNamara's sphere—from defense of cities to defense of "super-hardened" Minuteman silos.

WOULD THE PRESIDENT PUSH THE BUTTON?

If present trends are allowed to continue and U.S.-Soviet forces grow more asymmetrical, the situation by the mid-1970s could become menacing. An ABM defense lends itself superbly to bluffing and blackmail. The mere existence of Soviet defenses would exert psychological influence on both sides. It is easy to imagine a suddenly belligerent Soviet attitude toward Western Europe. Would the undefended United States react strongly if the defended U.S.S.R. appeared willing to risk war? It is possible to imagine a threat aimed directly at the United States itself, perhaps even the execution of the threat by the obliteration of a selected city. Would the President choose automatically to avenge the limited number of dead Americans by ordering a response certain to end civilized life in this country? Soviet planners, as they "war game" with the forces of the 1970s, surely ask themselves such questions.

The United States must soon recognize that a gradual but almost certainly irreversible change is occurring in the nature of deterrence. The assured destruction concept, founded on the superiority of the offense in modern warfare, has been challenged by technology and its application to defense. The technology of missile defense is now advancing more rapidly than

30

the technology of offense. The relative costs and effectiveness of ballistic missile defense are measured within the Pentagon through the "cost-exchange ratio." A few years ago, the high costs and ineffectiveness of defense were officially expressed in a cost-exchange ratio of between 10:1 and 100:1—that is, every $100 spent on defense could be offset by spending from $1 to $10 on increased offense. Now, however, by Secretary McNamara's own reckoning, the ratio is between 4:1 and 1:1, or parity. Of course, such numerical comparisons take no account of the relative burdens imposed on the U.S. and Soviet economies by higher arms spending. If the technological trend continues over the next decade, defense could gain a margin of superiority.

The improving prospects for defense are welcomed by the Russians, as their respected military commentator, Major General Nikolai Talensky, has written: "The creation of an effective antimissile missile system enables the state to make its defenses dependent chiefly on it own capabilities, not only on mutual deterrence, that is, on the good will of the other side." More is involved here than a Soviet state of mind that Secretary McNamara dismisses as "an absolute religious fanaticism on the subject of defense." Another Soviet military strategist has emphasized the balanced nature of the emerging Soviet offensive-defensive deterrent: "It must be remembered that victory in war is determined not merely by the character of weapons but by the *relationships of forces* of the combatant sides."

In future psychopolitical conflict, which uses weapons as manipulative symbols, the decisive advantage could lie with the side that possesses defenses. Even though these may be ineffective, the undefended side cannot determine this without exposing itself to mortal risk. A situation in which *both* sides had defenses would balance uncertainties and might well produce greater stability than the previous state of anxious nakedness.

The case for a prompt U.S. commitment to a limited deployment of Nike-X is compelling. Though Secretary McNamara argues that an antiballistic missile defense would not reduce American casualties "in any meaningful sense," a Nike-X system might save 30 to 50 million lives, and as General Wheeler testified, this would be "meaningful, we believe, in every sense." There is little time to act if the President in the mid-1970s, whoever he may be, is to have available a full range of policy alternatives. Clearly the effect of the present policy is to foreclose options for the future President.

From the moment of a decision to proceed, five to seven years would be required to deploy Nike-X around twenty-five major cities and key defense installations. Lieutenant General Austin Betts, Chief of R. and D. for the Army, who has overseen the development of Nike-X, believes the "optimum" moment has arrived for a decision to begin production. Further delay could mean the break-up of contractor teams and the onset of obsolescence in important components.

THE SYSTEM THAT'S READY

An argument can be made that it is better to postpone deployment of Nike-X if further R & D could produce a more advanced ABM—and it probably can. But Nike-X is the only defense system that can be deployed by the mid-1970s. Secretary McNamara's projected cost of $40 billion for a full-scale deployment of Nike-X includes such "damage limiting" measures as interceptor aircraft and shelters. However, this forbidding figure would be spent over ten years. Senator Russell describes it as "a sort of congressional deterrent." Beyond the question of how many billions of dollars are involved lies the uncertainty about the performance of Nike-X systems in a nuclear environment. These questions cannot be resolved entirely in the laboratory. A decision to go ahead might stir demands for a resumption of nuclear testing, which would surely arouse a world outcry.

But every objection to the limited deployment of Nike-X can be met with soundly based apprehensions about the grave risks of *not* having at least a measure of defense in the next decade. A light attack ("thin") defense has been estimated to cost perhaps $4 billion and could be modified or superseded by new technology. Such a defense would serve several purposes: it would at once restore strategic balance and reassure the Russians that the United States is not obsessed with the offense and tempted to strike first; it would cope with the accidental firing of a missile; it would counter the threat expected from Red China until well into the late 1970s; and it could help check the recent estrangement from our European and Asian allies by enhancing the credibility of our promise to defend them. Should the Soviet threat become more extreme, NATO might be rebuilt around a sharing of defensive nuclear weapons.

Perhaps most significant of all, the deployment of a limited Nike-X defense system, combined with the vigorous pursuit of an improved ABM, would signal the Soviet Union that the United States has not, after all, misunderstood the dynamic force of technology. The American will to lead the technological race and to maintain superiority is the most enduring deterrent.

CHAPTER 2

The Prudent Case for Safeguard

William R. Kintner

The antiballistic missile (ABM) controversy is now the most complex and vital issue confronting American security—as crucial as Franklin D. Roosevelt's decision to develop the atomic bomb. The gut question is whether the U.S. Safeguard operational development is essential for the future credibility of America's strategic deterrent force.

THE DEBATE AND THE DEBATERS

The debate is about the technological feasibility of a missile defense system; the effect of Safeguard on the forthcoming strategic arms limitation talks with the Soviet Union and, hence, on the "arms race" in general; and the allocation of funds for security and domestic needs.

The debate so far has been largely confined to the political and intellectual communities. In the intellectual community many natural scientists, social scientists, and national security scholars are opposed to ABM. On the other hand, most of those intellectuals who have professionally studied national security problems, for example, Herman Kahn, director of the Hudson

Institute, and Albert Wohlstetter, a leading U.S. strategic analyst and currently professor of political science at the University of Chicago, are in favor of developing an ABM system.

Many senators contend that the Pentagon has so far not established a clear and convincing case for the operational testing of a U.S. ABM system. One reason for this view is that the change in rationale from the defense of cities, as provided for by the Johnson administration's Sentinel system, to Safeguard's protection of the retaliatory Minuteman missiles (the present intercontinental ballistic missiles, ICBM), has not been persuasively presented. Questions most frequently asked by the "I'm from Missouri" senators include:

1. Will Safeguard adversely affect significant disarmament talks with the Soviet Union?
2. Will the Safeguard system weaken the Atlantic Alliance and subvert the aims of the Non-Proliferation Treaty?
3. Can Safeguard operate if its radars are blacked out?
4. If the Safeguard system cannot work perfectly, can it be effective?
5. Will it be obsolete before finished?
6. Don't we have enough retaliatory power even if all our Minuteman missiles are destroyed?
7. Will the continued escalation of offensive/defensive weapons cause the balance of terror to become unbalanced?

A systematic analysis[1] of the various issues implicitly or explicitly connected with the Safeguard decision must relate to

---

[1] The author is indebted to Richard B. Foster, director, Special Projects Office, Strategic Studies, Stanford Research Institute, for the substantial intellectual stimulation and exchange over many years which has helped the writing of this article.

(1) the extent and significance of the Soviet strategic arms build-up, (2) the character of Soviet leadership and Soviet military doctrine, (3) alternative military options open to the United States, (4) missile defense feasibility and effectiveness, (5) the impact of congressional action on the President's Safeguard decision on (a) Soviet strategic options, (b) arms negotiations, (c) U.S. strategy, (d) U.S. world image and influence, (e) crisis diplomacy, (6) the command nature of President Nixon's Safeguard decision, and (7) the President as "Negotiator in Chief."

THE PRESENT EMERGING SOVIET THREAT

During the past five years the Soviet Union has been spending almost twice as much in absolute terms as the United States in offensive/defensive weapons systems. Soviet military-oriented R & D (research and development) has already surpassed that of the United States and is estimated to exceed the U.S. R & D effort by some $2 billion to $5 billion annually. (See Table 1, U.S./U.S.S.R. RDT&E [research and development testing and engineering] Expenditure Trends.) President Nixon has revealed that U.S. estimates of Soviet SS-9 missiles (the largest Soviet ICBMs carrying warheads with yields as high as twenty-five megatons) and attack submarines indicate they are now 60 percent higher than estimates for 1967. The Soviet Union has a total of about 1,200 ICBMs in place or to be deployed —150 more than the number of U.S. land-based missiles. The Soviets now have almost 250 SS-9 missiles ready or under construction, capable of carrying twenty to twenty-five megaton warheads (explosive power sufficient to destroy Washington, D.C.); they have already tested multiple warheads for the SS-9. The SS-9 could be an excellent weapon for destroying a well protected striking force. A twenty-megaton weapon can destroy

36

TABLE 1

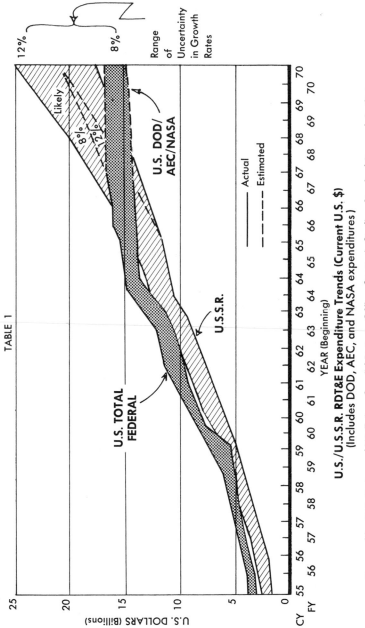

U.S./U.S.S.R. RDT&E Expenditure Trends (Current U.S. $)
(Includes DOD, AEC, and NASA expenditures)

Prepared by R. B. Foster and W. T. Lee, Special Projects Office, Strategic Studies, Stanford Research Institute

a Minuteman missile even if it explodes within .6 to .8 mile of its silo.

Soviet defense achievements may be discarded by critics of ABM, but the fact remains that the Soviets have ABM forces and we do not. They have been developing ABM systems for the past fifteen years and may soon have a more advanced model. There is some evidence that the Soviet Union is also seeking to develop an antispace defense. This capability, if the Soviets obtain it, could seriously limit U.S. intelligence capacity.

The total Soviet effort to acquire all the instruments of national power—in space, through a naval and merchant marine build-up—is more significant than advances in any particular sector, except strategic forces. The remarkable military commitment of the Soviet Union is shown in Table 2, which compares U.S./U.S.S.R. national security expenditure trends.

The Soviet Union is investing two to three times more in strategic military forces annually than the United States.

No official figures are available on Soviet strategic forces investment. The American Security Council estimated in 1967 that the U.S.S.R. strategic military budget for 1967 was about 14.7 billion dollars. We used roughly the same percentage for 1969 and 1970. The range of uncertainty, we believe, from reviewing all sources, is about 15-20%.[2]

Taking into account the increasing rate of expenditure, "The U.S.S.R. may invest at least $50 to $100 billion more in strategic forces between now and 1975 than the United States, unless the relative trends change substantially."[3]

[2] "The ABM and the Changed Strategic Military Balance U.S.A. vs. U.S.S.R.," a study prepared by the National Strategy Committee of the American Security Council, May 1969, p. 19.
[3] *Ibid.*, p. 20.

TABLE 2

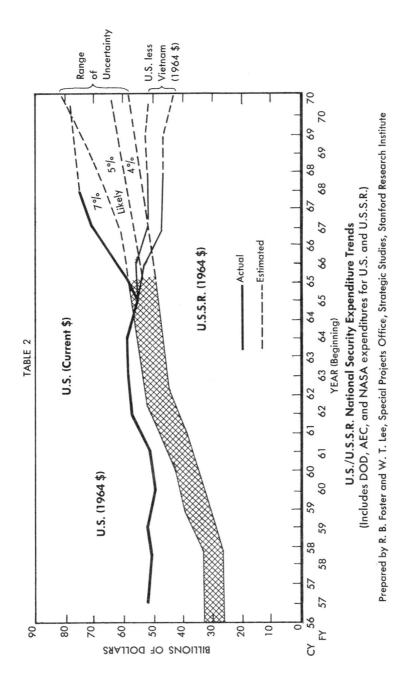

U.S./U.S.S.R. National Security Expenditure Trends
(Includes DOD, AEC, and NASA expenditures for U.S. and U.S.S.R.)

Prepared by R. B. Foster and W. T. Lee, Special Projects Office, Strategic Studies, Stanford Research Institute

From the Soviet point of view, support of Hanoi—which alone permits the Vietnamese war to continue—may be seen as a masterly diversion of U.S. resources. Soviet military assistance to Hanoi runs about one fifteenth to one thirtieth of the $30 billion per year that it costs the United States to finance that conflict. The military budget of the Soviet Union is already essentially equal to or considerably greater than the U.S. budget, especially when costs peculiar to Vietnam are excluded from the U.S. figures. Obviously, the conditions which *The New York Times* editorially described on May 13, 1969, as "the present moment of rare and precarious strategic balance" will not last very long if the Soviets continue their present rate of investment in strategic forces.

Despite the categorical statements made by President Nixon and Secretary of Defense Laird[4] concerning these trends and the magnitude of the Soviet strategic threat, Senator Stuart Symington rejects taking any kind of action, defensively or offensively, to counter what the Defense Department contends is an emerging Soviet capability of knocking out U.S. land-based retaliatory forces with huge SS-9 missiles by the early or mid-1970s. "I've been fooled badly in my time," the former Air Force Secretary said. "I was fooled in the early 1950s regarding the bomber gap, in the late 1950s by the so-called missile gap. It's not going to happen again."

The issue is not whether we were fooled in the past, but rather, are present estimates reliable? Admittedly, in the early 1950s, the Soviets did not build up their long-range bomber force to the numbers then predicted. The Soviets may have decided to shift to ICBMs while the bomber program was in midcourse. But in any event, U.S. intelligence gathering was woefully inadequate fifteen years ago because of the Soviet secrecy curtain and the U.S. lack of reconnaissance.

[4] See Chapter 3, "Secretary of Defense Melvin R. Laird Speaks Out."

By the end of the 1950s, U-2 flights over selected sectors of the Soviet Union had improved our intelligence collection. The U-2s uncovered a missile gap but not the kind discussed in the 1960 presidential campaign. The Soviets had begun to place some seven hundred to eight hundred intermediate-range missiles (IRBMs and MRBMs) and targeted them against Western Europe. In 1960, the Soviets had also begun to place big, inaccurate, unprotected ICBMs. In response to these Soviet moves, President Eisenhower dispersed SAC and put a portion of SAC bombers on airborne alert and simultaneously accelerated the development and production of the Polaris and Minuteman delivery systems. By so acting, Eisenhower minimized the danger.

In 1969 Joseph Alsop (Washington *Post*, April 7) cited the very end of 1960 as the beginning of satellite reconnaissance flights which proved that the Soviet Union had deployed only a few large unprotected ICBMs.

Since 1961 satellite reconnaissance over the length and breadth of the Soviet Union gives the United States a far more precise picture of Soviet offensive and defensive strategic weapons systems. Satellite reconnaissance has become so effective that many arms control advocates now assert that we can dispense with most, if not all, on-site inspections to police arms control agreements. We are thus placed in the quandary of either accepting President Nixon's public assessment of the Soviet threat or challenging the reliability of our satellite-obtained intelligence and the estimates concerning future Soviet deployments subsequently derived. These estimates are subject to modification as additional intelligence is obtained.

Looking back, it appears that the rapid U.S. build-up in ICBMs was not based on an accurate reading of how the Soviets had ordered their priorities between ICBMs and other strategic forces. Nevertheless, our wide range of superiority proved providential in the 1962 Cuban crisis.

With the memories of how President Eisenhower's Minuteman and Polaris decisions of the late fifties turned the tables on the Soviets in 1962 in mind, U.S. senators might ponder President Nixon's reason for making the Safeguard decision:

I determined that this limited offensive action—limited insofar as the Soviet Union is concerned—to defend our Minutemen missile sites was the best action that could be taken.

I still believe that to be the case. I believe it is essential for the national security and it is essential to avoid putting an American President—either this President or the next President—in a position where the United States would be second rather than first or at least equal to any potential enemy.

THE CHARACTER OF SOVIET LEADERS
AND MILITARY DOCTRINE

Critics of Safeguard believe that Soviet leaders conceive of strategic parity and stability in the same way that Americans do.[5] Yet both concepts are subjective and beyond empirical validation. Strategic stability is presumed to arise from the capability of both sides to produce very high fatalities and/or industrial damage and from neither having a marked advantage in striking first. For parity to exist there must be a sustained state of equilibrium when neither nation wishes to improve significantly its strategic position. Such equilibrium means that both nations are content with the strategic forces they have. The effort to maintain equilibrium is exceptionally difficult,

[5] See Chapter 6, "The Rationale Underlying Soviet Strategic Forces," and Chapter 9, "The Safeguard BMD Proposal and Arms Control Prospects for the 1970s."

even if both sides seek this goal. Yet agreement on goals does not exist. Soviet weapons are designed and deployed in accordance with doctrine and strategy that do *not* mirror comparable U.S. choices. Specifically, the Soviets apparently reject the U.S. "assured destruction only" strategy. The Soviets have not adopted this strategy despite repeated U.S. urging.[6]

The men now running the Soviet Union appear to be more interested in expanding Soviet influence than in accommodation and to have formulated their policy and nuclear strategy accordingly.[7]

In the spring of 1966 the 23d Congress of the Communist party muted the coexistence line and asserted that the fundamental policy of the Soviet Union was to secure favorable international conditions for the construction of socialism and communism. Specifically, at his closing speech to the Congress on April 8, L. I. Brezhnev stated:

> The congress has charged the Central Committee and Soviet Government with pursuing in the future a foreign policy aimed at creating most favorable conditions for the building of communism, the strengthening of the socialist system and giving all-out support to the peoples' struggle for national and social liberation, for consolidating peace and preventing a new world war, and for asserting the Leninist principles of peaceful coexistence of states with different social systems.

By way of creating most favorable conditions for the building of communism, the Soviet Union invaded Czechoslovakia in 1968 and has been for many years the principal supplier of

[6] See Chapter 6, "The Rationale Underlying Soviet Strategic Forces."

[7] See William R. Kintner and Harriet Fast Scott, *The Nuclear Revolution in Soviet Military Affairs* (University of Oklahoma Press, 1968).

arms to Hanoi and to Egypt and Syria. Since 1966, much evidence points to the return of Stalinism within the Soviet Union in a new form.[8] According to the authoritative Sovietologist, Wolfgang Leonhard, we are witnessing a change in Soviet policy as important as that introduced by the death of Stalin. There has been a resurrection of the KGB, mass arrests of political opponents, the establishment of forty-five new concentration camps, an increase in recruiting for the secret police, and the silencing of criticism against Stalin.

George F. Kennan, in his review of Robert Conquest's book, *The Great Terror*, has raised the fundamental question concerning the present Soviet leadership:

> Can men who can neither eradicate nor deny nor explain the blood that disfigures their own hands be fit leaders of a great country and a great empire today? Is not the inability to face one's own past a serious disqualification for the responsibility of government in the present?

Yet despite their commitment to a world outlook alien to our own, Soviet leaders deal pragmatically with problems confronting them.

We cannot presume to know how the Soviet leaders intend to use their growing strategic arsenal. We can logically surmise, however, that the present rate of Soviet strategic build-up, their extremely active development program in space and in both offensive and defensive weapons, their stated strategic doctrine,[9]

---

[8] See also Anatole Shubs's articles, "Russia Turns the Clock Back," which appeared in the Washington *Post*, mid-June 1969. Also, Chapter 5, "Negotiating the Future," by Senator Henry M. Jackson.

[9] See V. D. Sokolovsky, Marshal of the Soviet Union, *Military Strategy,* 3d ed., 1968. See also Appendix A, "Soviet Views of the ABM and Soviet Strategy."

44

and their major effort to build a naval force capable of projecting Soviet power into every ocean argue against the assessment that the Soviet Union is seeking and will be content with "strategic parity" with the United States.

In estimating an adversary's potential, it may be fruitless to devote effort to divining his future intentions, for these are rarely predictable. It is nevertheless necessary to attempt to divine his intentions over the next two or three years—as difficult as this endeavor is—and also to assess the full range of the adversary's capabilities and then to analyze the consequences for U.S. security if the adversary acquires certain kinds and levels of strategic forces. What we can do is assess his capabilities and then visualize the range of actions he might take, given certain kinds and levels of forces. Motivations and intentions can be judged retrospectively, however, with some confidence, since the capabilities that exist today reflect the past intentions that created them. If one looks at evolving Soviet strategic capability from this perspective, the most salient feature of Soviet military planning has been the *continuing search for decisive advantage.*

The Western goal of international stability is a concept alien to Soviet thinking. For the Kremlin's dialecticians, stability does not exist: the world is in constant flux. Strategic parity is therefore a midway point between inferiority to the United States and the opportunity to achieve superiority. The Soviet leadership places great emphasis upon the development of "correct concepts" of strategy, and unlike some American leaders has never renounced the concept of victory.

In 1957 a prominent partisan of the political order of the Soviet Union, the Polish economist Oskar Lange, publicly expressed his own carefully weighed judgment of the Soviet economic system in the following words: "I think that, essentially, it can be described as a *sui generis* war economy." The prime

45

purpose of this economy has been to nurture power. Some Soviet efforts in the strategic field can be interpreted as reactions to the U.S. threat; others cannot. There have been almost no crash Soviet weapons programs initiated in response to any specific U.S. development such as the Polaris missile. Instead, there has been a sustained, year-by-year, broad-front build-up.

The fact is that the Soviets have made their strategic weapons decisions independently of most U.S. decisions. For example: they have gone for much higher payload missiles and for much larger warheads; they have developed the fractional orbital bombardment system, FOBS (a delivery system of nuclear weapons for low-altitude orbital trajectories), which can strike U.S. SAC bases with little warning; and finally, although they started to deploy an ABM system over five years ago, we are still debating the merits of such a system. Moreover, although we have emphasized the superiority of the strategic offense over the strategic defense, the Soviets have generally sought a balance between the two for either policy or technical reasons. Their initial deployment of ICBMs was at a much slower pace than our initial Minuteman-Polaris deployment, although comparable to the U.S. Atlas and Titan programs. Subsequently they have accelerated their ICBM deployment, particularly of the SS-9 and SS-11. According to Defense Secretary Melvin Laird, "We now have hard evidence that the Soviets are testing an improved long-range ABM."[10]

Soviet military doctrine (and associated weapons systems) is open-ended.[11] They have created forces that will provide them with the fullest possible options for all contingencies. Soviet strategic doctrine is based on a war-winning concept. It is aimed at the destruction of opposing military and economic capabil-

[10] U.S., Congress, House, *Hearings* before Subcommittees of the Committee on Appropriations, 91st Cong., 1st sess., 1969, pp. 10–11. See Chapter 3, "Secretary of Defense Melvin Laird Speaks Out."

[11] See Chapter 6, "The Rationale Underlying Soviet Strategic Forces."

ities and the preservation of the Soviet Union as a political entity. Their rationale is quite different from ours; they adhere to a different scale of values, and employ different criteria for making decisions and calculations of risk. Most Westerners fail to recognize this fundamental difference. For this reason, the Soviet leaders may sense a critical and historic opportunity—in which they might undermine the credibility of the U.S. strategic deterrent and thus transform the global balance of power.

George W. Rathjens, visiting professor of political science, Massachusetts Institute of Technology, an opponent of the ABM, has unwittingly, so it seems, suggested this possibility:

> It is conceivable that one of the superpowers with an ABM system might develop MIRVs [multiple individually guided reentry vehicles] to the point where it could use them to destroy the bulk of its adversary's ICBM force in a preemptive attack. Its air and ABM defenses would then have to deal with a much degraded retaliatory blow consisting of the sea-launched forces and any ICBMs and aircraft that might have survived the preemptive attack.

> The problems of defense in such a contingency would remain formidable. They would be significantly less difficult, however, than if the adversary's ICBM force had not been seriously depleted. In fact, the defense problem would be relatively simple if a large fraction of the adversary's retaliatory capability were, as is true for the United States and to a far greater degree for the U.S.S.R. in its land-based ICBMs, most of which would presumably have been destroyed.

> It may seem unlikely that either superpower would initiate such a preemptive attack in view of the great uncertainties in effectiveness (particularly with respect to defenses) and the disastrous consequences if even a comparatively small fraction of the adversary's retaliatory force

47

should get through. With both MIRVs and an ABM system, however, such a preemptive attack would not seem as unlikely as it does now.[12]

The Soviet Union may be well on the way toward acquiring the capabilities required for what Rathjens described as the prerequisite for a preemptive attack. As V. M. Bondarenko expressed it: ". . . possibilities exist not to allow a surprise attack by an aggressor; to deliver nuclear strikes on him at the right time."[13] On the other hand, the deployment of BMDs by the United States would do much to thwart any such Soviet design.

Soviet strategic power is increasingly under the operational influence of the Soviet marshals. After the 1968 Soviet invasion of Czechoslovakia, Milovan Djilas, former vice-president of Yugoslavia, wrote that the Russian Revolution has degenerated into imperialism. It was Marshal Andrei Grechko, Soviet Defense Minister, who appears to have forced the liberal Czech leader, Dubcek, out of office. Many signs point to the fact that the Soviet marshals, with Brezhnev's willing or unwilling cooperation, are gaining an increasingly powerful hand in Moscow's national security decision-making machinery.

Within the party-military hierarchy controlling the levers of Soviet power there is a general acceptance among Soviet leaders that nuclear weapons can support a positive political policy. Bondarenko, writing in a magazine published under the aegis of the Presidium, made this point explicitly:

The new possibilities of conducting armed struggle have arisen not in spite of but because of nuclear rocket means.

[12] George W. Rathjens, "An ABM Doesn't Turn Off Easily," Washington *Post,* March 30, 1969.
[13] "Military-Technical Superiority is the Most Important Factor in a Reliable Defense of the Country," *Kommunist Vooruzhennykh sil,* No. 17 (September 1966).

They do not lower their combat effectiveness but most important, they do not exclude the possible use of this weapon. All this forces us to make the conclusion that the present situation is one of the features of the revolution in military affairs. It flows from this revolution, continues it, and does not contradict it.

Proceeding from this, we can define the modern revolution in military affairs as that sort of radical revolution in its development which is characterized by *new possibilities of achieving political goals in war flowing from the presence in the armaments of the troops of the nuclear rocket weapon.*[14]

U.S. OPTIONS

The differences in U.S. and Soviet strategic doctrine and deployment pose a paradox: The Soviet Union, pursuing a policy marked by offensive probes (in Cuba, Berlin, Vietnam, Indonesia, South Korea, and the Middle East), has opted for a defensive/offensive posture, while the United States, pursuing an essentially defensive, status quo policy, has opted for an almost exclusively offensive strategy. Yet as gaps in this posture become increasingly vulnerable to Soviet developments, the flexibility of U.S. policy diminishes.

Today we have sufficient strategic forces—missiles, bombers, and Polaris submarines—to respond to any attack that might be launched against the United States. Yet the Soviet Union is building at a very rapid rate the kinds of weapons that could be used to erode our deterrent.

In weighing now whether the Soviets are increasing their offensive strategic forces to achieve only parity in deterrent forces, we must take into account the fact that many of the

---

[14] "The Modern Revolution in Military Affairs and the Combat Readiness of Troops," *Communist of the Armed Forces*, No. 24 (December 1968). Emphasis added.

Soviet ICBMs are armed with significantly larger warheads than are the warheads on U.S. missiles.

Another important factor is that population and industry in the United States is far more concentrated than in the Soviet Union and, hence, more vulnerable. Dr. Eugene P. Wigner, distinguished physicist and Nobel Laureate, has testified before Congress that Soviet civil-defense preparations are far ahead of those of the United States. Soviet civil-defense doctrine calls for the evacuation of cities, which, lacking extensive suburbs, are more easily evacuated than those of the United States.

To sum up the growing Soviet strategic threat:

1. They already have an ABM system around Moscow. They are currently investing heavily in ABM R&D and may initiate a national ABM deployment at any time.
2. They are continuing to install very large missiles capable of destroying our hardened (emplaced in underground silos) Minuteman forces.
3. They are substantially increasing SLBMs (submarine-launched ballistic missiles).
4. They appear to be developing a semiorbital nuclear weapons system.
5. They are using mobile ICBMs, the numbers and location of which cannot be pinpointed by reconnaissance satellites.

Measures (1), (3), and (5) could be consistent with a strategy of deterrence, but when combined with measures (2) and (4), they correspond more closely with the potential for a first-strike strategy. Measure (2) indicates that the Soviets are buying massive and redundant instruments of destruction which would be an irrational waste of billions of rubles unless their strategy called for the targeting against U.S. retaliatory weapons. Measure (4) reveals that the Soviets are developing a capability of compressing the warning time of ordinary ICBMs so that they can strike and destroy U.S. strategic bomber aircraft *before* they can be launched in retaliation against a first strike. (Over-the-horizon radars may compensate for this "end-run" of our Distant Early Warning System.) Standard Soviet model ICBMs can deliver greater destructive payloads on SAC bases at far less cost, but with a longer warning period.

We could counter this growing Soviet arsenal (without judging Soviet intention to launch a first strike) by deploying more ICBMs and by accelerating the development and production of MIRVs (multiple, independently targetable reentry vehicles). Such action would greatly accelerate the offensive arms race and create greater strategic instability. Or, we might choose, as President Nixon has done, to develop Safeguard. Some opponents of ballistic missile defense (BMD) argue that if we were to deploy any BMD system, the Soviet response would be to increase their offensive system so as to maintain the same level of assured destruction against the United States as they could have achieved prior to the U.S. deployment of a BMD system. The net result, if the Soviets followed our logic, would be that both sides would restore the equivalent degree of assured destruction at a far greater cost—hence, the popularized spiraling-arms-race argument.[15] In retrospect, for the past five years the Soviets have been racing and we have coasted. If the Soviet

[15] See statement of Dr. Jerome B. Wiesner, Chapter 11. But this argument presupposes that Soviet strategic doctrine, values, and targeting concepts are mirror images of Dr. Wiesner's. Dr. Wiesner assumes that there is a predictable, repetitive pattern in U.S.-Soviet strategic interactions and that the Soviet Union has the technical and economic capabilities to match the United States in a spiraling arms race. The first two assumptions fly in the face of existing evidence. The third assumption is very doubtful, particularly if the first two assumptions prove invalid.

pattern persists, the Soviet response to a U.S. BMD deployment would probably be to increase not only their offensive systems but also their ABM system—which might, by enhancing the uncertainties of the outcome of a nuclear exchange, lead to a more stable strategic balance than the one that appears to be developing. Consequently, the deployment of Safeguard could bring our strategic posture into more meaningful correspondence with our defensive policy.

The heart of the problem of choice now confronting the United States is lead-time. If we wanted to maintain the survivability of our retaliatory forces, yet did nothing to enhance their safety until an advanced Soviet threat were actually deployed, we might not be able to protect our forces. To maintain a credible deterrent we must start to counter Soviet offensive improvements when we see their incipient development. There is no other solution to this problem than a major weapons system in anticipation of a technological advance, scored by the adversary, even before he proceeds to deploy the new weapon or before more existing weapons—that is, the SS-9—produce an overwhelming force.

President Nixon confronts hard choices in the face of the present and emerging Soviet threat. If he asked for more missiles rather than an ABM defense to meet the progressive Soviet strategic arms build-up, he could be escalating the arms race. When he attempts to limit the arms race by negotiation—as he will—negotiations concerning reductions in offensive and defensive strategic weapons will inherently be far more complex than the lengthy talks from which ensued the partial Test Ban Treaty and the Non-Proliferation Treaty.[16] Presumably the goal sought in the arms talks would be a stand-off between U.S. and Soviet strategic force capabilities. But how can President Nixon

---

[16] See Chapter 5, "Negotiating the Future" by Senator Henry M. Jackson.

ask the Soviet leaders to give up an ABM defense against the emerging Chinese Communist nuclear threat? With respect to nuclear weapons development, the Chinese, on a minimum number of tests, have made more rapid progress than any other people. The indications are that the Chinese Communists will have an initial ICBM capability by the early 1970s, which neither the Soviets nor we can ignore.[17] In the face of both the Chinese and the Soviet strategic threats, the currently most logical choice for a countervailing weapons system is Safeguard.

DEFENSE FEASIBILITY AND EFFECTIVENESS

In the past several years most critics of the ABM have conceded that it is technically feasible. (But not all. See Chapter 11.) The projected Safeguard system can achieve well over a 90 percent kill probability of incoming reentry vehicles with the expenditure of 1.25 interceptors. Admittedly, any defense system can eventually be defeated by the exhaustion of the interceptors: yet if the opposition employs exhaustion tactics against ABM, the costs favor the defense. The cost of the attack ICBMs exceeds that of the BMD radar-launcher complex. Consequently, a perfect defense is not necessary in order to contribute significantly to the preservation of strategic missiles. Further, there is no reason to believe that the technology of defense cannot advance to match improvements in the offense. Because of the high payload and increasing accuracy of Soviet offensive missiles, the U.S. land-based missile system will become increasingly vulnerable. It is questionable whether this vulnerability can be compensated for by the increased hardening (fortifying) of the silos (although this may be a desirable complement to

[17] See Chapter 7, "The Impact of Chinese ICBMs on Strategic Deterrence" by Harry G. Gelber.

53

missile defense), since the airborne debris created by the nuclear explosion would damage the very-high-velocity ICBM launched from that particular silo, even if the silo was not destroyed.

Opponents of Safeguard also charge that precursor nuclear explosions would blind the defensive radar. The problem of radar blackout is a worrisome one. Yet the netting of geographically dispersed radars provides a promising solution to this problem. The precursor approach is a low-confidence measure for penetrating an ABM system. In fact, every Secretary of Defense has favored the development of expensive penetration aids rather than relying upon precursor tactics to ensure the penetration of the Soviet defenses by our own missile system.

Few of the opponents of the Safeguard system have questioned the necessity of continued R & D in missile defense. In reality, the President's Safeguard decision might just as well have been described as operational development as deployment. The most important operational development required for Safeguard is in its radar system, together with the software of its computers, and the netting of the various radars into an operational system. This kind of development must be done in the field where the whole system can be exercised and tested. The operational development intrinsic to Safeguard should provide improvements in surveillance, warning, prediction, and display, which could be of incalculable value to American security.

Critics of the Safeguard BMD argue that it would not significantly enhance the protection of the land-based missiles. Ralph E. Lapp, in a recent study submitted to the U.S. Senate, stated that "protection of the Minuteman force is unwarranted and consequently the rationale for the Safeguard is indefensible." Yet a matrix of hypothetical attacks, based on Lapp's own assumptions, indicates a wide range of potential outcomes. The potential destruction associated with a force of 335 SS-9s

54

(Lapp's presumed Soviet force) could be awesome. Unless BMD defenses keep pace with the Soviet threat, the U.S. Minuteman force—even one employing Minuteman III (with multiple warheads)—could be seriously hurt. The total strategic deterrent force is composed of Minuteman, SAC bombers, and Polaris. The Safeguard can also provide some protection of SAC bombers against FOBS. One must remember that serious degradation of any one of the three components of the strategic offense could weaken the credibility of the whole deterrent. (We just do not know how vulnerable our submarines will become with respect to the expanding fleet of Soviet attack submarines.)

While it is true that all three components of the U.S. strategic retaliatory force (SAC bombers, submarine-launched Polaris missiles, and land-based ICBMs) are important, the land-based ICBMs comprise the backbone of this force. SAC bombers, for example, are the most vulnerable of all to a surprise attack. The command and control problem for the Polaris fleet is well known. Furthermore, the doctrine of freedom of the seas in peacetime makes the submarine force more vulnerable to unexpected mishaps, such as that which befell the *Pueblo.* In addition, it has been reported that:

> The Soviet Union is working hard to "neutralize or destroy" the United States' fleet of 41 Polaris missile submarines. As of today, the Polaris is safe from all-out attack, Admiral Rickover said. "However, there is no assurance that this situation will prevail for long," he said.
>
> He estimated that the Soviet Union might achieve the ability to wipe out Polaris, one of the three arms of America's nuclear deterrent force, by the mid-1970s.[18]

[18] *The New York Times,* June 16, 1969, p. 14.

The Minuteman missile poses the greatest interception problem to any Soviet ABM system, and the location of these missiles in the continental United States both guarantees their security and enhances the effectiveness of their command and control system.

It is also alleged by its critics that the runaway costs of Safeguard would incapacitate U.S. efforts to deal with its domestic problems, particularly the urban crisis. The total cost of the Safeguard system, over a several-year period, however, will be about a tenth of the $60 billion Major Social Programs budget for 1969. In terms of the 1968 dollar, the U.S. defense effort, except for the authorizations for the war in Vietnam, has remained almost constant for the past fifteen years; during a period of time in which the gross national product more than doubled. (See Table 3.) We need, of course, to strike a balance of needs between national security and the general welfare. But we must be able to defend the nation if we are to be permitted to enhance the general welfare. A false struggle between security and welfare can only confuse the issue.

The specter of the accidental explosion of the ABM's nuclear warhead has also been raised to frighten the American people into opposing the ABM. We have never had an accidental explosion of a nuclear weapon, although many of them have been stored near and have been flown over our cities for over a decade. Safeguard, however, is alleged to be a hazard to our cities.

THE IMPACT OF CONGRESSIONAL ACTION

If, in fact, Safeguard will be essential to the nation's security by 1973–74, congressional rejection of the President's request to proceed with Safeguard will permit degradation of the Minuteman force and will damage the credibility of the U.S. strategic deterrent. Conversely, congressional support for it will enhance

TABLE 3

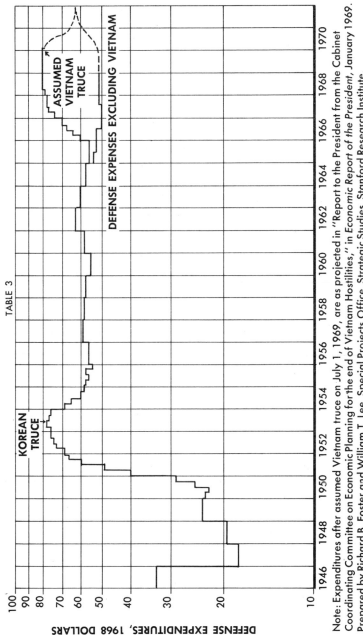

DEFENSE EXPENSES EXCLUDING VIETNAM

ASSUMED VIETNAM TRUCE

KOREAN TRUCE

DEFENSE EXPENDITURES, 1968 DOLLARS

Note: Expenditures after assumed Vietnam truce on July 1, 1969, are as projected in "Report to the President from the Cabinet Coordinating Committee on Economic Planning for the end of Vietnam Hostilities," in *Economic Report of the President*, January 1969. Prepared by Richard B. Foster and William T. Lee, Special Projects Office, Strategic Studies, Stanford Research Institute.

the credibility of the U.S. deterrent and will have the following beneficial consequences.

ON SOVIET STRATEGIC OPTIONS

The Safeguard system can help render obsolete the present Soviet offensive system because Soviet ICBMs now lack sophisticated penetration aids.[19] If the United States could neutralize the existing Soviet missile force and thus demonstrate the futility of the search for decisive superiority, we could pave the way for more meaningful arms control and disarmament negotiations; otherwise we could force the Soviets to invest in an entirely new offensive system which might also be neutralized.

Although already ahead of us in higher payload missiles and higher yield warheads, the present Soviet ABM lags some five years behind the technology of the Safeguard BMD system.[20] By capitalizing on our superiority in defensive technology, through the Safeguard system, we can negate much of the threat value of the Soviet Union's existing strategic arsenal. Consequently, Safeguard, more than any other action we can now take, might finally induce the Soviet leaders to abandon, or delay as profitless their efforts to gain decisive strategic superiority over the United States—if this is indeed their goal—and thus create the conditions for meaningful arms control

---

[19] In an article in *Partinay Zhizn,* a journal of the Communist party's Central Committee, published on the eve of the May Day celebration, 1969, Marshal Matvei V. Zakharov, chief of the Soviet General Staff, asserted that Soviet missiles could not only carry "colossal payloads but could also penetrate an enemy's antimissile defense." According to *The New York Times,* May 1, 1969, "Marshal Zakharov's article did not mention the missile debate in the United States, but implicitly entered into the discussion by saying that Soviet strategic missiles could penetrate an antimissile defense. This is also the view of those in the United States who are opposed to spending large sums of money for a defense they say will not work."

[20] See Chapters 3 and 4.

agreements. We should use our lead in defense technology for these high stakes rather than recklessly throw it away.

ON ARMS NEGOTIATIONS

After President Johnson announced in 1967 that he was going to deploy the Sentinel (far more extensive than the Safeguard system), the Soviets agreed to enter the arms limitation talks. They have never indicated that a U.S. BMD would escalate the arms race. Yet the widely cultivated fear of destabilization has become a factor in U.S. reluctance to deploy a BMD system. Presumably, destabilization ensues from changes made in the strategic force structure, either offensive or defensive— changes that tend to upset the balance of forces existing at any given time. Soviet strategists seem to devote little time to such sophisticated arguments. Apparently, they do not regard defense capabilities as either provocative or destabilizing, believing instead that a government should provide for the defense and safety of its people and property. Soviet General Talensky has written:

It is said that the international strategic situation cannot be stable where both sides simultaneously strive toward deterrence through nuclear rocket power and the creation of defensive antimissile systems.

I cannot agree with this view either. From the standpoint of strategy, powerful deterrent forces and an effective antimissile defense system, when taken together, substantially increase the stability of mutual deterrence, for any partial shifts in the qualitative and quantitative balance of these two component elements of mutual deterrence tend to be correspondingly compensated and equalized.[21]

[21] "Antimissile Systems and Disarmament," *Bulletin of the Atomic Scientists,* February 1965, p. 28.

During a February 1967 visit to London, Premier Kosygin held a press conference in which he reiterated long-held Soviet views on disarmament in general and ABM defenses in particular. When asked whether a build-up of a Soviet antimissile defense system was a new step in the arms race, Kosygin responded as follows:

> It seems to me that the system that warns of an attack is not a factor in the arms race. On the contrary, it is a factor that reduces the possibility of the destruction of people.
>
> That is why I think it is a mistake to look at this question the way some people do.

Soviet behavior is frequently unpredictable; yet it will issue from the Soviet leadership's pragmatic calculations of Soviet interest.

An effective BMD would enable the United States and the Soviet Union to engage in more meaningful arms control negotiations for the reduction of strategic capabilities. Both superpowers might be prepared to make greater concessions for major reductions in offensive strategic capabilities, since the possibility of either superpower launching a devastating nuclear attack on the other would be diminished. Thus, with respectively lower levels of strategic forces, both superpowers might gain an added measure of security.

The opponents of the BMD, nonetheless, assert that the installation of the system would escalate the arms race. The Soviets did deploy a BMD system; we did not. Far better than we, the Soviets know the worth of their system. Since we have no reason to doubt their scientific and technological ingenuity, we must assume that they can improve upon the system that they have and develop more advanced models. Of course, the

Soviets have noted our domestic debate and have begun to *comment approvingly* on the arguments advanced by the opponents in this country of the Safeguard BMD.[22] On the whole, the Soviets have been quite reticent about participating in this debate: certainly, they have not offered to scrap *their* ABM effort, which would be their one and only logical response if they agreed with the contention that an increase in defensive strategic weapons signifies the escalation of the arms race. Hence, the burden of proof is upon those who assert that the Safeguard system—which will not be operational for several years—raises a significant obstacle to fruitful negotiation on the reduction of strategic weapons. Such a proof could not be furnished until these negotiations have actually gotten under way.

Certain on-the-fence senators with respect to Safeguard are reviving Senator Eugene McCarthy's proposal of last summer for the United States to halt deployment of new offensive and defensive missiles pending "speedy agreement" on a mutual moratorium. After the jolting 1961 Soviet rupture of the tacit test-ban moratorium in which the Soviets tested the largest nuclear warheads ever developed, the risks for the United States to enter into a tacit understanding with the Soviet Union on a missile moratorium should be considered. Despite the amazing growth in satellite reconnaissance, satellites cannot peer into an ICBM nose cone to see how many separate reentry vehicles it carries. Without detailed, on-site inspection, we could be at the mercy of Soviet secrecy and deception in such uninspected agreements. The United States must compensate for errors in

[22] According to *The New York Times,* June 11, 1969, a commentary in the current issue of *Mezhdunarodnaya Zhizn,* a foreign affairs monthly, said that development of the Safeguard antimissile system and MIRV offensive system could only complicate future Soviet-American negotiations. "The development of these defensive and offensive systems would lead to a qualitative new step in the nuclear arms race and would add billions to the already large and burdensome military expenditures."

its intelligence resulting from Soviet secrecy if it seeks a long-term détente with the Soviet Union while at the same time preserving itself against Soviet military capabilities.

There is no way of telling whether the expressed Soviet willingness to discuss a halt in the strategic offensive/defensive competition is a tactical maneuver—taken to delay if not halt Safeguard's deployment. The prospects of a real U.S.-Soviet détente will, paradoxically, be higher if the United States can convince the Soviet Union that it has no intention of sliding into a state of strategic inferiority.

When the so-called scientific arguments against the Safeguard system are analyzed, it becomes apparent that these arguments are almost exclusively political and highly unscientific. Technical facts are being twisted and perverted to support a political point of view in much the same fashion as many scientists urged President Truman not to order development of the H-bomb by asserting that it just couldn't be done.

In an effort to keep the ABM debate both factual and logical, Dr. Albert Wohlstetter of the University of Chicago, one of the country's leading nuclear strategists, told Congress that many arguments of scientists opposed to a missile defense system ranged from mistaken to "plainly absurd." On May 25 Dr. Wohlstetter delivered a twenty-one-page report to the Senate Armed Services Committee in which he chided his colleagues on the other side of the antimissile argument for either not having done their homework or having done it sloppily. Wohlstetter spoke with the confidence of a man who was once described by Dr. Henry A. Kissinger, the President's National Security Adviser, as the man who more than any other "provided the intellectual impetus for the recasting of American military strategy in the 1960s." In particular, Dr. Wohlstetter chided Dr. George Rathjens, a former disarmament official, for computations that led to his conclusion that an all-out surprise attack by Soviet missiles on the one thousand American Minuteman missiles would destroy only 75 percent of the targets. Dr. Wohlstetter insisted the "correct" number is 95 percent.[23]

ON U.S. STRATEGY

The Safeguard debate is confused by the fact that we are still locked into the narrow and rigid strategy developed by former Defense Secretary McNamara and his assistants.

In April 1968, Dr. Alain C. Enthoven, the Assistant Secretary of Defense for Systems Analysis, told the Senate Preparedness Investigating Subcommittee why we would not and should not attempt to limit damage to ourselves:

> . . . any attempt we might make to achieve more than a fully adequate assured destruction capability must be considered in light of probable Soviet reactions . . . the Soviets *can* and *would* react to any steps we might take to achieve a full first-strike capability or to limit damage to ourselves significantly. Hence, forces bought for this mission would contribute little to our national security, and they would push the arms race one step further. Thus, we and the Soviets *should* accept a state of mutual deterrence. [Emphasis added.]

Implicit in this statement is the assumption that Soviet leaders think as we do and, too, want only offensive parity and have abandoned attempts to limit damage to themselves. Advocates of the "assured destruction only" strategy argue that any major war would result in mutual annihilation, because neither side *can* or *should* defend itself. When the McNamara strategy was

[23] Dr. Wohlstetter reaffirmed his calculations in a public exchange with George W. Rathjens which appeared in *The New York Times,* June 15, 1969. See Chapter 11.

fashionable, any attempt to plan for other possible contingencies came to be regarded as potentially provocative and disturbing to the Soviet Union.[24] The initiative in the deployment of other strategic weapons systems has been yielded to the Soviet Union. But U.S. reaction to any and all Soviet initiatives is very dependent on intelligence, since it is necessary for the United States to have a sufficient, highly accurate intelligence lead-time in order to take countervailing measures.[25]

To maintain parity in totally unacceptable casualty levels which the presumed stability of mutual deterrence through assured destruction requires, the United States has until now refrained from deploying any ABM because previous defense planners considered it provocative, destabilizing, costly, and/or useless in the long term. This underlying rationale is still accepted by most of the opponents of the Safeguard system. This simplistic concept of deterrence rooted in the assured ·destruction of a high percentage of both the American and Soviet people was premised on the naïve hope that the Soviets could be persuaded to give up their rational dedication to ensuring the survival of the Soviet Union. All U.S. efforts to convert the Soviet leaders to accept the mutual suicide pact have failed and for good reason—the McNamara concept flew in the face of the logic and common sense of Soviet leaders.

ON U.S. WORLD IMAGE AND INFLUENCE

The rejection of the presidential request on the Safeguard could be a disastrous blow to U.S. world image and influence abroad. It would also create uncertainties as to whether or not the United States really wanted to maintain its global stabilizing role. Although the Safeguard aims at the protection

[24] See Chapter 8, "The Case for Population Defense" by D. G. Brennan.

[25] William R. Kintner, *Peace and the Strategy Conflict* (New York: Praeger, 1967).

of U.S. missile sites against Soviet attack, it seems likely that much, if not all, of the protection against a Chinese missile attack proposed by Secretary of Defense McNamara in 1967 could also be accomplished by the Safeguard system. It seems likely, too, that once the Safeguard deployment had begun, the lead-time for an extension of its area cover capability would be less than the lead-time for China's missile deployment. There would be considerable advantages if this could indeed be done. It would weaken the Chinese capability of deterring the United States and inhibit the Chinese leadership from attempting to "spoil" the Soviet-American nuclear balance. Because such action would be unprovocative toward China, it should be politically attractive within the United States.[26]

By protecting our strategic capabilities, the Safeguard could also render more credible the U.S. nuclear guarantee to Western Europe and other countries whose security we have pledged, either in multilateral treaties or bilateral pacts, to defend. Failure to deploy Safeguard would raise European doubts about the credibility of the U.S. guarantee in NATO, especially if the Soviets continue to increase both their offensive and defensive capabilities. Moreover, the downgrading of U.S. strategic capabilities, as a result of a failure to create Safeguard, might give added encouragement to other nations to develop their own nuclear capabilities, or at least reduce the prospects for their signing the Non-Proliferation Treaty.

The security of the entire free world depends on the effectiveness of the U.S. deterrent. If scientific-technological advances in this country would result in the development of effective strategic defensive systems, then such a development might be of even greater importance to some of our allies than it is to us. Hardly anyone among our European allies, for

[26] See Chapter 7, "The Impact of Chinese ICBMs on Strategic Deterrence" by Harry G. Gelber.

example, doubts that we are anxious to conclude meaningful arms reduction agreements with the Soviets. If we now deploy a BMD system in order to restore the strategic symmetry, our European friends will not mistake such a decision for an irresponsible escalation of the arms race. On the whole, the European press is far more concerned with the war in Vietnam and the confrontation in the Middle East than with the modest proposal for the Safeguard system.

CRISIS DIPLOMACY

For the past two decades the United States has been best able to control a crisis when its conventional superiority in the crisis area operated under the umbrella of over-all strategic superiority. This combination has held the greatest potential for political bargaining at lesser crises.

In times of crisis it is not easy to determine how strategic superiority communicates itself, or is imparted, to policy-makers on opposing sides. Yet, examination of Cold War crises yields evidence that U.S. strategic forces played a part in inducing fear of unwanted consequences in the minds of Soviet leaders. In specific cases, interaction took a discernible pattern. Leaders of the Soviet Union often initiated or supported crisis policies despite their awareness of clear U.S. strategic superiority. But as the United States increased its resolve and readied itself strategically and tactically to deal with a crisis, the Soviet Union significantly modified its assessments of the relative merits, consequences, and costs of its policies and generally backed down from crisis-stirring actions.

Although power is always usable, at least in the psychological sense of influencing human behavior, it is commonly assumed that neither the United States nor the Soviet Union can consider resort to general nuclear war, or even the risk of such a conflict, a rational instrument of foreign policy. Nevertheless, the nuclear force possessed by both sides will influence actions taken in every important confrontation between the United States and the Soviet Union or Communist China.

The role that U.S. strategic as well as conventional power played in inducing the Soviet retreat during the Cuban missile confrontation amply demonstrates the relationship between crisis management and strategic sufficiency. It is not difficult to understand the implications for our worldwide position if, in some future confrontation, the United States were forced to make important political concessions to the Kremlin in the face of a clear strategic advantage. The United States would open itself to a series of humiliating political defeats.

When a revolutionary, expansionist power aims to upset the status quo, the loss of superiority by the defensive powers encourages instability. The *Pax Britannica* which prevailed throughout the globe during the nineteenth century flowed from a preponderance of British naval power. Only when, in the decades before the First World War, England's naval advantage became so narrow that it could be challenged was the *Pax Britannica* broken.

A revolutionary nation—believing itself equal in power to status quo powers and conceiving an offensive strategy to provide a decisive advantage—might well break the peace. Consequently, the best assurance for peace may lie in the possession of superior power by the defensive nations against an expansionist state. As Inis Claude has maintained, "A potential aggressor is likely to be deterred more effectively by confrontation with preponderant rather than merely equal power."

Strategic forces are not only useful in deterring nuclear attack, they play an ever present role in political bargaining. Would it make no difference, for instance, if the Soviet Union backed a surprise and successful Egyptian attack on Israel, and

Israel sent Washington an SOS, whether the United States or the Soviet Union had marginal superiority in nuclear weapons? If, for instance, in support of Egypt the Soviet Union launched a limited "demonstration" nuclear strike and we were unwilling to risk higher levels of exchange, might not the side that made the uncontested demonstration control the political bargaining that followed?

Inevitably, differences in strategic posture will influence Soviet decision-makers in determining their future policy. Consequently, America should possess a strategic force structure that reduces the likelihood that a crisis will be either deliberately created or deliberately escalated by the Kremlin.

For all the foregoing reasons, President Nixon stated at his press conference on March 16:

> I do not want to see an American President in the future, in the event of any crisis, to have his diplomatic credibility be so impaired because the United States was in a second class or inferior position. We saw what it meant to the Soviets when they were second. I don't want that position to be the United States' in the event of a future diplomatic crisis.

A COMMAND DECISION

President Nixon has properly described his decision to deploy the Safeguard BMD a command decision. The phrase is apt because in today's technological-military competition, choices regarding critical weapons systems have become as important as the decision to invade Normandy in the Second World War. Dr. Harold Brown, former Secretary of the Air Force, made this point in 1962:

> There have been a very few weapons system developments which have been critical in the sense that without them the

security of the United States would have been perhaps fatally impaired. These include in the nuclear weapons field the fission bomb and the thermonuclear weapon. Had we been forced to face an opponent which had either of these while we had not, our national survival might very well have been threatened . . . *the critical category also includes an antiballistic missile capability.*

Because the Soviet Union, over the past decade, has invested two to three times as much in strategic forces, we have lost strategic superiority, have entered a period of strategic parity, and may be facing the prospect of strategic inferiority. To prevent this development, President Nixon has made a command decision to deploy the Safeguard BMD system.

THE PRESIDENT AS NEGOTIATOR IN CHIEF

The choice before Congress is to support the President's decision on Safeguard or by rejecting it perhaps place the American people in greater future jeopardy. Can we afford to lose an immense lead-time-technology gamble, which may come back to haunt us in the future?

We are in an age of confrontation and negotiations. The U.S. strategic deterrent posture makes a contribution to our ability both to withstand confrontation and to coordinate negotiations. Accordingly, our research and development programs and our decisions to deploy weapons systems are part of our negotiation posture. One reason that negotiations must continue is to enable us to probe the real thinking of the Soviet leaders. If their real strategic doctrine is the one that is set forth in their public writings and that is being matched by their military installations, then our national security is already exposed to grave challenges.

In these circumstances, it is essential that the President, in

69

conducting his negotiations, carry with him coins of real value. The President—and no one else—has the responsibility for conducting negotiations. No senator can know as well as the President what counters he needs in order to negotiate advantageously with the Soviet leaders. It would be the height of folly for the United States Senate to tie the President's hands at this critical juncture in our history.

CHAPTER 3

Secretary of Defense
Melvin R. Laird Speaks Out*

In his testimony before the House Appropriations Committee, Secretary of Defense Laird gave the frankest revelation of what the United States government knows about Soviet strategic build-up ever to be made public. The statement was marked Top Secret when it was delivered.

Melvin R. Laird was nominated as Secretary of Defense by President Nixon on January 20, 1969, and was confirmed by the Senate the same day. When nominated, Secretary Laird represented the Seventh District of Wisconsin in the U.S. House of Representatives, where he had served continuously since 1952.

Secretary Laird served on the House Appropriations Committee, House Committee on Agriculture, and various subcommittees including Defense, Labor, Health, Education, and

---

* Hearings before Subcommittees of the Committtee on Appropriations, House of Representatives, Ninety-First Congress, First Session, May 22, 1969, GPO, pp. 5–39.

Welfare, and Military Construction. He was chairman of the House Republican Conference and a member of the Republican Coordinating Committee. He is author or editor of several books and articles dealing with public policy, including A House Divided *(Chicago: Henry Regnery Co., 1962).*

Mr. Chairman and members of the committee, I greatly appreciate this opportunity to discuss with you the administration's Safeguard antiballistic missile proposal. As a former member of this committee over a period of some fourteen years, I well know how thoroughly and conscientiously you review the defense programs and budgets presented to the Congress each year by the Executive Branch.

Let me say initially that I welcome the debate which is taking place on the ABM program. It is very·much in our tradition for major national issues to be widely discussed and understood. As a matter of fact, such debate is always a reassuring sign of the health of our free society.

Let me suggest, however, that at this point in the debate, the true perspective has been somewhat obscured by the literally millions of words that have been spoken and written on this subject in the past few months. Minor and major points have been mixed together indiscriminately. Facts and opinions have been stated without distinction. Emotion and wishful thinking, rather than reason and reality, have gained the ascendency in the current debate on this vital issue.

What I hope to do this afternoon is to assist this committee in identifying the crucial issues and factors that led President Nixon to propose the measured Safeguard ABM program at this time.

First, it is imperative for everyone to understand that the President's decision resulted from his recognition of the special responsibility he has as Commander in Chief for the nation's security. All of the essential facts concerning this matter were analyzed by those of us to whom this responsibility, or a portion of it, has been delegated. Our analyses were made and our judgments reached under the full weight of this responsibility. Accordingly, there was absolutely no place in this equation for expediency—political, economic, or otherwise.

Second, Safeguard is recommended by the President as the best step we can take *at this time* to fulfill the major requirements posed by national security and foreign policy considerations and domestic economic constraints.

I do not make this statement lightly, but I say it to emphasize that many complex factors entered into the Safeguard decision, any one of which taken by itself could have suggested a different approach. However, all of these factors taken together clearly justify the Safeguard decision as the best course available at this time for discharging the awesome responsibilities the President and the Congress share together.

For example, some opponents of ABM suggest that in response to the growing Soviet threat we should move forward with the deployment of additional strategic offensive weapons such as more Poseidon submarines, Minuteman III ICBMs, and so on. This could be a proper response to the rapid build-up in Soviet offensive strategic weapons, but it would probably also dim the growing prospects for arms limitation talks and exacerbate the strategic arms race. At the same time, it would not significantly enhance our position vis-à-vis the Communist Chinese if, as expected, they develop a small ICBM capability during the decade of the 1970s.

What the Nixon administration tried to do, successfully I believe, was devise a program that in all respects would advance the cause of peace and at the same time ensure the continued adequacy of our nation's strategic power should peace collapse.

Under our constitutional system, Congress shares the heavy burden of responsibility for our national security and for the

73

decisions which, in the final analysis, could tip the scales for either war or peace. It is the Congress which has the constitutional power to decide whether the Safeguard system shall be authorized. And it is the Congress which can deny the President the authority to go forward with the program or the funds needed to implement it.

Mr. Chairman, it is not the purpose of this administration to attempt to force congressional approval of a particular weapons system. It is the President's responsibility, however, to make recommendations for those programs he believes necessary for an adequate defense and a sufficiency of military forces, and to provide the Congress with the information and reasoning on which his judgment is based.

I would like to stress that the President's decision on Safeguard was based on the best judgment of those of us in the Executive Branch who bear the responsibility for making such a recommendation. In the final analysis, we can offer you no more than this—our best judgments, based on a careful analysis of all of the data available to us.

It is from this perspective that I would like to discuss the factors bearing on the President's Safeguard ABM recommendation.

To do this, I will attempt in my statement today to strip away from this problem the many interesting but irrelevant and marginal' arguments which now surround it, and return to the fundamentals involved:

A. The size and character of the threat to the continental United States projected over the next five to ten years.

B. The alternatives other than an ABM defense which might be available to meet that threat.

C. The purposes which an ABM defense system deployed in the continental United States could serve.

74

D. The origins of the ABM defense system, the concept of operation, and the state of development.

E. The basic elements of the Safeguard program proposed by the Nixon administration.

F. The anticipated effectiveness of the Safeguard program against the projected threat.

G. The estimated cost of the Safeguard program.

H. The strategic and foreign-policy implications of a decision to deploy the system.

A. ANALYSIS OF THE THREAT

The first question which had to be answered by the Nixon administration was whether an ABM defense should be deployed at all.

In order to explain to you how the administration answered this question, it is first necessary to examine the size, character, and timing of the actual and potential strategic threats which face the United States in the decade of the 1970s. These are (1) the Soviet missile threat against our population and cities, (2) the Soviet missile threat against our land-based strategic offensive forces, (3) the Chinese ICBM threat against our population and cities, (4) an accidental missile launch, and (5) a "demonstration" missile launch. Any ABM system we might deploy to meet the first, second, or third threat would be ample to cope with the fourth and fifth threats. Accordingly, we need to consider only the first three threats.

As this committee well knows, our intelligence projections over the near term, two or three years, are reasonably firm. But when we project five or six years ahead, we are getting into an area of considerable uncertainty, particularly insofar as actual deployments are concerned. Since it only takes eighteen to twenty-four months from the start of construction to the operational availability of an ICBM in a silo, it is clear that projections beyond that point involve estimates of decisions which may not as yet have been made. For this reason our national intelligence projections for the mid-1970s involve a large measure of judgment rather than hard evidence. This point should be kept in mind when I discuss our longer-range intelligence estimates.

1. THE SOVIET THREAT TO OUR CITIES AND POPULATION

The Soviet Union today has a force of more than one thousand ICBMs which can reach our cities. To protect our cities against even the present threat would require a very large and effective ABM system. This is so because even one 1-megaton warhead penetrating the defense could virtually destroy a medium-size city; one 10-megaton warhead could extensively damage even the largest city. But more important for the future, the Soviet Union has the technical and economic capability to develop and install large numbers of multiple independently targeted reentry vehicles (MIRVs) in each of its larger ICBMs, the SS-9 type, and perhaps several warheads in each of its smaller SS-11 and SS-13 ICBMs. And each of these warheads would require at least one ABM to ensure even a reasonable degree of protection.

Accordingly, it does not appear feasible, with existing ABM technology, to erect a defense against the Soviet missile threat to our cities which could preclude a catastrophic level of fatalities. But it is feasible to provide an effective defense for our land-based strategic offensive forces against the Soviet threat. This is so because in this case we do not need to intercept all of the incoming warheads, just enough of them to ensure that a sufficient portion of our strategic offensive forces survive to enable us to inflict unacceptable damage on the Soviet Union in retaliation. It is this threat that I now want to discuss in detail.

2. THE SOVIET THREAT TO OUR STRATEGIC OFFENSIVE FORCES

As this committee is well aware, the Soviet ICBM force has more than quadrupled in the last two and three-quarters years —from 250 operational launchers in June 1966 to more than 1,000 as of the end of March 1969. On the basis of the intelligence estimates prepared last fall, this force build-up was expected to level off after the Soviets had achieved a rough numerical parity with the United States in ICBMs excluding the older systems. However, if the Soviets were to continue to deploy ICBMs at the rate they deployed them in 1967–68, they could have as many as 2,500 by the mid-1970s. This is the area of judgment I referred to earlier. We have a very good estimate of the number of ICBM silos now under construction, but we can only conjecture as to the number they will start during the next two or three years.

Although these numbers are impressive in themselves, the real threat to the survivability of our strategic offensive forces lies in the accuracy and kinds of payloads these missiles might carry in the future. At the present time, the only serious threat to our ICBM force is the large SS-9 ICBM which, with a warhead yield of up to twenty-five megatons and its presently estimated accuracy, could destroy a Minuteman in its silo. The Soviets now have more than 230 of these missiles operational or under construction. According to the latest intelligence estimates, they are expected to have somewhere around 400 SS-9 types operational by the mid-1970s, including a new version with considerably greater accuracy.

Currently, about two thirds of the Soviet ICBM force consists of SS-11s, a small, Minuteman-size, liquid-fuel missile. With its currently estimated warhead yield and accuracy, this weapon does not pose a threat to our Minuteman force. The Soviets have just started to deploy a new solid-fuel ICBM, the SS-13. But, again, this missile, with an even smaller warhead yield and no better accuracy, constitutes even less of a threat than the SS-11 to our Minuteman force.

Our real concern at this time is the prospect that the Soviets might install highly accurate MIRVs on their large ICBMs and greatly improve the accuracy of their small ICBMs. If they were to do so, the survivability of our Minuteman force would be gravely endangered.

The Soviets have already begun to test multiple reentry vehicles (MRVs) on their SS-9, three RVs (each with payload equivalent to a five-megaton warhead) per missile, and it is estimated that they might start deploying these weapons in existing silos in the next year or so. A number of these vehicles have been launched thus far, three out to 5,100 n.mi. into the Pacific. (The third was launched just the other day.) Although we still have no conclusive evidence that these multiple reentry vehicles are independently aimed, the intelligence community considers it likely that the Soviets will go on with the development of MIRV's and install them in a new version of their SS-9 type ICBMs. Should they also greatly improve the accuracy of their small ICBMs, which the intelligence community considers possible, the survivability of our Minuteman force as presently deployed would be virtually nil by the mid to late 1970s.

It is also possible that the SS-9 with the three reentry vehicles will turn out to be a MIRVed missile. If that should be the case and if the Soviets were to back-fit all of their SS-9's with this new payload, three 5-megaton warheads each, the more than 230 SS-9s now operational or under construction would in themselves constitute a severe threat to our Minuteman force. And, if the Soviets were to increase this force to even 420 missiles and improve the accuracy to a quarter of a mile, they could probably destroy 95 percent of our Minuteman force, leaving only 50 surviving. (I should point out that this calculation assumes a failure rate of 20 percent and a capability to retarget a second missile for those that fail.)

For example, one reliable arriving twenty-megaton warhead with an accuracy of 0.5 mi. would have about a 90 percent probability of destroying a Minuteman in its silo. But one five-megaton warhead with an accuracy of 0.25 mi. would have a kill probability of about 95 percent.

That our Minuteman force might become vulnerable in the 1970s we have known for some time. In fact, this possibility was raised by Mr. McNamara before this committee in early 1966, and it has been restated in each annual posture statement since then. Now, three years later, we are fast approaching the time when this threat may be upon us.

As already noted, the Soviet Union has come abreast of us in numbers of ICBMs; evidence is now accumulating that they intend to match us in numbers of submarine-launched ballistic missiles (SLBMs). We knew more than a year ago that they were constructing a new class of nuclear-powered ballistic missile submarines with sixteen tubes, and that they were testing a new storable liquid fuel submerged-launched ballistic missile out to a range of about 1,500 n.mi. We now know that this submarine (designated the Y-class) is in full-scale production at a very large facility near Archangel, Severodvinsk, and possibly at another smaller yard. These two facilities can accommodate a total of twelve complete hulls. The intelligence community estimates that the two facilities can produce as many as eight submarines per year. I think that as production experience is gained the rate of output from these two facilities might very well increase significantly.

Eight or nine Y-class submarines have already been launched and several are believed to be operational. (They also have a number of H-class nuclear-powered submarines which carry three to six shorter-range SLBMs.) Even at a rate of construction of only six Y-class submarines a year the Soviet SLBM force could equal our own, in terms of numbers, by 1975. Nevertheless, with their currently estimated warhead yield and accuracy, these SLBMs would not constitute a threat to our Minuteman force. But, given our present radar coverage of the seaward approaches and no ABM defense of our bomber bases, they could constitute a severe threat to the survival of our bomber forces—even those aircraft held on ground alert.

This would be especially true if the Soviets design their SLBMs for depressed trajectory launch, which is not very difficult to do. If they were to do this with their SLBMs the flight time to large number of bomber bases could be considerably reduced.

If we had adequate warning against an SLBM launch, which we do not now have, twelve to fifteen minutes would be enough to get our alert bombers (40 percent of the operational inventory) airborne before the warheads detonated. (Our current and planned early warning systems promise to provide at least the twelve to fifteen minutes needed to get our alert bombers off their bases before the Soviet ICBMs or fractional orbit bombardment system, FOBS, could reach their targets.) With considerably less warning, we would have to be able to intercept at least the first few salvos of SLBMs in order to ensure that most of the alert bombers could get off their bases.

Accordingly, we are convinced that the Soviet strategic offensive missile forces could well pose a very serious threat to the survival of our own land-based strategic offensive forces by the mid or late 1970s. We would then be dependent upon our Polaris and Poseidon forces, unless we were willing to launch our Minuteman force on warning. While I do not want to foreclose this possibility, I do not believe we should allow ourselves to get into a position where the President would have no other choice.

I want to make it very clear that we have the greatest confidence in the survivability of our SLBM force, at least through the early to mid-1970s. But, in my judgment, it would be entirely too risky to rely upon only one of the three elements in our strategic offensive forces. We cannot preclude the possibility that the Soviets in the next few years may devise some weapon, technique, or tactic which might increase the vulnerability of our Polaris/Poseidon submarines. In that event, our strategic deterrent could be dangerously eroded, with all the consequences which would follow such a development.

Furthermore, we cannot preclude the possibility that the Soviet Union might deploy a more extensive and effective ABM defense. Such a defense, in combination with a substantial hard-target kill capability in the form of highly accurate small ICBMs or MIRVed large ICBMs, is what has been characterized by my predecessors as the "greater-than-expected threat" which could seriously degrade our assured destruction, or deterrent capability. As you know, the Soviets are now completing the deployment of some sixty Galosh ABM missiles on launchers around Moscow.

But more important, we now have hard evidence that the Soviets are testing an improved long-range ABM, which apparently has a "loiter" capability. In other words, after the initial firing, the missile can coast or "loiter" for a period of time until a specific target is selected, at which point it can then be restarted and maneuvered to the target.

We have already begun to provide a hedge (i.e., Poseidon and Minuteman III, both equipped with MIRVs) against the possibility that the Soviet Union might deploy an extensive and effective ABM defense. But we must be sure that both of these systems survive in sufficient numbers to saturate such a defense and inflict unacceptable damage on the Soviet Union. Otherwise, the credibility of our strategic deterrent might become questionable, and that we cannot afford.

In summary, the potential Soviet threat to the survival of our strategic offensive forces in the mid-1970s is clearly evident. How fast and how extensively it will develop is still uncertain. But, considering the lead-times involved on our side, it seems perfectly apparent to me that some action must be taken very soon to place ourselves in a position where we can respond promptly to that threat as it actually emerges.

3. THE CHINESE COMMUNIST ICBM THREAT

Because the Chinese ICBM development program has not progressed as rapidly as estimated a year or two ago, there has been a tendency in the current debate on the ABM issue to overlook this potential threat. Accordingly, I would like to take this opportunity to review that threat with you in the detail which I believe it warrants.

Late in 1965, and again in late 1966, the intelligence community estimated that the Chinese Communists had the technical and industrial capabilities required for the deployment of ballistic missiles and that they were making an intensive effort to develop a missile in the 700-1,000 mile range. It was estimated at the time that the first of these medium-range missiles could be deployed as early as 1967–68, and that by the mid-1970s they could have as many as eighty to one hundred operational in fixed soft sites.

Although there was no direct evidence in late 1965 that the Chinese Communists were developing an ICBM, it was assumed that they were. This assumption was strengthened in the following year (late 1966), when the intelligence community stated that the Chinese were pursuing such a program with a high priority. On the basis of the evidence then available, it was estimated that they might conduct either a space launch or an ICBM flight test before the end of 1967.

Inasmuch as the Chinese Communists have not yet launched their first ICBM (or space shot), and we still have no evidence that they are deploying an MRBM, Mr. Packard and I decided to make a complete reassessment of the available data on the progress of their ballistic missile programs. We did so in order to determine for ourselves if a potential Chinese ICBM threat does, in fact, exist.

There are four major elements involved in preparing for deployment of an ICBM force: (a) nuclear materials production, (b) nuclear weapons development and testing, (c) ballistic missile development and testing, and (d) the construction of missile production facilities.

a. Nuclear Materials Production. The Chinese Communists have been producing U-235 since about 1963. We now believe they are also producing plutonium. (The use of plutonium showed up for the first time in the December 1968 test.) Sources for other materials used by China in its thermonuclear weapons, such as deuterium and lithium-6, also appear to be available. And the Chinese have an ample supply of natural uranium.

The amount of U-235 now estimated to be available for stockpiling is still fairly limited. Continued production of U-235 and plutonium will help to increase the supply of fissionable material. But any sizable production of nuclear weapons will require the further expansion of production facilities for fissionable materials, especially U-235. Once construction of a new U-235 plant is started, we estimate that at least three years would be required before production could begin. Thus, China's nuclear capabilities can be expected to grow gradually, at least over the next few years.

b. Nuclear Weapons Development and Testing. From October 16, 1964, to December 27, 1968, in a period of three and a quarter years, the Chinese detonated eight nuclear devices, one of which was delivered by a missile. Five of the eight tests involved thermonuclear materials. The first of these was detonated in May 1966 and produced a yield of more than two hundred kilotons. The second device, detonated in December 1966, produced a yield of a few hundred kilotons. The third, detonated in June 1967, produced a yield of about three megatons. The fourth, detonated in December 1967, was a probable failure since it produced only ten to twenty-five kilotons. The last, detonated on December 27, 1968, was another device which produced a yield of about three megatons.

Thus, on a minimum number of shots the Chinese have made more rapid progress than any other nation. The first three-megaton device was relatively heavy, but the latest device could be considerably lighter for the same yield. Either of these devices could be delivered by an ICBM, but the lower weight would be an obvious advantage.

The last three thermonuclear devices were probably air-dropped by a medium-range bomber. Inasmuch as the Chinese have a few of the Soviet TU-16-type jet medium bombers, the early three-megaton weapon may be designed for aircraft delivery. In any event, the TU-16 has an operational radius of only about 1,650 nautical miles and therefore does not represent a threat to the United States.

The nuclear device delivered by a missile in the fourth test had a yield of less than twenty kilotons and used a primitive fission technology. Unless they intend to deploy an MRBM very soon, they would most likely develop a thermonuclear warhead with a yield of a few hundred kilotons for this missile.

c. Ballistic Missile Development and Testing. The Chinese Communists have been working on an MRBM for a number of years. By 1965, activity at the principal missile test range had become very noticeable. And, as noted earlier, they actually delivered a nuclear device with a missile in the October 1966 test. By the summer of 1967, the rate of test firings greatly exceeded the level considered normal for an R & D program, leading the intelligence community to believe that deployment might be imminent. Yet, almost two years later, we still have no evidence than an MRBM is actually being deployed.

The program may have been delayed by technical problems with the missile itself. Or, it may have been disrupted by the Cultural Revolution. There is even the possibility that the Chinese never intended to deploy their first-generation MRBM, choosing to wait for a more advanced missile and warhead. In any event, MRBM testing is continuing up to ranges of about one thousand miles. The intelligence community continues to believe that the Chinese intend eventually to deploy the current MRBM system. If they were to do so soon, they would have to use a warhead based on the fourth test (*i.e.*, the less than twenty-kiloton device delivered by a missile). Even so, they would probably not have an operational MRBM force until sometime in 1970. By the mid-1970s they could have a force of eighty to one hundred operational missiles. However, this system does not pose a direct threat to the United States.

(Although the Chinese have one Soviet-type G-class diesel-powered missile launching submarine, we have no evidence that they have developed a missile for it. Moreover, diesel-powered submarines with their limited endurance and high noise levels do not offer much of a threat against the continental United States).

Given the experience already acquired with the MRBM, there is no reason to believe that the Chinese cannot in time develop and deploy an ICBM. The United States and the Soviet Union have both moved from the shorter-range to the longer-range ballistic missiles, and the Chinese are probably following the same course. We know that a large ballistic missile launch facility already exists. In fact, it was the construction of this facility that led the intelligence community in late 1966 to estimate that the Chinese Communists could launch their first ICBM (or space shot) before the end of 1967.

Thus, assuming that test vehicles are available, which we as yet have no way of knowing, flight testing of an ICBM could begin sometime this year. At least three years would then be required to achieve an initial operational capability (IOC), *i.e.*, sometime in late 1972. In the light of Chinese inexperience, their limited technical and scientific base, and considering general political and economic conditions in China, more time will probably be required. Thus, an IOC is more likely to be achieved later than 1972, perhaps as much as two or three years later. Even assuming an IOC in late 1972, it is doubtful that the Chinese could achieve a force of more than ten to twenty-five operational ICBM's on launchers by 1975.

We would almost certainly detect ICBM firings to full range, which would necessarily be to an area outside China. Monitoring of these tests should not only provide one year advance warning of IOC, but should also provide useful data on the missile characteristics as well.

We believe the Chinese have already constructed a solid propellant plant, and it is possible that they are looking ahead to a solid fuel ICBM. Such a missile could be more easily emplaced in hard silos, but it could not be deployed before 1975 at the earliest.

d. Construction of Production Facilities. We have known since 1963 that the Chinese Communists were constructing a large ballistic missile production facility. Whether ICBMs are now being produced there is still not known, but MRBMs probably are.

In summary, the Chinese Communists seem to have all of the major elements required for the production and deployment of ICBMs. After examining the available data, we have concluded that the potential threat is very real, and that the Chinese will ultimately deploy a force of ICBMs. What is still uncertain is when they will start deployment and how large and how good a force they will have by the mid-1970s and beyond. We believe, especially because of the work being done on the launch facility, that they will begin flight testing ICBMs (or a space booster) within eighteen months. If they do, we will soon know much more about the other questions.

B. ALTERNATIVES TO THE DEPLOYMENT OF AN ABM DEFENSE

1. AGAINST THE SOVIET THREAT TO OUR STRATEGIC OFFENSIVE FORCES

The alternatives to an ABM defense for our strategic offensive forces fall under two general headings. First, we could increase the size of our strategic offensive forces, *i.e.*, the number of sea- or land-based missiles or of bombers—or all three. Second, we could improve the survivability of our existing forces by placing our Minuteman missiles in harder silos and further dispersing our bomber force, increasing the number on ground alert or placing a portion of the force on continuous airborne alert.

Many of the alternatives in the first group might, as my predecessors would have phrased it, be equally "cost/effective" in ensuring the survival of a sufficient force to inflict unacceptable damage to the Soviet Union. But all of these alternatives could be misconstrued by the Soviets as an attempt to threaten their deterrent, and thereby stimulate the arms race. In other words, the Soviets might interpret a major expansion of our strategic offensive forces as an attempt on our part to achieve a low-risk first-strike capability against them.

The second group of alternatives runs up against cost and

physical limitations. We do intend to further disperse our bomber force, but as we increase the proportion on ground alert the costs begin to mount. The alternative of maintaining a portion of our bomber force on continuous airborne alert has, as you know, been considered off and on for a period of at least ten years. It has always been rejected because of the very high cost and the wear and tear on both crews and aircraft. Nevertheless, as I am sure you are aware, we still have on the statute books, in the annual Appropriations Acts, a provision to do just that in an emergency and to pay for it on a deficiency basis.

Placing our Minuteman missiles in harder silos involves a somewhat different problem. As you know, we have requested funds in the fiscal year 1970 budget to continue with the development of hard rock silos. But this increase in the hardness of the silo could be offset by a reduction in the accuracy of the attacking missile. For example, an increase in accuracy from one mile to one half mile is equivalent to an eight-fold increase in the warhead yield against a hard target.

Moreover, there appears to be a limit to how hard we can make a Minuteman silo. While we can add concrete and steel to the top of the silo, there is little we can do about the geology of the area in which the silo is emplaced. Where the limits of the geology lie, we just do not know at this time. Nevertheless, we plan to proceed with our program to develop hard rock silos. But we all must recognize that hardening alone would not be enough to solve the problem of survivability if the Soviet MIRVed SS-9 threat develops to the full extent I described earlier.

2. AGAINST THE CHINESE THREAT TO OUR CITIES

Given our present commitments in Asia and the Western Pacific, and assuming the Chinese do indeed deploy an ICBM force in the 1970s, there is really only one alternative to an

ABM defense against that threat to our cities and population. That alternative is to rely on the deterrent power of our strategic offensive forces, just as we do against the far larger Soviet threat to our cities. However, in considering this alternative, we must keep clearly in mind a number of interrelated factors—demographic, technical, economic, social, and political.

First, we must recognize the major demographic differences between the Soviet Union and Communist China. As shown on the following table, the thousand largest Chinese cities account for only 11 percent of the total population, compared with 47 percent for the Soviet Union and 63 percent for the United States. Thus, the thousand largest Chinese cities contain considerably less than the one third, one fourth, or one fifth of the population Mr. McNamara has postulated at various times as the level required for "assured destruction" against the Soviet Union.

The fact that a large proportion of Chinese industrial capacity is concentrated in a relatively small number of cities does have a bearing on the problem of deterrence. But China is predominantly a rural society where the great majority of the people live off the land and are dependent only to a limited extent on

CUMULATIVE PERCENTAGE DISTRIBUTION OF POPULATION AND INDUSTRIAL CAPACITY IN 1970

[Number of cities in order of population rank]

Number of cities	United States		Soviet Union		Communist China	
	Population	Industrial capacity	Population	Industrial capacity	Population	Industrial capacity
10	25.1	33.1	8.3	25	3.7	30–35
50	42.0	55.0	20.0	40	6.8	50–60
100	48.0	65.0	25.0	50	8.6	65–75
200	55.0	75.0	34.0	62	9.0	80–90
400	60.0	82.0	40.0	72	10.0	85–90
1,000	63.0	86.0	47.0	82	11.0	

urban industry for their survival. Furthermore, as Mao Tse-tung is reported to have said, China with its huge population (now estimated at 800 million) could survive (*i.e.*, as a people but not as a twentieth-century nation) even with a loss of hundreds of millions from a nuclear attack. And we know from past experience that the Asian Communists are tenacious opponents and are willing to take great losses of life in achieving their objectives. Therefore, it is reasonable to conclude that our ability to deter Communist China with our strategic offensive forces is considerably less certain than in the case of the Soviet Union.

Second, because our population is heavily concentrated in a relatively few large cities (42 percent in the largest fifty cities compared with 6.8 percent for Communist China), we would be highly vulnerable to an attack by even a relatively few ICBMs—if we had no defense against them. If deterrence should not work, our only recourse would be retaliation. However, we would have to withhold a large part of our strategic offensive forces as a deterrent to the Soviet Union, and the fatalities that we could inflict on Communist China would be relatively small in proportion to its total population. We could, however, destroy most of their urban industry and population with a relatively small number of weapons.

Third, given the character of the present regime in China, their ambitions in Asia, and their implacable hostility toward the United States, it would seem extremely foolhardly on our part to rely on deterrence only—if we had any better alternative. The President of the United States, no matter who he may be at the time, could find himself in an extremely difficult position in a serious confrontation with a Communist China armed with a force of even twenty-five relatively primitive ICBMs. Our cities would be hostage to the Chinese ICBM force, and the President would have no other alternative but to back down or risk the destruction of several major U.S. cities and the death of millions of Americans.

90

Thus, the issue resolves itself into a matter of judgment. If one believes that a Communist China armed with a force of ICBMs could still be deterred by our overwhelmingly greater strategic offensive forces, then an ABM defense need not be deployed against that threat. If, however, one believes as I do that the Chinese leaders might not be deterred, then the Safeguard system would be well worth its cost for that purpose alone.

C. PURPOSES WHICH AN ABM DEFENSE SYSTEM COULD SERVE

It may be useful, at this point, to review briefly the various purposes which an ABM system could serve, given the nature of the actual and potential threats. There are at least three major purposes and two minor ones.

Major purposes:

1. Protection of our population and cities against the kind of heavy, sophisticated missile attack the Soviets could launch in the 1970s.
2. Defense of our strategic offensive forces and their command and control (*e.g.,* bomber bases, Minuteman silos, the National Command Authorities, etc.) as a substitute in whole or in part for the further expansion of those forces in the event a Soviet threat to their survival clearly emerges in the next few years.
3. Protection of our population and cities against the kind of limited, unsophisticated ICBM attack the Chinese Communists might be able to launch in the 1970s.

Minor purposes:

1. Protection against the improbable, but possible, accidental launching of an ICBM toward the United States.

2. Protection against an unlikely, but possible, "demonstration attack," *i.e.*, one or two missiles launched against our homeland as a sort of "shot across the bow."

The Sentinel system proposed by the preceding administration and approved by the Congress was primarily intended to serve the third major purpose—defense of our population against a Chinese ICBM attack, and, to some extent, the second major purpose—defense of our strategic offensive forces. In fact, a more comprehensive defense of our Minuteman force was included in Sentinel as an option that could be exercised at any time. Beacuse of its nationwide coverage, it would have also fully served the two minor purposes. Finally, given the mode of deployment proposed (*i.e.*, placing most of the radars and missile launcers in or near the major urban areas) it could have served as a foundation for a greatly expanded system for the defense of our prinicipal cities against a Soviet missile attack.

But, the important point to keep in mind is that the Sentinel system was designed primarily to defend our population and cities against a Chinese Communist ICBM attack in the 1970s, and not an all-out Soviet attack. It would have had very little value against the latter, as the following table drawn from previous posture statements well illustrates:

U.S. FATALITIES FROM A CHINESE *OR* SOVIET FIRST STRIKE IN THE MID-1970S

[In millions]

	Chinese[1]	Soviet
With no defense	7–23	110–120
With Sentinel	0–1	100

[1] The range of fatalities shown for a Chinese attack reflects a force of 10–75 ICBMs.

92

Unfortunately, this point has been obscured by the fact that many of the Sentinel sites (with Spartan missile launchers and the associated radars) were to be located in or near the major urban areas. We understand that this mode of deployment was selected so that in the event a decision was made at a later time to provide a terminal defense, the Sprint missiles could be installed at the same sites. Because the Sprint has a much shorter range (approximately twenty-five miles) than the Spartan (several hundred miles) it must be installed in or near the city to be defended.

I will have more to say about this matter of siting when I discuss the deployment alternatives.

D. STATUS OF THE ABM DEFENSE SYSTEM

I would now like to turn to the status of the ABM defense system. I know you are all familiar with the major components of this system, but I think it would be useful at this point to review briefly the origins of the system, the concept of operation, and the state of development.

1. ORIGINS OF THE SAFEGUARD SYSTEM

Many people have lost sight of the fact that the Safeguard program is the culmination of more than thirteen years of research and development effort and the expenditure of about $5 billion, including all the various projects related to ballistic missile defense. During the entire period, as this committee well knows, the ABM program has proceeded under the continuous scrutiny of the Congress. Much thought and study has gone into its formulation since it was first presented to the Congress and this Committee in 1955. You will recall, Mr. Chairman, that the program did not move into full-scale development until 1958, and that by 1959 there was already considerable sentiment in the Congress, not to speak about the Department of the Army, to start the deployment of the system then known as Nike-Zeus. In fact, the Congress added $375 million to President Eisenhower's fiscal year 1960 budget request "for the acceleration of Nike-Zeus and/or the modernization of Army firepower." President Eisenhower, as later events demonstrated, wisely rejected this proposal in favor of continued development and test.

In fiscal year 1963, the Nike-Zeus system as such was abandoned because, with the mechanically steered radars which it employed, it could not cope with the kind of attack the Soviets could mount in the late 1960s. Accordingly, a new, improved system, known as the Nike-X, was placed in development. The Nike-X was to consist of a new family of phased-array radars and a new high-acceleration terminal defense missile, the Sprint. This system promised to be much more effective against a sophisticated missile attack employing penetration aids, and much less susceptible to saturation. However, even if the system were deployed around all our major cities, a large part of the nation would still be left undefended. Moreover, the attacker would still have the option of ground bursting his warheads outside of the defended areas, thereby producing vast amounts of lethal fallout which could be carried by the winds over the defended areas. While the second problem could be ameliorated by a nationwide system of fallout shelters, something more would be needed to deal with the first problem. The solution adopted in December 1964 was the initiation of development of a new, long-range interceptor with a high-yield warhead which kills by X ray. With this missile, called the Spartan, the Nike-X system offered the possibility of a defense in depth— an area defense for the entire nation, as well as a terminal defense for our major cities with the Sprint missile.

Consequently, the Congress in the summer of 1966 appropriated $168 million over and above the President's fiscal year 1967 budget request to prepare for the production of the Nike-X system. This action, together with a number of other developments which occurred during that year,[1] brought the Nike-X deployment issue to a head.

In response to these events, President Johnson, on January 24, 1967, made the following recommendation to the Congress:

"Continue intensive development of Nike-X but take no action now to deploy an antiballistic missile (ABM) defense; initiate discussions with the Soviet Union on the limitation of ABM deployments; in the event these discussions prove unsuccessful, we will reconsider our deployment decision. To provide for actions that may be required at that time, approximately $375 million has been included in the 1968 budget for the production of Nike-X for such purposes as defense of our offensive weapon systems."

However, later in that same year (in a speech in San Francisco on September 18, 1967) Secretary of Defense McNamara announced the Johnson administration's decision to move forward with the deployment of an antiballistic missile defense system against the potential threat of a Chinese Communist ICBM attack in the mid-1970s. It is pertinent to note the

---

[1] Among these developments were the following:

(1) The Soviet Union had accelerated the deployment of hard ICBMs beyond the rates forecasted by the U.S. intelligence community and had initiated the deployment of an antiballistic missile defense system around Moscow.

(2) The Chinese Communists had launched and demonstrated a nuclear-armed medium-range ballistic missile and had detonated their first two thermonuclear devices.

(3) The Nike-X had reached a stage of development where the start of concurrent production and deployment had become feasible.

(4) The Joint Chiefs of Staff had strongly urged a prompt decision to deploy the system.

reasons given by Secretary McNamara for this decision. He stated them as follows:

"There is evidence that the Chinese are devoting very substantial resource to the development of both nuclear warheads, and missile delivery systems . . . indications are that they will have medium-range ballistic missiles within a year or so, an initial intercontinental ballistic missile capability in the early 1970s, and a modest force in the mid-1970s.

"Up to now, the lead-time factor has allowed us to postpone a decision on whether or not a light ABM deployment might be advantageous as a countermeasure to Communist China's nuclear development.

"But the time will shortly be right for us to initiate production if we desire such a system."

*   *   *   *   *

"The system would be relatively inexpensive—preliminary estimates place the cost at about $5 billion—and would have a much higher degree of reliability against a Chinese attack, than the much more massive and complicated system that some have recommended against a possible Soviet attack.

"Moreover, such an ABM deployment designed against a possible Chinese attack would have a number of other advantages. It would provide an additional indication to Asians that we intend to deter China from nuclear blackmail, and thus would contribute toward our goal of discouraging nuclear weapon proliferation among the present nonnuclear countries.

"Further, the Chinese-oriented ABM deployment would enable us to add—as a concurrent benefit—a further defense of our Minuteman sites against Soviet attack, which means that at modest cost we would, in fact, be adding even greater effectiveness to our offensive missile force and avoiding a much more costly expansion of that force.

96

"Finally, such a reasonably reliable ABM system would add protection of our population against the improbable but possible accidental launch of an intercontinental missile by any one of the nuclear powers."

As you know, this Chinese-oriented ABM system was called the Sentinel. By January 1969, production of many of the components of that system was already under way, and the acquisition of operational sites had been started. Indeed, the Johnson administration's fiscal year 1970 budget included $1.8 billion to carry forward the full-scale deployment of the system, with an initial equipment readiness date of October 1972 for the first site at Boston and completion of the entire system by January 1975.

Thus, the Nixon administration was confronted with a going program, and not just a proposal. A choice had to be made. The alternatives open to the new administration from this point of view can be summarized as follows:

1. Permit the Sentinel program to move forward as planned by the preceding administration.
2. Halt production and deployment and continue research and development only.
3. Terminate all work on the Sentinel system as such, and continue only research and development on more advanced ABM technology.
4. Reorient and rephase the entire Sentinel program.

For reasons which I discussed earlier, the fourth alternative was chosen.

2. CONCEPT OF OPERATION AND STATUS OF DEVELOPMENT

Mr. Chairman, there are two basic concepts involved in the kind of ballistic missile defense systems we are discussing here today—area defense and terminal defense. Area defense involves the detection and tracking of the incoming reentry vehicles with long-range radars, and the interception of those vehicles with long-range defense missiles while they are still high above the atmosphere. Terminal defense involves the interception of enemy reentry vehicles with short-range, high-acceleration defense missiles, after these vehicles have reentered the atmosphere and after they have been sorted out by the atmosphere from decoys, chaff, and other confusion devices. By using both concepts in combination, a defense in depth can be provided.

Both the Sentinel and Safeguard systems involve the same basic technology and utilize the same major components: Perimeter Acquisition Radars (PARs), Missile Site Radars (MSRs), Spartan missiles, Sprint missiles, and a data processing center associated with each of the radars. These components serve the following basic functions: The PAR is the long-range radar which first acquires and tracks the target, while the MSR is the shorter-range radar which continues to track the target and also guides the interceptor missiles. The Spartan is the long-range area defense missile, and the Sprint is the high-acceleration terminal defense missile. The data processing centers provide the necessary calculations for the entire intercept operation.

The Perimeter Acquisition Radar (PAR) is a relatively low-frequency, phased-array radar which is capable of simultaneously detecting and tracking a large number of objects at a range greater than a thousand miles. The PAR provides information to the data processing center which computes the track of the incoming missile and the probable point of intercept. (When the target missile comes within range of the MSR, the MSR tracks it and provides the guidance for the Spartan interceptor missile.) The PAR radar must be large in order to provide the long range and high resolution required for the system. It will be housed in a building about 200 feet square, 130 feet high, and will have an antenna with a diameter of 116 feet.

The principles, functions, power level, and frequency of the PAR are quite similar to existing operational space and air defense radars. Hence, there is no need to build a complete R & D PAR, and the first PAR can be assembled directly at an operational site. The status of the work on this radar is as follows: The equipment configuration has been chosen, the design and performance specifications have been prepared, a partial prototype test model has been started and is now 40 percent complete, the design for the PAR structure has been finished, and the PAR computer is 25 percent complete. In short, work on the PAR is well along and no major problems are anticipated.

The Missile Site Radar is also a phased-array radar which controls the Sprint and Spartan interceptor missiles during an engagement. It has a range of several hundred miles and can simultaneously track multiple incoming objects and guide missiles to intercept them. After the MSR has been alerted to the incoming target by the PAR, it and its associated computers provide the capability to ready interceptors for launch, launch them, guide them to intercept, arm their warheads, and fire them.

Because the functions of the MSR are more complex than those of the PAR, a prototype system has been installed at Meck Island in the Kwajalein Missile Range, where its operational capabilities are being tested. The installation was completed in May 1968 as scheduled, and the radar was successfully brought up to full power in November 1968. Work on the data processing center associated with this MSR, including the programming, is now progressing well. The first MSR-directed Spartan intercept of a single ICBM is expected to take place in the spring or summer of 1970, and an intercept with a Sprint later in that year. The first intercept of multiple targets at Kwajalein is scheduled for early 1971.

The data processing function, which I just mentioned, is an extremely important element in the ABM defense system. Powerful computers and sophisticated "programs" are needed to control the radars, compute trajectories, differentiate the incoming warheads from other objects, guide the defense missiles, and so forth. Moreover, the "programs" must be designed in advance to reflect every conceivable eventuality the system may confront, and this represents a very complex problem. While each of the PARs and MSRs has a data processing center associated with it, the entire system will be tied into a ballistic missile defense center located at the underground headquarters of the Continental Air Defense Command.

The MSR computer has the more difficult data processing requirement, since it must not only track the target but also guide the interceptor missile. It utilizes a multi-processor with several units which can operate in parallel on different tasks or different parts of the same tasks. Two processors out of an eventual total of four have been installed and are now operating with the MSR at Kwajalein. (Installation of the third is now under way.) The two operational processors have been integrated with the radar and are being used to test the radar "hardware" and to develop the "software" computer programs. The data processing system, including the computer programs, should be ready for use in the first live intercept scheduled for 1970.

The three-stage Spartan missile is used for area defense and can intercept objects at a range of several hundred miles and at altitudes high above the atmosphere. This missile is a scaled-up version of the Nike-Zeus. The latter was fired 154 times, and it made 10 successful interceptions out of 14 attempts against ICBMs fired from the West Coast in 1962 and 1963, during its system test phase.

The first Spartan was fired in March 1968, and there have

100

now been a total of eight firings. Six were completely successful, and two only partially successful. However, the deficiencies in the latter two have been identified and corrections have been made. Additional t st firings will go on at a rate of about one per month.

The Spartan multimegaton warhead is being developed and tested by the Atomic Energy Commission. A successful scaled-down developmental shot was fired underground in Nevada in December 1968. It should be noted that this Spartan warhead is being designed so that it cannot detonate below a certain minimum safe altitude, and because of the high altitudes where the interceptions will take place, there will be no significant effects on people or property on the ground.

The very fast Sprint missile makes its intercept in the atmosphere. It is used for terminal defense where the incoming enemy warhead is not destroyed by the Spartan missile, either because of a miss or malfunction, or a failure of the radars to discriminate between an armed warhead and a decoy or other confusion device. Once the actual warhead has emerged from its accompanying confusion devices as they enter the atmosphere, the high speed of the Sprint enables it to make the intercept before the warhead descends to its detonation altitude.

Test firings of the Sprint began in 1965. Out of a total of twenty-nine launches, there have been fourteen successes, seven partial successes, and eight failures. However, eight out of the last ten firings have been fully successful. Moreover, the exact causes of the two failures have been identified and corrective action has been taken. On the basis of these recent flight tests, we believe the Sprint will meet its performance specifications.

The Sprint's warhead is designed to use two kinds of phenomena to kill an incoming reentry vehicle—an air blast which destroys the vehicle, and neutrons which penetrate the vehicle. The warhead will be provided with a safety device which will

101

prevent it from detonating below a minimum safe altitude. At this altitude there should be no adverse effects on people or property on the ground. Testing of the development warhead by the AEC has indicated that the proposed design can meet the requirements. Design and fabrication of the operational warhead is proceeding as planned.

Mr. Chairman, I believe it is clear from my discussion of the status of the major components, that the system as a whole is ready for production and deployment. In fact, as I noted earlier, some of the components are already being manufactured, and a total of about $434 million has been obligated for procurement alone. Included in this total is about $70 million for the first PAR; about $120 million for data processors; $59 million for advance procurement of an MSR; about $146 million for production facilities, production engineering, etc., for various major components of the Safeguard system. As of March 30, 1969, about $103 million in procurement funds has already been expended. We estimate that a total of about fifteen thousand employees in the prime and major subcontractor plants, alone, are engaged in this ABM development and production effort.

Mr. Chairman and members of the committee, I must tell you very frankly that if the Congress, this year, does not approve the deployment of Phase 1 of this system, we would not only have to terminate production, but also drastically revise the R & D effort uniquely related to the deployment of this particular system. We have been advised by very knowledgeable people in the business that we have probably gone as far as we can in the development of some of the components of this system. In any event, we would, of course, continue R & D work associated with the Kwajalein test program and on more advanced ABM defense technology.

Nevertheless, a large portion of the work force presently engaged in this effort would have to be disbanded, and if we should

102

later decide to go ahead with the Safeguard program in fiscal year 1971, it would take not just one more year, but at least two more years to complete the full deployment. In other words, the system would not be fully operational until the spring of 1978 instead of 1976. This is so because the work force would have to be rebuilt and all of the production processes restarted, and this would take at least an additional year. To delay this program for another two years would, in my judgment, be gambling with the nation's survival—unless we adopt some of the other alternatives (*e.g.*, increasing our strategic offensive forces) which I discussed earlier. And I want to make it perfectly clear that those measures would have little effect on the situation which would prevail if the Chinese ICBM threat were to emerge in the mid-1970s.

*   *   *   *   *

I would now like to turn to the Safeguard program specifically proposed by President Nixon.

E. BASIC ELEMENTS OF THE SAFEGUARD PROGRAM

Before I discuss the Safeguard program, I believe it would be useful to review briefly the main characteristics of the ABM program proposed by the preceding administration and the reasons why we felt it should be reoriented.

The Sentinel system, as I noted earlier, was oriented primarily against the Chinese ICBM threat. It involved the deployment of seventeen sites; fifteen in the forty-eight contiguous states and one each in Alaska and Hawaii. The plan called for the deployment of six PARs (with one face each) along the northern border of the United States facing the Chinese ICBM threat corridors. Each site was to be equipped with an MSR, some with more than one face each, for a total of thirty-eight faces. (The four sites in the Minuteman fields and the one in Washington, D.C., would each have had a four-face MSR to give them an all-around defense capability.) All of the sites except Hawaii were to have Spartan missiles. The Hawaiian site was to be equipped with Sprints only because of the small area to be protected. All sites at which the PARs were to be located were to be equipped with Sprints for defense of the radars.

There were several elements of this plan which we felt could be considerably improved. First, the plan was too heavily oriented to the Chinese ICBM threat. For example, all of the PARs faced north only, providing no warning or tracking capability against the SLBM threat from the sea. Many MSRs had no terminal defense, and no Sprints were specifically provided for the defense of the Minuteman force. This last requirement was simply held open as an option, to be exercised if needed. Yet the Soviet threat to our land-based ICBMs and bombers was growing more rapidly than was forecast only a year or two ago, while the Chinese ICBM threat was evolving more slowly.

Second, ten of the fifteen Sentinel sites in the contiguous forty-eight states were to be located in or near major metropolitan areas. This particular pattern of deployment could well appear to the Soviets as a threat to their deterrent, since it could serve as the foundation for a thick ABM defense of our cities. We would, of course, all wish to defend our cities if that were technically feasible, which it is not. Thus, placing the Sentinel sites in or near the major metropolitan areas might have simply resulted in an increase in the Soviet ballistic missile threat to our cities.

Furthermore, since the public is well aware that Spartan will be equipped with a large, megaton-class warhead, many people became gravely concerned as to their safety in the event of an accidental detonation. We cannot, from a strictly technical point

104

of view, absolutely preclude that very remote possibility, but the control techniques employed heretofore clearly show that the chance of an accidental detonation is virtually nil. We can point with great confidence to our record on nuclear safety, which includes the safe deployment of Nike-Hercules air defense missiles around our major cities for more than a decade.

Third, the entire Sentinel system was to be deployed on a fixed, predetermined schedule, instead of on a step-by-step basis which would allow for a periodic reassessment of the international situation and the need to continue the deployment.

The Safeguard program, in contrast, is based on a different concept. It is to be deployed in a manner which will make its defensive intent unmistakable. All of the sites will be located well outside the major urban areas, except for Washington, D.C., which is the control center of the National Command Authorities. This site will be provided a heavier defense than was planned in the Sentinel program, since protection of the NCA is essential if we wish command and control of our nuclear weapons to continue to reside in the hands of the constituted authority.

By properly locating the twelve sites, we can provide reasonable coverage for our manned bombers against the SLBM threat from the sea. To provide the all-around radar coverage required, seven PARs with eleven faces would be installed, instead of six PARs with six faces. Six of these eleven PAR faces would cover the seaward approaches, including the Gulf of Mexico. And, even though the Safeguard sites would be located away from the cities, a good area defense of virtually the entire country against the kind of threat the Chinese Communists might pose in the 1970s could be provided with twelve instead of fifteen sites (excluding in both cases Alaska and Hawaii).

The Safeguard system, if all Phase 2 options are exercised, would require somewhat fewer Spartans but more than twice as many Sprints on launchers than the Sentinel system. The increased number of Sprints is principally for the protection of the Minuteman fields, and the four Safeguard sites planned for these fields would account for almost two thirds of the Sprints. More than half of these Sprints would be deployed at so-called remote sites around the MSR to provide better coverage of the Minuteman force.

Another important feature of the Safeguard proposal is that the deployment would be implemented in stages in a manner clearly related to the actual development of the threat and the international situation generally. All we are asking the Congress to approve this year is Phase 1 of the program, which includes only the first two sites in the Minuteman fields—Grand Forks Air Force Base in North Dakota and Malmstrom Air Force Base in Montana. Each of these sites would be equipped, initially, with a one-face PAR, a four-face MSR, and Spartan and Sprint missiles, plus the required data processors, communication facilities, and so forth. How we would propose to proceed from there would depend upon the outcome of the forthcoming talks with the Soviet Union on strategic arms limitations and, ultimately, on how the threats, both from the Soviet Union and Communist China, actually evolve.

There are several reasons why we feel it is extremely important that we move ahead with Phase 1 at this time. First, as I already noted, if we do not proceed with production and deployment of the ABM components in fiscal year 1970, we would probably have to put the entire project on the shelf for the time being, thus delaying the availability of an operational system for at least two years. Second, although we plan to install an R & D prototype system (except for the PAR) at Kwajalein, that system would still not be the one we would install at an operational base. We feel it is absolutely essential to deploy at an operational site in order to check out the entire system under realistic conditions and work out the problems that inevitably arise in the deployment of any new major weapon system. This work must be done in any event if we ever want to deploy this system. If we don't do it now, we will have to do it later, thus depriving the President of the option to move forward rapidly with the Phase 2 options should the need arise within the next few years.

The reason we have proposed two sites instead of one is that they would be mutually supporting in an area defense role since the PAR and the Spartan coverage would overlap to some extent. Furthermore, we have to begin somewhere, and these two sites would provide protection for at least a limited portion of the Minuteman force. Accordingly, even if we don't go beyond Phase 1, we would still get some value out of the deployment of the first two sites. To protect our population against the Chinese ICBM threat, in contrast, would require the deployment of all twelve sites.

Because most of the start-up costs must be incurred in the beginning of the production program, the DOD investment cost (procurement, construction, and installation) of Phase 1 is estimated at $2.1 billion. About $800 million of these funds are already available; another $360 million is included in the revised fiscal year 1970 budget request, making a total of about $1,160 million. The balance of the $2.1 billion DOD investment cost for Phase 1 would have to be financed in subsequent years.

The initial equipment readiness date of the first site at Grand Forks is estimated to be January 1974, and the second site at Malmstrom, July 1974. It is pertinent to note that the initial equipment readiness date of the first site in the Sentinel plan discussed in Mr. Clifford's fiscal year 1970 posture statement was October 1972. Thus, we have already slipped the ABM deployment program by more than one year. That is how we have been able to reduce the total fiscal year 1970 budget request for

107

.ABM deployment—including RDT&E [research and development testing and engineering] and so forth—by almost $1 billion.

I want to make it clear at this point that these cost figures pertain only to the Defense Department budget; they do not include the nuclear warhead costs which, as you well know, are financed in the Atomic Energy Commission's budget. This has always been the case insofar as DOD weapon system costs are concerned. For example, the fiscal year 1970 Sentinel budget request figures cited in Mr. Clifford's statement also exclude warhead costs, as do the figures cited in Mr. McNamara's last statement.

I should also caution that the term "DOD investment cost" excludes RDT&E. Although I think it is more logical to include RDT&E in investment costs, and I have taken action to see that this is done in the future, the practice in the Defense Department in the past has been to include only procurement and military construction. In order to maintain comparability with the Sentinel costs used in the past, we have continued to apply this more narrow definition of investment costs to the Safeguard program. As a result, the cost figures I am using with regard to Safeguard are directly comparable to the figures used for Sentinel.

If the Soviet ICBM threat to our Minuteman force evolves in the manner I described earlier, but the Chinese ICBM threat does not develop, then we might propose to proceed with option 2A. This would involve adding two more sites in the Minuteman fields—Whiteman Air Force Base in Missouri and Warren Air Force Base in Wyoming. It would also involve a substantial increase in the number of Sprints in the Minuteman fields (plus more Spartans) and the installation of a Safeguard site at Washington, D.C. (with one four-face MSR, Spartans and Sprints) for the protection of the National Command Authorities. The exercise of option 2A would bring the total DOD investment cost for Safeguard up to $3.4 billion (including Phase 1).

The relative effectiveness of Safeguard option 2A in defending our Minuteman force can be measured in terms of the threat I mentioned earlier; namely, the large Soviet SS-9-type missile equipped with three independently targetable five-megaton warheads with an accuracy of one quarter of a mile. With a force of 420 of these missiles on launchers and an assumed failure rate of 20 percent, the Soviets could place over the Minuteman fields about one thousand warheads. Without any ABM defense, it is possible that only about fifty Minutemen would survive. (A mixed force made up of fewer large missiles but including a number of highly accurate small missiles could produce similar results.) With Safeguard Phase 1, perhaps two or three times as many Minutemen would survive and with Safeguard option 2A perhaps five or six times as many. (The actual number surviving would vary, depending upon both the offensive and defensive tactics employed.)

I cannot state as a fact that the Soviets will actually develop a MIRVed missile of this type or deploy a force of 420 of them. But I think you will agree, in the light of the information already in hand, that it is well within the realm of the possible. And if they should do so, our Minuteman force as presently deployed could be virtually wiped out—unless we provide some ABM defense.

Safeguard option 2B is designed to meet the growing Soviet SLBM threat to our bomber force. This option would involve the installation of all twelve sites and the deployment of the improved Spartan. The total DOD investment cost would amount to $6.3 billion (including Phase 1). Without an ABM defense, only a relatively small portion of our bombers and tankers would survive if the Soviets could place as many as fifteen Y-class submarines off our coasts, especially if the Soviet SLBMs are fired on a depressed trajectory. With the option 2B deployment, most of our alert bomber force could be expected to survive. Thus, the expected payoff from an option 2B deployment would be very substantial under these particular circumstances.

Option 2C is designed specifically against the Chinese ICBM threat, and assumes that the Soviet threat to our strategic offensive forces falls short of the levels postulated under options 2A and 2B. In this case, we would install all twelve sites and deploy the improved Spartan. But we could probably omit the PARs planned for Florida and southern California, since we would not have to defend against the Soviet SLBM threat to our bomber force. Moreover, some of the multiple MSR faces could probably also be omitted, since we would not have to defend against the Soviet ICBM threat to our Minuteman force. The DOD investment cost of this option would be $6 billion (including Phase 1).

The effectiveness of option 2C against the Chinese ICBM threat is expected to be very high. If the Chinese deploy a force of only thirty ICBMs on launchers by mid-1976, they could inflict about 15 million fatalities on us—if we had no ABM defense. With option 2C deployed, fatalities could be held to less than one million. And, even if they were to deploy as many as seventy-five ICBMs on launchers by the end of the decade, fatalities could still be held to less than one million, particularly if the improved Spartan is deployed. Here again, the deployment of Safeguard would have a very large payoff, if the Chinese ICBM threat should, in fact, emerge.

If we fully deploy the Safeguard system against all three of the threats I have discussed, the total DOD investment cost would be $6.6 billion, about $600 million more than currently estimated for the Sentinel system. Adding the estimated $2.5 billion of RDT&E costs specifically associated with the Safeguard program, the total DOD cost would amount to $9.1 billion. This leaves the warhead costs to be considered. According to the AEC, these costs would amount to about $1.2 billion, including the costs of all of the facilities required for development and test. The incremental investment cost incident to the deployment of the system, *i.e.,* the cost of producing the warheads alone, would only amount to about $0.2 billion. What proportion of the remaining costs should properly be charged to the Safeguard program is problematical. Some of the new AEC facilities being constructed for the Safeguard program can be used for other development and test programs. Moreover, the special nuclear materials involved are recoverable. But, even if we charge off the entire $1.2 billion of AEC costs to the Safeguard program, the total would amount to $10.3 billion.

If we should later decide to extend the Safeguard system to Alaska and Hawaii, another $450 to $500 million would have to be added to this total.

The annual operating cost of the fully deployed system is estimated to be about $350 million a year.

F. STRATEGIC AND FOREIGN-POLICY CONSIDERATIONS

For many years, and over several administrations, this nation's strategic nuclear war policies have been squarely based on the proposition that the other great nuclear power in the world, the Soviet Union, must under all foreseeable conditions be deterred from ever attempting a first strike on the United States. The terminology employed in describing this policy has varied over the years, but its essence has remained unchanged: we must always be in a position where we can inflict unacceptable damage on the Soviet Union, even after absorbing the first blow. In more recent times, this capability has been labeled "assured destruction," and I am sure that the members of this committee understand the meaning of that term: it was certainly pounded home to us often enough by my distinguished predecessor, Robert McNamara.

The issue that now confronts the nation is how best to ensure that deterrent (or assured destruction) power through the 1970s. If the Soviets continue on the course they are now following, and I am speaking here of what they are actually doing and not what we think they intend to do, the survival of two of the three major elements of our strategic offensive forces, namely, the bombers and the land-based ICBMs, could be gravely endangered. To rely on only one of the three major elements would, in my considered judgment, be far too risky, considering the stake involved, which is the very survival of our nation. It is perfectly apparent, therefore, that something more must be done, and in view of the lead-times involved, done fairly soon.

One possibility, of course, is an agreement with the Soviet Union on the limitation of strategic armaments. I wholeheartedly support that objective, and we should do everything in our power to achieve a suitable agreement. But we must recognize that the issues involved are extremely complex and, even with the best of goodwill on both sides, it will be very difficult to work out an arrangement which truly safeguards the security of our respective nations.

Meanwhile, we have to deal with the world as it is today. Until an acceptable arrangement is achieved, we must continue to ensure the sufficiency of our deterrent. As I noted earlier, we can do this by increasing our strategic offensive forces. But we feel that this course would simply accelerate the arms race with the Soviet Union. And it would not solve the problem of the other threat looming on the horizon; namely, the prospect that the Chinese Communists will deploy an ICBM force. Nor would it provide protection against the possibility of an accidental

ICBM launch against the United States, or an intimidation attack with a few missiles.

The only single program which can cope with all of these contingencies is Safeguard. It can ensure the survival of the minimum required number of land-based ICBMs and bombers; it can provide a very high degree of protection for our population against the kind of attack the Chinese Communists may be capable of launching in the 1970s; and it can defend the nation against an accidental ICBM launch or an intimidation attack. While there might be some question as to whether it would be worth $10 billion to place ourselves in a position to defend against any one of these potential threats, there can be no question but that it would be well worth that amount of money to be able to defend ourselves against all of these threats.

We see no reason why a decision to move forward with Phase 1 of the Safeguard program should in any way impede the forthcoming talks with the Soviet Union on strategic armaments limitation. Let me remind you that only a few days after the Senate had approved the Sentinel program last year, following many dire warnings that such an approval would wreck the chances for strategic arms talks, the Soviets announced their readiness to start such talks. And, they have displayed no loss of interest in the ratification of the Non-Proliferation Treaty.

Furthermore, as I noted earlier, the Soviet Union has been deploying an ABM system around Moscow, and they are continuing their work on more advanced ABMs. I think it is entirely possible, therefore, that the Soviet Union may want to provide for some minimum ABM defense in any agreement they reach with us on the limitation of strategic armaments. The Soviet leaders have traditionally laid great stress on defense, particularly the defense of Moscow, and I doubt very much that they would be willing to dismantle the existing Galosh ABM system around that city.

113

Thus, it is entirely possible that a Soviet-United States agreement on strategic arms limitations might provide for a limited ABM defense on both sides. I myself can see no objection to such an arrangement, especially in the face of a situation where our cities could become hostage to the Chinese Communists. I recognize that we plan to continue to rely on our deterrent to protect our cities against a Soviet attack in the 1970s, but that is because we have no better alternative. Against the Chinese Communist ICBM threat, however, we do have a better alternative, and that is the deployment of the Safeguard system. I think we would be foolhardy not to employ it, if that threat does indeed begin to emerge.

With regard to other foreign-policy implications of a decision to deploy Safeguard, we believe that "on balance" the advantages far exceed the disadvantages. This would be particularly true with respect to the free world position in Asia. Once Communist China acquires a force of medium-range bombers and/or ballistic missiles, all of her neighbors would be open to nuclear blackmail. Should Communist China then also acquire an ICBM force with which it can threaten our cities, and we have no defense against it, the President of the United States would have no alternative but to back down or risk the destruction of several of our major cities in any serious confrontation with Communist China.

Furthermore, as former Secretary of Defense McNamara pointed out last year in his discussion of the Sentinel program, "It would provide an additional indication to the people of Asia that we intend to support them against nuclear blackmail from China, and thus help to convince the nonnuclear countries that acquisition of their own nuclear weapons is not required for their security."

With regard to our allies in Europe, the Johnson administration's decision to deploy the Sentinel system did not have any important repercussions one way or the other. The issue of an

ABM defense for Western Europe was discussed with our allies and it was concluded that the threat was so great and varied that even an extensive deployment might not be able to prevent great damage from the kind of attack the Soviets could mount over the next several years.

However, some of our NATO allies have expressed concern about the impact of such a decision on the prospects for a détente in Europe. But, as I just pointed out, the decision of the U.S. Congress last year to support the Sentinel program did not have any perceptible adverse effect on the Soviet Union's attitude toward the Non-Proliferation Treaty or the strategic arms limitation talks. I doubt that a decision to proceed with Safeguard will have any bearing on their attitude toward a détente in Europe.

Canada, on the military level, has shown great interest in our ABM defense program, although it is not considered a part of the United States–Canadian NORAD system. But at the political level the interest is less pronounced. It is my impression that the Canadian government has decided to adopt a noncommittal position on this issue. We do have an obligation to keep the Canadian government, and our other NATO allies, informed of our ABM defense plans, and we are meeting that obligation.

Thus, from a foreign-policy point of view, we see no adverse implications in a decision to go forward with the deployment of Safeguard. And, certainly, this is true with respect to Phase 1, the deployment of which would simply place us in a better position to move forward promptly if it should later become necessary to deploy the whole system.

G. SUMMARY AND CONCLUSIONS

Mr. Chairman and members of the committee, I have outlined here today the reasons why the Nixon administration has reached the conclusion that we should move forward at this time with the deployment of at least Phase 1 of the Safeguard system. I have presented to you the facts and the analyses upon which that conclusion was based. The choices now open to you are the same ones which President Nixon had to confront in reaching his decision in March:

1. Continue the Sentinel program proposed by the preceding administration two years ago and approved by the Congress last year.
2. Cancel that program and revert to R & D only.
3. Modify that program to bring it into better balance with the threats as they now appear to be developing.

The President rejected the first choice because the Sentinel program was not geared to the threats as they were actually evolving. He rejected the second choice because he was convinced that the Soviet threat to our bombers and land-based missiles was more imminent than previously assumed, and that the Chinese threat to our cities would ultimately emerge, albeit later than originally estimated. He adopted the third choice because the deployment of an ABM defense at this time would be the best response to both of these threats, and, in addition, would provide protection against an accidental ICBM launch or an intimidation attack on the United States. Because neither of these threats might develop as fast or to the full extent presently estimated, he decided to pace the deployment of the Safeguard system to the actual emergence of these threats and request the Congress to approve only Phase 1 of the system at this time.

I can assure this committee that we have carefully considered the feasibility of delaying the deployment of Phase 1. In fact, initiation of deployment has already been delayed by more than a year compared with the Sentinel schedule. I have, on my own initiative, held up all construction work on ABM sites and any further acquisition of land for these sites, pending a congressional decision on this program. But production had already been started by the time the Nixon administration took office. Had we terminated production, we would, in effect, have preempted the congressional decision on deployment. The labor force would have had to be laid off and the contractors reimbursed for costs already incurred. As a result, we would not now be in a position to start deployment promptly, even if the Congress approves the program in the current session. Aside from the waste of public funds involved, this course of action would have delayed the program by at least one extra year.

If we put off the deployment decision until next year, we would delay the completion of the program by at least two years, from the spring of 1976 to the spring of 1978. This choice appears to us to be far too risky since both the Chinese threat to our population and particularly the Soviet threat to our bomber and land-based missile forces are likely to emerge considerably before that time, perhaps as early as 1974–75. Furthermore, it would entail all of the waste and delays involved in terminating production.

It has also been suggested by some people that we complete the test program at Kwajalein before we initiate deployment. The thought here is that we would know much more about the effectiveness of the system, and thus be in a much better position to decide whether it is worth deploying. Aside from the fact that we would have to cut back drastically the Safeguard R & D effort as well as terminate production, it would delay completion of deployment until the end of the 1970s, far too late in relation to our current estimates of the threat.

Moreover, the Kwajalein tests will not answer all the questions involved in the actual deployment of an operational system. Only a prototype operational site can answer those questions.

117

So, to those who are concerned about whether the Safeguard system will work, I would say let us deploy Phase 1 and find out. Only in this way can we be sure to uncover all of the operating problems that are bound to arise when a new major weapons system is first deployed. Since it will take five years to deploy the first two sites, we will have ample time to find the solutions through our continuing R & D effort to any operational problem which may arise. And only then will we be in a position to move forward promptly, and with confidence, in the event the threat develops to a point where deployment of the entire system becomes necessary.

With regard to technological obsolescence, let me assure you that we have carefully explored all of the various systems which have been proposed by the Navy and Air Force as well as the Army. The radar guided intercept concept, which the Safeguard system employs, is the latest and best technology presently available. No other technology on the horizon promises any better system. With improved terminal guidance, we might be able to substitute nonnuclear for nuclear warheads. We are pursuing this path, but there is a great deal of work yet to be done to prove the feasibility of this concept. We have also looked at the lasers, but they are still quite a way off in the future. Even then, we would still need the Perimeter Acquisition Radars. A number of other advanced technological concepts have been explored, but none of them lies within the required time frame.

In conclusion, Mr. Chairman, we have reviewed very carefully and conscientiously all of the criticism that has been leveled against the Safeguard program and I can assure you that all of the major points raised have been considered at one time or another during the many years this system has been in development. The deployment of Phase 1 would involve a DOD investment cost of $2.1 billion, excluding R & D and AEC costs which would have to be incurred, for the most part, even if we postpone deployment for another year. This represents an average annual expenditure of about $400 million over the next five years. I submit that in view of the great stakes involved, this is a very modest insurance premium, roughly one half of 1 percent of the total defense budget, and considerably less than one twentieth of 1 percent of our current gross national product. Notwithstanding the severe budget stringencies under which the government will have to operate in the next fiscal year, President Nixon found it necessary to recommend this program to the Congress.

Congressional approval of the Phase 1 deployment will give the President the flexibility he needs at this critical juncture in our history. It will strengthen his hand in the forthcoming negotiations with the Soviet Union on the limitation of strategic armaments. If these negotiations do not produce an acceptable agreement, he will be in a position to move promptly to protect our strategic deterrent. In short, the deployment of Phase 1 of the Safeguard program is the very least that we should do at this time to ensure our security in the 1970s.

CHAPTER 4

The Safeguard Decision
before Congress*

John S. Foster, Jr.

John S. Foster has served as Director of Defense Research and Engineering for Defense Secretaries McNamara, Clifford, and now Laird. A physicist and former director of the Lawrence Radiation Laboratory at Livermore, California (1961–63), Dr. Foster has also been a panel consultant of the President's Advisory Council since 1959. His outstanding scientific experience and years of activity as both worker and administrator in vast research and development programs qualify Dr. Foster uniquely to discuss professionally the ABM decision.

My purpose in discussing the Safeguard ballistic missile defense system is to describe briefly why we need it; the issue before Congress and what it turns on; and then to attempt to

---

* Adapted from an address by Dr. John S. Foster, Jr., Director of Defense Research and Engineering, before the Aviation/Space Writers' Association, Sheraton-Dayton Hotel, Dayton, Ohio, May 12, 1969.

set the record straight on some of the technical questions that have tended to dominate public debate.

First the whys of Safeguard.

During the last four years we have observed a rapid growth in the Soviet Union's strategic forces. This growth has resulted in an improvement and expansion of their already massive anti-aircraft defenses, the deployment of a small ABM system, the start of more than one thousand ICBM launchers, and the rapid deployment of more advanced nuclear submarines—both attack and ballistic missile launching. The expansion is continuing.

As we have watched this expansion during the last few years, most of us assumed that the Soviet Union was attempting, logically, to gain strategic parity with the United States. We ourselves have not significantly expanded our forces during this period.

However, more recently the character and number of Soviet offensive weapons have tended in directions that cause us now to doubt most seriously our previous less disturbing assumptions. A continuation of these trends could constitute a threat to our strategic forces—to our land-based ICBMs and to our strategic bombers. The phased development of Safeguard is intended to give us a minimum necessary "hedge" to protect against these contingencies.

The first phase of this operational development is limited to the location of Safeguard at two Minuteman bases. Location at these two sites provides an opportunity to "shake down" such a system—to find and remove those technical and operational bugs that are not likely to show up in research and development efforts. We would be prepared to move to the second phase should the threat continue to increase. We could move in the direction of giving greater coverage to the ICBM force, or to protect our alert B-52s against a submarine-launched ballistic missile attack, or to protect the National Command Authority

121

in Washington, D.C., or to protect our population against a Communist Chinese ICBM attack, or some combination of these options.

If the threat stabilizes, lessens or is negated by arms control talks, the system could be halted. Still, it is extremely important that we understand clearly the issue before the Congress and the consequences of its decision one way or the other.

The question of operational development rests on three key points. First, we are requesting just under $900 million in the 1970 fiscal year to continue development, test, and initial installation. Of this, about half of the money is for development, test, and the necessary supervision; and the remainder for installation of equipment. The Safeguard decision, therefore, involves the authorization and appropriation of an incremental, $450 to $500 million—less than 1 percent of the Defense Department's budget request for this year. In fact, expenditures for 1970 would be reduced by only about $250 million, but the ultimate over-all Department of Defense cost for the completed Phase I would increase some $250 million.

Second, it is important to maintain continuity of this hedge against the still evolving threats. Ever since the approval by Congress, and Secretary McNamara's decision in 1967, to proceed with the development of a ballistic missile defense system (this system was named Sentinel and was conceived primarily as a defense of American cities and primarily oriented against a possible Chinese Communist nuclear attack), we have been building up our capability to produce and install these components. If authorization to continue selection of sites were delayed until next year, the current capability would decay, and we would lose not just one year but two or more years. Without authority for production and deployment, we would have to close our developmental production lines, discharge our production personnel and cease our engineering at installation sites.

Later, if authority was granted to reinitiate production, site acquisition, and on-site engineering and construction, we would have to reengage the necessary personnel and train them before productive work could be accomplished. This means that the first two sites could not be in operation until 1976 at the earliest, instead of 1974. If at the same time, the Soviets continue on their present course, they could have another hundred SS-9 missiles making a total perhaps of 500, with up to 1,500 warheads to attack our 1,000 Minuteman. We would then be defending with too little too late.

The third and final key point on which the ABM issue rests is our desire to negotiate with the Soviet Union and end the strategic nuclear arms race. President Nixon has been quite clear on this point:

I have taken cognizance of the view that beginning construction of a U.S. ballistic missile defense would complicate an agreement on strategic arms with the Soviet Union.

I do not believe that the evidence of the recent past bears out this contention. The Soviet interest in strategic talks was not deterred by the decision of the previous administration to deploy the Sentinel ABM system—in fact, it was formally announced shortly afterwards. I believe that the modifications we have made in the previous program will give the Soviet Union even less reason to view our defense effort as an obstacle to talks. Moreover, I wish to emphasize that in any arms limitation talks with the Soviet Union, the United States will be fully prepared to discuss limitations on defensive as well as offensive weapons systems.

In summary, the President has decided that we should take this minimum step consistent with preserving our security and

123

enhancing the chances for meaningful negotiation with the Soviet Union. Failure to take the step could not only endanger our security in the mid-seventies but also weaken our negotiating position in the immediate future.

The Safeguard issue is complicated by genuine uncertainties over Soviet intentions, and unnecessary confusion over technical and tactical problems. What is most remarkable in the public debate is the high level of confusion and misunderstanding which exists in the minds of some professionals, as well as some nonprofessionals. For example, regarding the Soviet threat, the following quotation is from the recent book *ABM,* edited by Professors Chayes and Wiesner.[1]

It is important to understand that these assertions by Secretary Laird are not based on any intelligence about new Soviet weapons systems. They represent his interpretation of facts that have, in the main, been known for some time, but have not been viewed heretofore by the responsible officials as signaling a Soviet attempt to attain a first-strike capability.

On the other hand, former Secretary of Defense Clark Clifford concluded in his January 1969 statement on the budget for the 1970 fiscal year: "It is quite apparent from the foregoing review of the threat that the Soviet Union is moving vigorously to catch up with the United States at least in *numbers* of strategic missiles—both land-based and sea-based."[2]

[1] Abram Chayes and Jerome B. Wiesner, eds., *ABM: An Evaluation of the Decision to Deploy an Antiballistic Missile System* (New York: Harper & Row, 1969).

[2] Statement prepared for Congress by outgoing Secretary of Defense Clark M. Clifford, on January 15, 1969, providing "the general setting and rationale for the major program proposals contained in the FY 1970 Defense Budget."

Implicit in Secretary Clifford's conclusion is that the Soviets would level off when they "catch up." The subsequent evaluation of intelligence obtained earlier than his statement and intelligence received subsequently reveals both that the Soviets are moving even faster than anticipated and that, having passed the assumed leveling off point, their expansion programs are continuing unabated.

Secretary Laird's statements are based upon intelligence data on which there is general agreement. I know of no disagreement on the approximate number of SS-9s being built by the Soviet Union, nor of any significant issue in the size of its payload. Intelligence and policy specialists agree on the existence of new submarines and their approximate rate of deployment. No person who has seen the data objects to the conclusion that the SS-9 has been tested with multiple warhead reentry vehicles, and the community agrees on an approximate weight of these vehicles.

We do not know just how effectively these could attack the present U.S. land-based Minuteman silos since we do not know precisely their accuracy. But, their testing is continuing.

Also, we do not know how many SS-9s the Soviets will finally build. Perhaps the Soviets themselves haven't decided. But we do have a good idea of the number they could build in any given time at the recent rate, and we do have a good idea of the accuracy they might achieve.

President Johnson and Secretary McNamara saw only the beginning of the SS-9 build-up when the Sentinel system was started in 1967, but even at that time the option to defend the Minuteman was designed into that plan. To quote Mr. McNamara in September 1967: "Further, the Chinese-oriented ABM deployment would enable us to add—as a concurrent benefit—a further defense of our Minuteman sites against Soviet attack."

125

Secretary Clifford requested, and the Congress granted, funds to maintain that option.

The Chayes-Wiesner ABM book also argues that "a successful first strike against United States retaliatory forces is today an impossibility." To make this argument the book seems to play a strange numbers game. At one point the book states: "With our Minutemen in hardened silos, it would take at least two attacking ICBMs to be reasonably sure of destroying one Minuteman."

An ICBM with three independently aimed warheads can attack three silos. The United States has designed, but not deployed, a system that allows a missile to signal the launch-control point if it has launched its reentry vehicle properly. With this system, the control point could reprogram another missile to make up for failures. For example, a missile system having a 20 percent failure rate and carrying three reentry vehicles per missile would require only 420 missiles to attack one thousand silos.[3] If the yield of each reentry vehicle was a reasonable five megatons and the accuracy a reasonable quarter of a mile, about 95 percent of the silos could be destroyed. This would mean fifty of the thousand Minutemen would survive. It would be foolish to attack half of the silos twice as the book advised, rather than all of them once.

The same strange numbers game is played relative to one missile site defense. To quote from the Chayes-Wiesner book again:

It would take three missiles with 30 percent failure probability to destroy an incoming warhead with 97 percent certainty. Some such requirement must be incorporated

[3] Such a force would have 1,260 reentry vehicles. With a 20 percent failure rate one reentry vehicle would reach each of a thousand silos.

into the firing doctrine for any ABM defense of cities, radars, or bomber bases, and this uses up the defensive missiles at a fearsome rate.

Professor Steven Weinberg indicates in his contribution to the Chayes-Wiesner book that sequential firing of the interceptors would eliminate this problem in that if the first interceptor destroyed the incoming reentry vehicle, no other need be fired. He considers this very difficult. It is not. This is just the tactic which we will use and we have planned to use for many years. It is feasible. Furthermore, we expect a missile failure rate that would be considerably less than his assumed 30 percent. Results of Nike, Spartan and Sprint missile firings to date support our expectation. Of those missiles that fail, almost all occur early in flight. Should one fail, we would fire another. Sufficient time is available.

We also find the statement: "But that system [Sentinel] was designed for a wholly different purpose. . . ."

This quotation is part of a much longer charge implying that the Safeguard components were not designed to defend Minuteman. This is just not true. The Nike-X R & D program upon which both Sentinel and Safeguard were based, always had a Sprint missile for point defense of targets, specifically Minutemen and cities. We have, from time to time, examined specialized systems, designed only to hard-point defense, with the hope that we could find something much cheaper or much better. But we haven't found it. Sprint was designed for this job and will do it.

Another statement reads: "It has been authoritatively suggested that it just may be impossible during the next years to write a computer program for dealing with the various forms of attack that can be anticipated."

Programming (the instruction built into the computer which

analyzes the attack and provides appropriate responses) of large computer-controlled systems is difficult. But, we have had considerable relevant experience, and our experience shows us that it can be done. The systems cited as horrible examples were pioneering new ground, but they eventually worked quite well. A recent example is the Air Force Space Track Radar recently completed. It is very similar to the Perimeter Acquisition Radar (PAR) radar in its operation; it has one of the largest real time computer programs ever written and contains almost a million instructions. It was built on schedule and within cost estimates—including the computer programming. The radar and its computer program are now operational, and the system is being operated and maintained by Air Force crews. In the case of Safeguard, we are allowing a year to test and assure operability of the hardware with the computer.

The Chayes-Wiesner book in many places also claims that a defense can be easily countered by simple penetration devices or by "blackout" attacks.

These "simple" devices simply are not simple. We know that the United States has attempted to field operational penetration aids for the last decade, and we are only now beginning to have workable ones in our forces. We use them to force the Soviets to install a complicated and more expensive defense—we do not depend on them to assure our penetration capability. The devices—and the tactics—will require more resources than the Communist Chinese will have available for a considerable time. Also, the Chinese have yet to achieve their first-generation ICBM. They do not know and do not yet have what it takes to develop and deploy penetration aides and tactics against a system as advanced as Safeguard. In regard to the Soviets, the penetration tactics are not very useful for an attack on the Minuteman force, and for that reason the Soviets would be wasting their time with them. Light penetration aids and extensive high-altitude blackout will not have much effect on a Sprint defense which takes place in the atmosphere.

Professor Wolfgang Panofsky, professor of physics at Stanford University, has recently asked how many Minutemen could be saved by Phase I of Safeguard.

There are attacks for which the testing phase will save a respectable number of missiles. The maximum number is associated with the number of interceptors—a number that is classified for obvious reasons. However, I think it is a mistake to consider Phase I in just such terms. Phase I has two basic functions. It is first a step that will prepare us to react rapidly to any further development of the threat. It prepares sites and production facilities necessary for increasing the number of interceptors and possibly radars, if a threat continues to develop.

Secondly, the testing phase of Safeguard provides a checkout, a shakedown, of an integrated ABM system. What we learn here will affect future improvements of the system.

Professor Panofsky recently inquired whether the Safeguard system forms an economically feasible defense against a heavy threat to the Minuteman force. Various estimates of the cost of an interceptor, including its assigned fraction of the radar and other systems cost, have varied between $2.5 million and $7 million. The present cost to the United States and probably the Soviet Union for an offensive RV is in excess of $10 million. The advances which we expect in our forces over the next few years may reduce these to about $3 million. There is little hope they will ever get as low as $2 million. In other words, the cost to attack and to defend in the 1970s appears roughly one to one. Whether or not it turns out in, say, 1975, to favor the offense or the defense depends on just what improvements the Soviets achieve, as well as on our own experience with the actual production and operation of our defensive system.

The Safeguard system has been designed by competent people

129

—the best that are available. Its design has been reviewed by outside experts. Those who do study the aspects of the system that are within their area of technical expertise are convinced it will do what it is designed to do. There are some eminent scientists who, for one reason or other, claim it won't work.[4] On that, I would like to state, first, that they have offered no problem which we have not long since addressed and resolved. Second, I want to point out that one does not obtain a meaningful technical judgment by taking a vote of the scientific community. This would go to the second warning against misplaced power mentioned by President Eisenhower in his often quoted farewell message: "Yet, in holding scientific research and discovery in respect as we should, we must also be alert to the equal and opposite danger that public policy could itself become the captive of a scientific-technological elite."

[4] See Chapter 11 Dr. William G. McMillan and Dr. Albert Wohlstetter for analysis supporting the feasibility of Safeguard and Dr. Jerome B. Wiesner for contrary analysis.

CHAPTER 5

Negotiating the Future

Senator Henry M. Jackson

*Henry M. Jackson has earned a national reputation as an
informed leader in military and foreign affairs. Highly respected in defense debates, he is a member of the Senate
Armed Services Committee (member of the Central Intelligence Agency "watchdog" Subcommittee); the Joint Atomic
Energy Committee (chairman of the Subcommittee on Atomic
Weapons); and the Government Operations Committee (chair-
man of the Subcommittee on National Security and International Operations). With his congressional inquiries of the
National Security Council, the State Department, the Atlantic
Alliance, and Planning-Programming-Budgeting, Senator
Jackson has become a leading Senate authority on the con-
duct of national security policy. Known, too, for his vigorous
sponsorship of progressive legislation, as chairman of the
Senate Interior and Insular Affairs Committee since 1963,
Senator Jackson has been instrumental in the passage of
much key conservation legislation. Senator Jackson has been
Democratic U.S. Senator from Washington since 1953 and*

was for twelve years before that a member of the House of Representatives.

Negotiation with adversaries is difficult and dangerous. If we are going to negotiate successfully in the future, we must learn how to take advantage of opportunities for dealing with adversaries while avoiding the pitfalls and booby traps of negotiation.

I can think of nothing more important at this time than clear thinking about this subject. One cannot read the newspapers these days without finding evidence of some dangerous misconceptions about negotiation.

Negotiation with Communists is a form of struggle. If need be, I could cite the usual sources to show that this is how the high priests of communism describe negotiation. For example, Lenin, who had obviously studied his Clausewitz; put it this way: ". . . every war is the continuation of the policy conducted in peace, only by other means; . . . the concessions which we grant, which we are forced to grant, are the continuation of war in another form, by other means."

Stalin was pithier. In contemptuously dismissing a suggestion that had been made on behalf of the Pope, he asked: "How many divisions does the Pope have?"

I would not attach importance to such statements just because they have been made. The Communists say many things for effect. But on reading of the historical record this view of negotiation finds expression and confirmation in communist practice in the conference room. This is borne out in a fascinating collection of analytic papers entitled "The Soviet Approach to Negotiation: Selected Writings," compiled by the Subcommittee on National Security and International Operations, which I chair. The Soviets do, in fact, behave as if negotiation were a form of struggle and discuss the art of negotiation in military terms.

The Communist takes pride in his realism and on the power of Marxism-Leninism to explain historical development. Through Marxist-Leninist spectacles he sees the history of our times as a continuing struggle between the forces of reaction and the forces of revolution. Although victory for the latter is assured, he believes, in the long run the Communist expects to suffer reverses as well as to score advances along the way to utopia. On occasion negotiation is a useful tactic or maneuver. Sometimes conditions call for retreat, sometimes for an armistice, sometimes for the dictation of terms of surrender to an enemy. In skillful hands negotiation may gain time, when that is desirable, or make possible an orderly retreat to new positions, when that is necessary, or, whatever the circumstances, help to prepare the ground for the next phase of the struggle.

We need to recognize a fundamental philosophical division between ourselves and our adversaries on this matter. We are less likely to make mistakes if we understand that while our side is trying to end conflict and make peace, the other side is continuing and waging conflict. It does not follow, of course, that we should not negotiate or that successful negotiation is not in the cards. A number of satisfactory agreements prove the opposite—for example, the Austrian Peace Treaty and the limited nuclear Test Ban Treaty. For if the Kremlin sees no advantageous alternative to a negotiated settlement in a given situation, it may accept a limited, expedient arrangement.

Sir William Hayter, former British Ambassador to Moscow, has said: "The Russians are not to be persuaded by eloquence or convinced by reasoned arguments. They rely on what Stalin used to call the proper basis of international policy, the calculation of forces." Stalin's view remains authoritative. Valerian Zorin recently wrote that "as a rule, the success of the diplomatic activity of the Soviet Union is determined above all by a correct Marxist-Leninist analysis of the situation and of the correlation of forces. . . ."

In all conflict the target is the will of the adversary. This is as true of the conference table as of the battlefield. To defeat an adversary is to bring him to an inner conviction that he cannot do what he wants to do and that he has no better course open to him than the acknowledgment of this fact of life. Defeat may be defined as the lack of an advantageous alternative to settlement on the adversary's terms.

In 1948–49 the success of the Berlin airlift led to the lifting of the Berlin blockade. Over the course of a year it became clear to Stalin that more drastic measures than a blockade would be required to cut off the flow of essential supplies to the city. Such measures, he decided, entailed too great a risk of war. Furthermore, the psychology of the situation was working against him. The blockade was accelerating the formation of the Atlantic Alliance, the strengthening of Western defenses, and the shift of West Germany from the status of an ex-enemy to that of a potential Western ally. The Soviets wanted, then as now, to get the West out of Berlin, but as it dawned on them that they could not do what they wanted at a price they were prepared to pay, they looked for and quickly found a way out. A footnote might be added: Once they had made up their minds, they were not held back by considerations of "face."

In mid-1951, U.S., South Korean and allied U.N. forces were driving the Chinese and North Korean forces north and inflicting heavy losses. The enemy made known his willingness to talk about an armistice. We agreed, and once talks began, we relaxed the military pressure. Admiral Joy has described the consequences of this decision as follows:

> On orders from Washington we eventually agreed to a provisional truce line with a thirty-day time limit, thereby giving the Communists a respite from United Nations Command military pressure. This allowed the Communists

a sorely needed breathing spell in which to dig in and stabilize their battle line. Consequently, they were able to haggle and delay in respect to subsequent agenda items, free from the compulsion of impending military disaster.

More recently, we have witnessed the tragic drama of Czechoslovakia "negotiating" the continuing subjugation of her people with the Soviet Union. In the spring and summer of 1968 the Soviet Union applied mounting pressure to Czechoslovakia. Talk did not produce results satisfactory to the Soviets, and they intervened with force. But the use of force, even in such circumstances, is risky and may be counterproductive, remembering that the target is the enemy's will. Informed Czechs knew what to expect. The visibility of the Soviet military forces was reduced, and the Soviets began to apply pressure to the helpless victim, though slowly enough, as one Czech put it, that no one would hear the bones crack. The process is now virtually complete, for the time being. It is an example of the application of the Brezhnev doctrine that the rest of us might well ponder. Czechoslovakia, a rueful Czech observed, is the most neutral country in the world; it does not even intervene in its own affairs.

One example after another could be cited—from Iran in 1945–46 to Vietnam in 1969—to demonstrate that the Soviets are not to be persuaded by reason or eloquence but by their calculation of forces, by their correct Marxist-Leninist analysis of the "objective conditions." In this sense they are realists, bending when circumstances are unfavorable, demanding when the correlation of forces favors them, seeing one move in relation to others in a single game, using negotiation to retreat there and advance here, there to cloak their purposes and here to confuse and divide their adversaries, there to heat things up and here to cool them while they quietly intensify their efforts

135

to produce conditions conducive to the accomplishment of their ambitions.

What is surprising is how many citizens of our free society are taken in by all this. Bargaining is such a familiar part of our day-to-day experience that we should have, one would think, an intuitive understanding of the problem of dealing with the Soviets—or others.

Over and over again, however, we have heard and read that before deciding to go ahead with the Safeguard ABM program, we should negotiate with the Soviet Union.

Why one or the other?

Why not both?

It is of the greatest importance that a way be found to halt the further evolution of strategic armaments. I see no way to do it other than through mutual, reciprocal action by the Soviets and ourselves. As Paul Nitze says, the assumption that if we refrain from taking an action, the Soviets, in the absence of an agreement to do so, will refrain from taking a similar action is not supported by any experience we have had in the past with the Soviets or any reasonable forecast of their future action. I see no good alternative to taking the actions necessary to give the United States unquestioned assurance of deterrence in the absence of an agreement with the Soviet Union for reciprocal limitations on offensive and defensive nuclear systems.

There are two current Soviet developments that threaten the credibility of our land-based missile deterrent in the time period of 1974–76—the Soviets' ballistic missile defense systems, and their steady installation of the big SS-9 missile with a capacity of twenty to twenty-five megatons, on which they are testing multiple warheads.

The huge Soviet SS-9 carrying multiple warheads each aimed precisely at a different target could be used against the U.S. land-based Minuteman system. The hard truth is that by the

136

mid-1970s, unless we continue to make appropriate decisions to meet technological change, the viability of a very important part of our second-strike force will be put in question.

Given the lead-time factor for the ABM system of five to seven years, continuing research and development only, without any start now on site preparation, would leave us with no option to provide defense for our deterrent on the schedule that may be essential if we do not reach an agreement with the Soviets on limiting or reducing strategic forces. If the Soviets should slam the door on a strategic arms limitation agreement, the Safeguard ABM program would permit us to continue orderly steps toward protection of vital elements of our retaliatory forces.

The Safeguard ABM system is designed and planned to meet the threats as they may develop, without overreacting, and is subject to annual review. The major components of the Safeguard system have received elaborate study and testing. Ideas for brand-new ABM systems to defend hard points are not serious competitors in the time period we are talking about. We can expect, as in the tests of every other offense and defense system, that we shall learn a great deal from experience in controlled tests, and we should expect to make some changes and improvements as we go along. As Dr. William McMillan said to the Senate Armed Services Committee: "We can ill afford to allow an important gap to develop in the learning process concerning such an important capability."

Furthermore, why is it difficult to understand that President Nixon would be in a much stronger position in the arms negotiations with the Soviet Union if we proceed with the Safeguard ABM program? To arrive at successful, reciprocal, and mutually acceptable agreement involving both offensive and defensive nuclear systems will, in any event, be enormously difficult. The negotiations are bound to be long-drawn-out and will involve

137

the most rigorous bargaining by Moscow for relative advantage. Does anyone really believe that the Soviets will agree to limit or reduce their ABM deployment if we unilaterally abandon all deployment of our ABMs? If we do not have *our* ABM system moving along, what incentive would we give the Soviets to negotiate with us on a freeze or a reduction in *their* ABM deployment? If American negotiators are confronted with a situation where the Soviet negotiators believe time is running on the Soviet side, our negotiators will be up against extremely adverse odds.

Under these circumstances, I see no sensible alternative to proceeding with the ABM Safeguard system.

President Nixon believes he has the best chance of arriving at an agreement satisfactory to the United States in arms control negotiations if we go ahead with Safeguard. I agree with that analysis.

I am a Democrat. But I am proud that over the years I have supported our President, whether he was a Democrat or a Republican, in the critical decisions to promote the security of our country and to try to halt the further evolution of strategic armaments by mutual agreement with the Soviet Union.

As a general proposition, I suggest that if you want to get an agreement with an adversary, do those things that would be necessary and desirable in the absence of agreement. This is really a corollary of the ancient dictum "Who would desire peace should be prepared for war." That was said in 375 B.C. The ancients knew some things that only Bartlett seems to remember.

The United States needs to learn to do two things simultaneously: to seek agreement with the Soviet Union where its interests and ours converge and, at the same time, to maintain the strength and the resolve to discourage and deter Soviet adventurism.

If I were to award a prize for the most foolish criticism of American foreign policy, I would nominate the *critics* of negotiating from strong positions. Do they recommend that we negotiate from weak positions? The idea is absurd. Preparation for negotiation is always more difficult than the negotiation itself, painful and frustrating as that often is, for preparation requires the creation of conditions in which one has an acceptable alternative to agreement and in which one's adversary can find no advantageous alternative to a negotiated agreement.

Obviously, one should not ask for more than one needs. In that connection our requirements are small. They are that the outcome of negotiated agreements should improve, not worsen, the chances for building a peaceful world.

I confess to a strong predisposition in favor of prudence in providing for our national defense—given the nature of the Soviet adversary. I do not know how to assess the Soviet Union except as an opportunistic, unpredictable, dangerous opponent with rapidly expanding military capabilities.

The U.S.-Soviet relationship is not symmetrical. The West has been, and is, on the political defensive. The Soviet Union is on the political offensive in respect to the noncommunist world. I do not think they look at their problem from the point of view of *deterring* the United States. Their problem is that, knowing they are on the political offensive, they see the risk that there may be of a nuclear war in the future. If there is to be a nuclear war, they want to see to it that the outcome of that nuclear war is basically favorable to them and unfavorable to us. They are hard at work on all kinds of military programs, including the very large SS-9 missiles, in order to be in the most favorable position possible if a nuclear war comes.

In this connection, one gets no comfort from this year's chilling article by General Alexei Yepishev, chief political commissar of the Soviet armed forces who was Stalin's assistant

139

minister of state security in the dreadful Doctors' Plot period. Yepishev, writing in *Kommunist*, the official Communist party journal, says that "classical Leninist teaching" on the inevitability of "a series of frightful clashes" between communism and the West still applies in the nuclear age and that World War III would "guarantee the construction of socialism and communism."

If anyone had any doubt about the importance of Moscow's modern weaponry in implementing its political purposes, the tragedy of Czechoslovakia should dispel the doubt.

In military terms the Soviet thrust into Czechoslovakia proved what they can do overnight—when unopposed. The Soviet capability that was exercised so impressively in Czechoslovakia—under the protection of the powerful and expanding Soviet nuclear-missile forces—is ready for employment on other tasks. And it is now clear that this Soviet military capability is available for use not only against long-acknowledged adversaries in the free world but against communist comrades as well.

Also disturbing are the increasing signs in the Soviet Union of a move to the reactionary right and to a Stalin-like suppression of dissent. Jews, scholars, writers, poets and others, are being subjected to vicious denunciation and censorship in the name of communist orthodoxy. There are more intellectuals in Soviet prisons now than at any time since Stalin's terror. The influence of the Stalinist-type political commissars appears to be on the rise in Moscow.

The policy in Moscow which prompted the invasion and subjugation of Czechoslovakia was not undertaken by rulers confident of the stability of their so-called commonwealth in Eastern Europe or of their regime at home. On the contrary, it suggests a deep fear that the urge for freedom that has appeared in Eastern Europe might spread within the Soviet Union itself. The Soviet rulers have a bear by the tail. We cannot discount the danger that an harassed, nervous, and temporarily

140

ascendant Kremlin faction will take dangerous risks and make serious errors of judgment in its conduct of foreign affairs.

Hence, there is everything to be said for steady strength on our part.

It is clear to me that World War II might have been avoidable had the Western democracies stood firm and taken the precautionary defensive steps to persuade Hitler to take their firmness seriously. This is what Winston Churchill had in mind when he called World War II the "unnecessary war." In the nuclear age the world cannot afford another unnecessary war.

General George Marshall wrote in 1945:

We finish each bloody war with a feeling of acute revulsion against the savage form of human behavior, and yet on each occasion we confuse military preparedness with the causes of war and then drift almost deliberately into another catastrophe.

These are words that all Americans should take to heart.

CHAPTER 6

The Rationale
Underlying Soviet Strategic Forces

William T. Lee

William T. Lee has been program manager of the Threat Analysis studies of the Strategic Studies Center of Stanford Research Institute. His academic training was in Russian and Chinese area studies at the University of Washington and Columbia University. As a member of the interdisciplinary Strategic Studies Center, Mr. Lee has headed the "Red Planning Team" portion of the Center for five years. During this period he has been a major contributor to many SRI and Army Studies, including the Threat Analysis Study of 1964; DEPEX, a twenty-year projection of Chinese nuclear capability; the X-66 Study of 1966, in which the first model of a potential Soviet MIRV-equipped SS-9 was generated; and the annual series of Army Strategic Posture Analysis studies, 1966 through the present. Mr. Lee has therefore been intimately acquainted and involved with strategic doctrine, effectiveness calculations, costing of Soviet and Chinese forces, and the economic allocation decision process of both China and the Soviet Union. This document does not constitute an official report of Stanford Research Institute.

Much of the recent public debate on the ABM issue has taken place in a peculiar milieu of Americans talking to Americans. Too often the Soviets have been depicted either as other Americans (albeit in red hats), or as very sinister demons indeed. Projecting one's own values, idealism, guilt feelings, darkest fears, atavistic urges, criteria, and behavior patterns into other societies is not a new phenomenon. It is probably part of the human condition, so nothing final can be done about it. But we can do something to alleviate the problem, and to do one's best in this respect, imperfect as that may be, is much better than nothing.

The problem of understanding people in other cultures has been the subject of recent hearings before the Senate Foreign Relations Committee. In the course of these hearings, Senator Fulbright asked Professor Edward T. Hall of Northwestern University: "If we want the Russians to slow down the arms race, how do we do it?" Professor Hall responded: "It is quite obvious if we read them the way we read ourselves the chances are we are going to read them wrong or, at best, are taking a very great risk." [1]

This paper attempts to read the Russians the way they are, not the way we wish they were, nor the way we wish they were not. The most important thesis of this article is that the Soviet strategic concepts are not mirror images of our own, nor do the Soviets apply identical criteria of weapons system effectiveness. On the subject of the ABM, Premier Kosygin had this to say in 1967:

Q. Doesn't the Soviet Prime Minister share the view that a build-up of a Soviet antimissile defense system is a new step in the arms race? Do you consider that a mora-

[1] The Washington *Post,* June 12, 1969.

torium on antimissile defense build-up is feasible and on what terms?

A. It seems to me that the system that warns of an attack is not a factor in the arms race. On the contrary, it is a factor that reduces the possibility of the destruction of people.

That is why I think it is a mistake to look at this question the way some people do.

According to some theories that are gaining ground in the world, the question is posed in the following way: Which is cheaper, to destroy man, that is, to have an offensive weapon that destroys people, cities, entire states, or to have a weapon that prevents such destruction?

According to these theories, the cheaper system should be adopted. As you know, in some countries they figure in arming the country how much it costs to kill a person $500,000 or $100,000.

The antimissile system probably costs more than an offensive weapon. But these questions are unrelated.

You see, there are other ways of solving this problem, more serious ways that would really help mankind.[2]

In 1964 General N. Talensky, who is generally not considered a Soviet "hardliner," wrote:

There is no need to go into any technical description of these weapons. What is important is that antimissile rockets are designed exclusively for the destruction of enemy rockets and not for hitting any other objectives on the enemy's territory. They are designed to destroy enemy rockets in flight in such a way as to prevent the destruc-

[2] *The New York Times,* February 10, 1967.

144

tion of a nuclear-warhead-carrying rocket from inflicting. damage on the population of one's own country or of allied and neutral states.

Thus, antimissile systems are defensive weapons in the full sense of the word: by their technical nature they go into action only when the rockets of the attacking side take to their flight paths, that is, when the act of aggression has been started. The advantage of antimissile systems in the political and international law context is that their use is caused by an act of aggression, and they will simply not work unless an aggressor's rocket makes its appearance in flight over a given area. There will be no difficulty at all in deciding who is the aggressor and who the attacked.

While nuclear rockets offer only one solution to the problem of attack and defense, namely a nuclear strike, antimissile systems are a new form of nuclear rockets, namely their specifically defensive form. Their task is to destroy the nuclear rocket means of attack as soon as these are set in motion, that is, without striking at the enemy's territory. This is a new factor which must be taken into account.[3]

It is all too easy to mistake a monologue with a mirror, or with a stereotype, for a dialogue. If we really want to get a dialogue going with the Soviets on strategic weapons, we might be well advised to listen to what they say—a common American failure when dealing with foreigners, according to Professor Hall—and to pay attention to what they do.

[3] Reprinted in the *Bulletin of the Atomic Scientists,* February 1965. (General Talensky engaged in a bit of "rocket rattling" in earlier years but seems to have softened a good deal by the 1960s.)

CONTRASTING VIEWS OF THE ADVERSARY

Those who argue the pros and cons of U.S. ballistic missile defense usually have different perceptions of the Soviet Union and to a lesser extent the Chinese Communists, as adversaries. Those who argue against U.S. BMD generally have the following perceptions of the Soviet Union, its nuclear strategies, and policies.

1. The Soviet Union is following the same strategy of assured destruction and pursuing similar policies of limiting the arms race as are advocated (for the United States) by the opponents of U.S. BMD.

2. With the exception of the admitted Soviet preoccupation with air defenses, the Soviet Union has been deploying the same types of weapons systems, and for the same or similar objectives, as has the United States. To the extent the Soviets are different, or would attempt to be different in the future, they can be forced or cajoled into adopting the strategy and policies advanced by U.S. opponents of BMD either by tutoring the Soviet leaders in what is the proper and desirable strategy, or by maintaining an overwhelmingly superior U.S. offensive force, or some combination of the two.

3. Those who advance these arguments implicitly or explicitly think that the Soviets measure their ability to inflict damage on the United States in the same way that we measure our ability to destroy them. This is to argue that both the United States and the Soviet Union have an "equal appetite for fatalities."

4. The Soviet Union is rapidly evolving from a totalitarian into a pluralistic society having virtues, vices, and values similar to those of the United States. Hence, the cold war is over unless the United States forecloses the opportunity for agreement on arms control by going ahead with BMD and MIRV.

146

The Soviet Union is alleged or assumed to have the same view of BMD as do those who oppose it in the United States.

5. The Soviet leaders are interested in stopping the arms race. The only reason they have not been willing to come to an agreement thus far is their inferiority in number of offensive weapons. Hence parity is a prerequisite for successful arms control negotiations. Closely related to this is the argument that the Soviet Union can be counted on to respond in a predictable manner to U.S. initiatives. Thus, if the United States voluntarily limits its offensive and defensive forces, the Soviet Union will follow suit in what has been described as "sympathetic parallelism."

Those who favor the U.S. BMD tend to have the following perception of the adversary.

1. The Soviet Union has quite a different view of strategic objectives and nuclear policy, including the desire to be able to conduct a nuclear war for rational ends (such as survival of the society) should deterrence fail for any reason; having a strategic offensive force capable of significantly reducing the weight of an attack on the Soviet Union should the Soviet leaders become convinced that such an attack is imminent; a belief in the utility and nonprovocative nature of defense (in all forms) against nuclear attack from any quarter.

2. The Soviet Union pursues its own objectives and initiatives in accordance with its own values, strategic objectives, and institutional propensities. Thus, the Soviet Union does not merely respond to U.S. initiatives. Instead of following a course of "sympathetic parallelism" in response to U.S. unilateral initiatives, the Soviet Union may attempt to gain a significant advantage with superior offensive and defensive forces.

3. The Soviet leaders still see a great deal of political utility in nuclear weapons, even if the risks involved are such that the Soviet Union cannot plan to use nuclear war at some predeter-

147

mine'd moment in time as an instrument for bringing the benefits of "Soviet socialism" to other nations.

4. It is not at all certain that the Soviet Union will evolve into a pluralistic society, even though there are identifiable elements that would like to move in this direction. Moreover, even if the Soviet Union is headed for pluralism, the kind of fundamental changes in the regime that are required for mutual confidence and "horse trading" with the United States are at least one generation, and possibly two generations, away.

While this article cannot fully explore all the arguments, particularly the question of convergence, it can attempt to throw some light on Soviet strategic thinking, to note similarities or differences between U.S. and Soviet views on some of the fundamental issues, and to provide some preliminary answers to the question of the consistency of theory and practice in Soviet force posture planning. Hence the article begins with a review of the development of Soviet strategic nuclear doctrine over the past fifteen years.

There are some puzzling anomalies in the Soviet debate on nuclear weapons and in their formulation of strategic doctrine, anomalies that seem to be resolved by a relatively simple concept, namely, the fundamental uncertainty as to which side would be the first to use nuclear weapons in a deep crisis. Soviet formulation of strategic nuclear doctrine is designed to express this uncertainty while avoiding the connotation of premeditated "surprise attack" or "preventive war." To provide as many hedges as possible against the uncertainty as to which side may exercise the initiative if mutual deterrence fails, the Soviets have bought not only a balance of strategic offensive and defensive forces (SOF and SDF) but also have deployed an SOF mix of hard and soft target (capable) systems. In this sense Soviet doctrine and planning appear to be increasingly "open-ended" while U.S. strategy and force planning in the mid-1960s became less flexible and began to foreclose options.

148

THE PASSING OF THE
PERMANENTLY OPERATING FACTORS

In 1954–55, after the death of Stalin, the Soviet military engaged in an extensive debate on the role and effect of nuclear weapons in warfare and what changes in strategy and doctrine were required as a result. Prior to that time Soviet thinking on the subject, or, to be more exact, public thinking on the subject, had been effectively stifled by Stalin's rejection of nuclear weapons as a revolutionary event. This was expressed in his line about the "permanently operating factors" being much more important than any single type of weapon, even thermonuclear bombs.[4]

When the post-Stalin debate on the implications of nuclear weapons for strategy and doctrine appeared in the unclassified journals, two basic schools of thought emerged. One stuck with a slightly modified version of the Stalinist dogma; the other saw the need for fundamental change and formulated a doctrine of "preemption." This debate was reported and analyzed by H. S. Dinerstein, then at Rand.[5] Dinerstein's conclusion was that the "preemptive" school had won out when the debate appeared to have concluded in April 1955. I do not think anyone could argue with this conclusion on the basis of the evidence available.

Nevertheless, a curious anomaly appeared in the fact that the new line was not widely publicized. In the Soviet Union when a debate ends in a decision that one side or the other is right, the winning line is normally promulgated by one

---

[4] Stalin's factors were the stability of the rear; the morale of the Army; the quantity and quality of divisions; the armament of the Army; the organizational ability of the commanders.

[5] *War and the Soviet Union,* R–236, August 1958. This initial post-Stalin debate on nuclear weapons lasted about eighteen months, closing in April 1955.

and all. In this case, there was a curious lack of repetition of the "preemption" line after 1955. During the debate the principal spokesmen for a "preemptive" strategy had been careful to draw the distinction between preemption, in the sense of seizing the initiative, and the surprise attack "out of the blue." Since the term "preemption" acquired the latter connotation in U.S. strategic literature, it is often suggested that the Soviets subsequently avoided the word for that very reason. Nevertheless, it is striking that very little was said on the subject, one way or the other, between mid-1955 and late 1961, at least not in the open press. The principal substantive issues debated at some length during these years were the effect of surprise on the outcome of the war, the possibilities of survival after a nuclear war, and the role of the General Purpose forces. Everyone now agreed that surprise was important, but the degree was the subject of considerable controversy,[6] as was the size of the Ground Forces required.

THE DOCTRINAL DISCUSSIONS
FROM 1955 TO 1961

The published doctrinal debate between mid-1955 and the 22d Party Congress revolved around two questions: the danger of a surprise nuclear attack on the Soviet Union and whether nuclear war would mean the "destruction of world civilization." Discussion of both of these questions was inextricably bound up in the leadership struggle during this period; the public formulations were used as instruments in that struggle, notably by Khrushchev and his allies.

The arguments on the heightened threat of an attack on the Soviet Union by the United States (with or without NATO)

[6] *Ibid.,* Chapter 6.

150

were advanced in the 1955–58 period while Khrushchev and his associates also pushed the line that a nuclear war would be the graveyard of capitalism. Malenkov was forced to recant on his line that nuclear war means the "destruction of world civilization" before his initial demotion. Those political leaders who argued that the socialist camp would inherit the world after a nuclear war did not claim that the Soviet Union would escape unscathed. What they seemed to have in mind was that having emerged from the enormous destruction of World War II as one of the two superpowers, the Soviet Union could hope to do so again even after suffering much heavier damage.

These arguments were not prominent in the military journals in the form of extended debates along the lines of the 1953–55 exchange. Nor did the military leaders come forth with a new military doctrine for the Soviet Union in the nuclear age until 1961. Yet debate and discussion surely continued among the military leaders who, among other things, must have formulated their targeting doctrine prior to 1958 while planning the deployment of some six hundred to seven hundred I/MRBM (intermediate / medium range ballistic missiles) launchers and the initial ICBM deployments. The trends in the military budget and the changes in the size and composition of the military establishment during the period also provide some insight into the Soviet approach to the nuclear age behind the scene of the public polemics.

MILITARY BUDGET STABILITY AND
MANPOWER RETRENCHMENT, 1955–58

Those who have analyzed the Khrushchev-Malenkov arguments, the light and heavy industry dispute between *Pravda* and *Izvestia,* and who followed the debate on the threat of war and its consequences in these years, have usually concluded that Khrushchev and his partisans were increasing the national security budget regularly after 1954. In fact, total national security outlays, which are significantly larger than the explicit item labeled "defense" in the Soviet budget, leveled off during this period and did not begin to increase significantly over the 1954–55 level until 1959.[7] There is no reason to believe that this trend was contrary to Khrushchev's policies. Indeed the change in the military establishment for which he and his intimates appear to have been primarily responsible in the 1955–58 period were designed to reduce all but the R & D outlays in the near term, while laying the ground work (R & D) for the expansion of the missile forces that did require much higher total budgets for the military establishment beginning in 1959.

The Soviet Union reacted rather strongly to the unexpected outcome of the North Korean attack in June 1950 by accelerating the enormous air defense program already under way and roughly doubling the size of the Ground Forces between 1950 and 1955. In part this may have been a reaction to a genuine fear that the United States would use the NATO alliance and its own reconstituted forces in Europe to attack the Soviet Union. In part the growth of the Soviet military estab-

[7] Total national security outlays here (and subsequently in this paper) refer to the U.S.S.R. equivalent of the Department of Defense (DOD), the military portion of the Atomic Energy Commission (AEC), and the space program of the National Aeronautics and Space Agency (NASA) (because the costs of these programs cannot be separated on the Soviet side) in the United States.

The trends in U.S.S.R. expenditures are based upon two SRI studies: RM 5205–54, *Probable Trend and Magnitude of Soviet Expenditures for National Purposes* (by S. A. Anderson, W. T. Lee, I. M. Oakwood and J. H. Alexander) and TN 5205–76, *Production and Allocation of Hardware to Military, Space, and RDT&E Programs, 1955–65* (by W. T. Lee, I. M. Oakwood, and J. H. Alexander).

152

lishment may have been designed to exploit almost the only counter the Soviet Union had to overcome U.S. nuclear superiority during this period, namely, the capability (probably more credible in Washington than in Moscow) of the Red Army to overrun Western Europe. Holding Western Europe as a hostage for U.S. behavior was widely credited to the Soviet Union by the West at this time, and also proclaimed later by Khrushchev, but only after he had built up a substantial MRBM force.

Despite all the statements about the increased danger of war and the need to "strengthen" the country's defense, the Soviet Union proceeded to reduce the Red Army to very nearly the pre-Korean manpower levels during 1955–61.[8] In contrast to the 1950–54 period when national security outlays increased very rapidly, when almost all the growth and the output of machinery and equipment was given to the military at the expense of investment for economic growth, Soviet expenditures for national security purposes were more or less constant from 1954–55 through 1958.[9] In contrast to the Korean war years, almost

---

[8] Personnel on active duty increased from 2.874 million at the beginning of 1948 to 5.763 million in 1955. See Marshal V. Sokolovsky and Maj. Gen. M. Cherednichenko, "Certain Questions of Soviet Military Construction in the Postwar Period," *Military Historical Journal*, March 1965, pp. 4 and 9. As far as can be determined, most, perhaps all, of this increase in military manpower occurred during 1950–53. By 1958 the forces had been reduced to 3.623 million and the planned reduction to 2.423 million was probably stopped (in 1961) at just above 3 million.

[9] The fluctuations in the explicit "defense" item in the Soviet budget—up from 8.28 billion rubles in 1950 to 10.74 billion in 1955, then steadily declining to 9.3 billion in 1960—are not a reliable guide to either the trend or the magnitude of total expenditures. The rise in 1950–55 and the subsequent decline until Khrushchev's dramatic "increase" of some 2.3 billion rubles in 1961, when demobilization ceased, were probably largely the result of change in pay, maintenance, and operations costs. Estimated actual expenditure trends are from RM 5205–54 and TN 5205–76.

all the growth in the output of machinery and equipment was devoted to new investment from 1954 through 1958.[10] Giving first priority to capital investment for machinery and equipment meant that the military procurement bill was constant, or even decreased slightly, from 1954–55 through 58.

This pattern of resource allocations was facilitated by the decision not to build a large heavy bomber force on which the U.S. continental air defense programs of the period were predicated, and to cut back on the surface ship building program for the Red Navy. Other major cuts, particularly equipment for the Ground Forces and the Tactical Air Armies, which seem to have borne the brunt of the demobilization, probably occurred but cannot be documented. Judging from the indicators available, air defense budgets probably showed some growth during these years as savings were made elsewhere. RDT&E outlays also were rising as the Soviets laid the basis for the shift to missiles and nuclear weapons.

MILITARY FORCES AND BUDGETS IN THE SEVEN YEAR PLAN

One of the overlooked aspects of the Seven Year Plan (1959–65) announced by Khrushchev in 1958, when he seems to have been firmly in command for nearly two years, was the provision for a substantial increase in military spending. The anticipated growth in the production of machinery and equipment in 1959–65 was to be divided roughly equally between investment for economic growth and the military establishment

---

[10] This interpretation of the trends in national security outlays—based on economic data, manpower trends, and displays of new weaponry—appears to be supported by the periodization of Soviet military programs provided by Sokolovsky and Cherednichenko, *loc. cit.*, pp. 3–7.

154

(to which the space program soon became a major addition as the Soviets joined in the lunar landing race). Output of many consumer durables was to increase absolutely, but the consumer's share of the total final product was to remain constant or even decrease slightly. In terms of the over-all national security budget, this implied an average growth of at least 5 percent per annum 1959–65, depending on what happened to the Ground Forces.

Meanwhile the Soviet Union had reorganized and was in the process of reequipping the Ground Forces for tactical nuclear warfare. Judging from the parade displays of new missiles (ballistic and cruise types), and allowing for nominal production runs, the reequipment and reorientation of the Ground Forces for tactical nuclear war was probably largely accomplished by 1961–62.

Much more far reaching consequences ensued from the decisions taken with regard to strategic nuclear forces. Khrushchev in particular seemed to have little faith in aircraft, an attitude that may have been shared by some of his political opponents as well.[11] Thus while the Soviet leaders decided not to produce a large heavy (intercontinental) bomber force, they did build a large medium (Eurasian) bomber force in the interim before the ballistic missiles were available. Since the Soviet stockpile of nuclear weapons may have been very limited during the early and mid-1950s, the small number of heavy bombers reinforced by a portion of the medium bombers not only gave the Soviets a modest nuclear deterrent against the

[11] Whatever the disagreements on other issues, the preference for missiles as a means of nuclear delivery seems to be very widespread in the political as well as the military leadership of the Soviet Union. In fact, the long tradition of artillerymen in Russia ("Artillery Is the King of Battle") has its natural heir in today's Strategic Rocket Troops (SRT).

155

United States but also was probably more than adequate to deliver the number of weapons actually available during those years.

There is, of course, no direct evidence on the size of the Soviet stockpile. Even the United States with its relatively liberal (formal and informal) dissemination of classified information has released little or no data on this subject. But occasional glimpses behind the scenes are possible and it is possible to draw some inferences from the nature of the weapons themselves. The U.S. weapons stockpile in 1949–50, some five years after the initial test, was apparently very small. And nuclear weapons, particularly the thermonuclear models, safe enough for military use are not easy to manufacture in quantity even now. Thus the usual assumption that the Soviets acquired a substantial stockpile of weapons, first fission then fusion, soon after the tests in 1949 and 1952 appears highly questionable in retrospect. It is more likely that the era of nuclear plenty in the Soviet Union roughly corresponded with the availability of tactical and strategic missiles, that is, beginning in 1957–58.[12]

With the benefit of 20/20 hindsight, the information released by Western officials on the status of Soviet forces over the years, the parades through Red Square, and Soviet statements, a number of key strategic nuclear decisions embodied in the Seven Year Plan (1959–63) can be identified: to build a very large medium- and intermediate-range ballistic missile force targeted against NATO Europe and peripheral targets in

[12] It is interesting to note that Sokolovsky and Cherednichenko (*loc. cit.*, p. 3) speak of 1954–58 as the period in which nuclear weapons were "perfected and stocked." In general, the Soviets seem to experience long delays between technological achievement in the laboratory and large-scale production. Did surprise at Soviet R & D progress in the nuclear field—first the fission device in 1949 and then the fusion test in 1952 several months before the first United States theromonuclear device in 1953—cause the United States to overestimate the growth of the Soviet weapons stockpile in the 1950s?

the Far East; to forego any attempt to build a large ICBM force with their first-generation missile;[13] and to deploy a force of second-generation ICBMs comparable to the combined U.S. Atlas and Titan programs. Since U.S. decisions to proceed with the Polaris and Minuteman programs were already taken (and publicized), the Soviet leaders in 1957–58 committed themselves to gross inferiority in the numbers of intercontinental delivery vehicles until the late 1960s. This pattern of decisions really should have been predictable, given the traditional fear and concern of Soviet leaders of attack from Europe, particularly after rearmament of West Germany was approved and that country included in NATO (1954–55).

The "ICBM gap" concept was the joint product of a very real lack of evidence on the part of the United States and a deliberate Soviet bluff. Both Khrushchev and Malinovsky made very explicit statements designed to mislead the United States into believing that a large ICBM deployment was under way in 1959–60, thus covering up for the earlier decision to put their money into medium- and intermediate-range systems rather than intercontinental missiles.[14] What is often forgotten, how-

[13] This was probably the same basic missile as the space booster deployed at the Paris Air Show in 1967. Although apparently rather reliable, this large and clumsy design would have been very expensive to deploy and was probably impossible to place in hardened launch sites. Its large size was probably dictated by the status of Soviet thermonuclear weapon technology in 1954–55.

[14] The key statements were that the Soviet ICBM had been put into "series" and then "mass" production (Khrushchev, November 1958–January 1959 and January 1960) and Malinovsky's statement that Soviet troops "had been equipped" with ICBMs (February 1959). These three statements stand apart from normal boasting. Both the timing and the precision were deliberate falsifications comparable to the subsequent denial of any intent to place offensive missiles in Cuba. For an excellent treatment of Soviet strategic deception during the period, see Myron Rush and Arnold Horelick, *Strategic Power and Soviet Foreign Policy* (Chicago: University of Chicago Press, 1966).

157

ever, is that there was—and still is—a strategic "missile gap" in Europe. By the early 1960s the Soviet Union had fielded some six hundred to seven hundred I/MRBM launchers, most of which were targeted against the NATO countries. The credibility of holding Europe in hostage for U.S. behavior with this missile force was probably much higher (in Soviet eyes) than previously with the medium bombers. The MRBMs were complemented by the newly acquired tactical nuclear capabilities, large armor formations, and high degree of mobility of the Soviet Ground Forces. And initially the Soviet leaders probably counted on keeping the United States in the dark for many years as to the number of ICBMs deployed.

These I/MRBM forces provide some insight into the Soviet thinking on strategic doctrine as it developed in private between 1955 and 1961. First, the MRBM force was much larger than needed simply to destroy enough cities to hold Europe as a hostage for U.S. behavior. Second, as the Institute of Strategic Studies has pointed out, the available evidence suggests that this force was aimed at U.S. and NATO military targets. As Khrushchev was wont to say, "Of course our missiles are aimed at this or that military installation but unfortunately some damage will be done to the nearby city." Although Khrushchev made such public statements primarily for political effect, he was probably expressing the actual targeting doctrine. The objective was to destroy all the key military forces and installations in Western Europe (large enough to warrant an I/MRBM strike) with as little collateral damage as possible. The strategic nuclear strikes would be followed up by the Red Army, relying on tactical nuclear fire power to mop up the remaining military forces and thus to occupy Western Europe in a short period of time.

Hence the I/MRBM force combined with the restructured

158

Red Army was designed to limit damage to the Soviet Union and to disarm, seize, and occupy a relatively intact Western Europe with severe constraints placed on the use of nuclear weapons.[15] These were war fighting forces and did not fit into the conceptual framework of "simple" or "finite" deterrence, nor into the later U.S. formulation of assured destruction. At the same time, there is nothing to suggest a timetable for surprise attack, although Khrushchev apparently did count on using his improved strategic position to support his German policies and to weaken the credibility and cohesion of NATO.[16]

On balance, the Soviet strategic force posture decisions taken in 1957–58 were consistent with the logic of the doctrinal debate as it had concluded in 1955, suggesting that a rationale was being worked out behind the scenes. In 1961–62 the new

[15] This military objective also made sense economically and ecologically. The Soviets not only wanted Europe's resources but also wished to minimize fallout from an attack on Europe (prevailing westerly winds carry fallout back to Russian soil, or on the advancing Russian troops).

[16] One foreign-policy corollary of this analysis runs as follows: The campaign to take over West Berlin was paced in accordance with the MRBM build-up and the growing tactical nuclear capabilities of the Ground Forces. The Cuban missile gambit was the last move in the Berlin campaign. The fatal flaw was the United States discovery in 1961, probably years before Khrushchev and company expected it, that the Soviet Union had but a handful of ICBMs. Why, then, did Khrushchev proceed with the Cuban venture in 1962 if he knew his strategic deception had failed? Two compatible hypotheses can be advanced. First, Khrushchev had come to realize that only overt military action, with all the dangers of escalation entailed therein, could force the West out of Berlin unless some new factor were introduced into the situation. The impulsive Khrushchev seized upon I/MRBMs in Cuba as the answer. Second, Khrushchev may have considered that the Soviet Union was now sufficiently powerful to play the game of foreign bases as well as the United States. Moreover, the experience with the Berlin Wall may have convinced Khrushchev that a *fait accompli* would be easier for the United States to accept, hence the repeated formal and informal denials of any Soviet intent to place missiles in Cuba.

Soviet doctrine for the nuclear age was published by Marshals Malinovsky and Sokolovsky.[17]

SOVIET MILITARY STRATEGY AND NUCLEAR TARGETING DOCTRINE, 1961 TO THE PRESENT

The next major public event in the doctrinal discussion after 1955 was Marshal Malinovsky's speech to the 22d Party Congress in October 1961 at which he spelled out the new Soviet doctrine for the nuclear age as it had evidently evolved after 1955. Malinovsky's speech was followed by the publication of Marshal Sokolovsky's *Military Strategy,* first published in 1962, revised in 1963 and again in 1967. The book contained the same formulation of doctrine that Malinovsky had just stated in 1961, but at much greater length. It also spelled out the targeting priorities that went with the doctrine.

The essential points in the new military doctrine (or nuclear strategy) as enunciated by Marshals Malinovsky and Sokolovsky were:

1. The Soviet Union would retaliate against any attack with its own second strike no matter what.
2. The Soviet forces would attempt to "disrupt" or to "frustrate" the surprise attack expected from the enemy.
3. In accord with Khrushchev's theses, nuclear war cannot be used to spread communism. But a surprise nuclear attack by the United States (with

[17] Marshal Malinovsky was Minister of Defense from 1957 until his death in 1967. Marshal Sokolovsky was Chief of Staff in 1956–60 and according to official biographies was noted for his "brilliant new creative approach" in military affairs.

160

or without NATO) is possible, although not "fatally inevitable."

4. Should nuclear war occur, the Soviet Union wishes to be able to conduct it toward rational ends. At a minimum the ends are survival as a viable, recuperable national entity and cessation of hostilities on terms favorable to the Soviet Union.

The phrasing of the "answering blow" in retaliation, then and now, amounts to saying deterrence is one objective. The Soviets do not use the word "deterrence," nor do they specify a desired number or percentage of fatalities required for deterrence. They simply say that they will retaliate.

The objective of disrupting (or frustrating) the enemy's surprise attack is also expressed in phraseology that varies from time to time. The word "preemptive" is almost always avoided; it has been used rarely by a few minor writers since 1955. Neither the top military people nor the prominent colonels nor the political leaders have used the term since about 1958. The phraseology employed instead varies from "disrupt," to "nip in the bud," to "repulse," to "frustrate" the enemy's "surprise attack" and "criminal intent." So the logic is clearly that the Soviets would attempt to get in the first lick if they were sure the attack was coming. But they carefully avoid any words suggesting that they would plan for and then initiate a surprise or preemptive ("out of the blue") attack in the sense that the term has come to be used in U.S. literature.[18]

In 1966 Marshal Sokolovsky and his collaborator, Major

---

[18] The most pertinent passage in Marshal Malinovsky's speech appears on p. 118 of Vol. II of the Stenographic Report of the 22d Congress proceedings. In the first two editions of Marshal Sokolovsky's book, see pp. 232 and 253.

General Cherednichenko, took the argument one step further, but still avoided the use of the word "preemptive": "Together with increasing possibilities of surprise there are growing possibilities of timely detection not only of the beginning of an attack, but also the initiation of direct preparations for an attack by the adversary, that is, it is possible not to permit a surprise attack." [19] What these statements seem to be saying is that at best the Soviet Union will have adequate warning to catch the adversary's missiles and aircraft on the ground; at worst the Soviet Union will receive enough early warning in order to launch before the enemy missiles and aircraft arrive. The possibility of not permitting a surprise attack because the adversary's preparations can be detected is even more suggestive of a counterforce strike than the implicit logic of "disrupting" or "frustrating" the attack in the earlier formulations. Again, the vagueness may reflect fundamental uncertainty about which side will succeed in exercising the initiative rather than just reluctance to say "preemptive strike."

If retaliation and, at least under some circumstances, counterforce strikes are the principal missions of the Strategic Rocket Troops, is there a role for the defense? The answer is emphatically yes. The air and missile defense troops are to defend the country and the armed forces from the nuclear strikes of the enemy. While differences in opinion on such matters as resource allocation and the roles and missions of force components can be discerned from time to time, both within the military establishment and between the military and civilian

[19] Marshal V. Sokolovsky and Maj. Gen. M. Cherednichenko, "On Contemporary Military Strategy," *Communist of the Armed Forces,* No. 7 (1966), p. 65. The same argument was repeated in the third edition of *Military Strategy* (published in 1968), p. 337, where detection, surveillance, and reconnaissance capabilities are referenced.

162

leadership, there does not appear to be a single instance where the role of air and missile defense is questioned. Moreover, the Soviets continue to believe that the coordinated, combined operation of all arms and branches of the military is essential:

In a nuclear-missile war the essentially new forms of strategic operations advance to the forefront—strategic nuclear strikes on the military, political, and economic targets of the adversary, that is, the operations of the Strategic Rocket Troops, nuclear submarine launched missiles, and long-range bombers. One of the chief forms of strategic operations is the operations of the air and missile defenses (PVO) in defending the country and the military forces from the nuclear strikes of the adversary. . . . As has been observed in the press, the development and mastering of such forms of [military forces and operations] as the nuclear strikes of the strategic forces, the operations of the air and missile defense (PVO and PRO), strategic offensive operations on the ground and at sea, and also vertical assault operations, have the greatest significance. . . . Insuring the highest state of readiness in the nuclear [attack] forces, the PVO and PRO forces and facilities, and all intelligence, reconnaissance, and warning systems is of particular significance at the present time. Victory in contemporary war can be achieved only through active, decisive operations and the full utilization of the military capabilities of all forces and means of combat, operating in efficient coordination together.[20]

[20] Sokolovsky and Cherednichenko, "On Contemporary Military Strategy," pp. 64, 65.

Soviet economic planning must take into account strategic considerations not only in the choice of weapons to be produced but also in such matters as the economy under the conditions of nuclear war, the development of technology, the creation of reserve stocks, and so on.[21]

That nuclear war is not an acceptable means of carrying the benefits of the Soviet system to other nations is an interpretation of Khrushchev's 1956 formulation that war is not "fatally inevitable" in the nuclear era when "socialist" and capitalist states coexist.[22] Others may give this formulation (and some subsequent statements) a much broader interpretation concerning the doubtful political utility of nuclear weapons in general. In the 1960s Khrushchev did make a number of statements suggesting the broader interpretation, but these latter utterances appear to have been in the context of replying to the Chinese, who were apparently urging the Russians to go ahead and finish capitalism off then and now, or at least to run a much greater risk of war in support of various political (and perhaps limited military) initiatives—for example, Berlin. But when all of Khrushchev's statements are taken into account, when one considers how he initiated and conducted the campaign to take over West Berlin, reviews his elaborate use of strategic deception and frequent "rocket rattling," and reflects on the weapons system programs he approved at the expense of his economic goals, then the more limited interpretation seems the more reasonable one. In other words, Khrushchev could very well reply to his Chinese critics in all sincerity that "to unleash a modern, thermonuclear war is simply madness" while continuing to attach political utility to nuclear forces and

[21] "On Contemporary Military Strategy," p. 61.
[22] For a similar interpretation, see Thomas W. Wolfe, *Soviet Military Policy at the Fifty-Year Mark* (Rand RM–5443–PR), p. 2.

accepting the military argument that the Soviet Union should attempt to defeat the enemy in the event of such a war.[23]

Although Malinovsky did not expound at length on the targeting philosophy associated with the new nuclear strategy (or doctrine) at the 22d Congress, Marshal Sokolovsky and his collaborators did. Over and over, the book (both the 1962 and 1963 editions) repeated that the priority targets were the enemy's nuclear weapons and delivery systems and other military targets, key industries supporting the military establishment, and command and control. The most succinct statement of Soviet nuclear targeting doctrine and basic military objectives (should deterrence fail) was provided in 1967 by Marshal Krylov, commander of the Strategic Rocket Troops.[24] According to Marshal Krylov:

- Objective
  Military Defeat of Enemy
- Targets
  Delivery Systems, Weapons Storage and Fabrication Sites
  Armed Forces—Military Installations
  Military Industries
  Centers of Politico-Military Administration, Command and Control

This is fully consistent with all previous declaratory policy and with the aforementioned characteristics of the MRBM force.

---

[23] Khrushchev is one of those prolific people who can be quoted on somewhat different sides of a number of subjects over the length of his career. This and other pertinent quotations in reply to Chinese pressure can be found in Roman Kolkowicz, *The Red "Hawks" on the Rationality of Nuclear War* (Rand RM–4899–PR), p. 11.

[24] Marshal N. Krylov, "The Strategic Rocket Forces," *Nedel'ya*, No. 36 (September 1967).

From Malinovsky's speech to date, the line of the Soviet military has been very consistent. The first objective is to be able to retaliate under any conditions. The second objective is to "disrupt" or "not to permit" the enemy's surprise attack. And the final objective is to achieve "victory," or, as often stated, the military defeat of the enemy. The military do not think that the Soviet Union could escape heavy damage, so there are no arguments for building up for a surprise attack to be launched by the Soviets. However, the combination of the doctrine, the reiteration of "victory" as the final objective, the nuclear targeting doctrine, and the characteristics of the Soviet Civil Defense Program, all suggest that what the military has in mind is a concept of national entity survival.[25]

The civilian leaders from Khrushchev to Kosygin and Brezhnev appear to have gone along with the above formulation, with some differences in emphasis. But the civilians have not contradicted the military formulation on any occasion. Generally, the civilian leaders avoid stating victory as the objective; they usually prefer to talk about retaliation and general improvements in all aspects of Soviet military capabilities. Occasionally, however, the civilian leaders return to the "victory" theme, as Mr. Brezhnev did in 1967.[26] Their differences with the military appear to be more a matter of reservations concerning feasibility than the substance of what is the desired objective should deterrence fail.

CONSISTENCY OF THEORY AND PRACTICE

It may be objected that declaratory policy is one thing, but the actual choice of weapons system, the level of expenditures

[25] Sokolovsky and Cherednichenko, "On Contemporary Military Strategy," pp. 61, 65.

[26] 50th Anniversary Speech, November 4, 1967, *The Current Digest of the Soviet Press,* Vol. XIX, No. 44.

for strategic forces, quite another. It behooves us, therefore, to review both the pattern of decisions on strategic forces taken in the early 1960s and the price the Soviet leaders have been willing to pay for improvements in their military capabilities.

As was indicated in the previous discussion of the Soviet I/MRBM force, in the years 1958–62 the Soviet Union installed a Eurasian strategic nuclear force very much in line with the new military doctrine promulgated publicly in 1961–62.[27] But in the intercontinental forces they were stuck with the consequences of their previous decision not to deploy their first-generation ICBM, so that in 1961–62 the Soviets were just beginning to acquire (at best) the first operational units of the 200 to 250 second-generation ICBMs force credited to them in 1965–66. Even if the targeting doctrine of the I/MRBM force was applied to the second-generation ICBMs, it was more or less irrelevant.[28] Unlike the war-fighting capability provided by the medium-range systems in Eurasia, a similar capability was many years away for their ICBM and SLBM forces. Hence one test of the seriousness with which the

[27] One of the little-noticed barriers to understanding Soviet military policy is the definition of what is "strategic." Americans tend to think only of weapons capable of striking (or defending) the United States or the U.S.S.R. as "strategic." Hence the "ICBM gap" is equated to the "missile gap" without taking into account the Soviet I/MRBM force. To the Soviets, with their continental historical perspective, questions of "strategic" offensive force capabilities begin with those Eurasian missiles and then move on to the ICBMs.

[28] By this time there were nearly 1,200 land-based ICBMs in the United States force (later reduced to 1,054). The Soviets may have thought the SS-9 was a short cut to the problem if they designed it to attack the Minuteman Launch Control Centers, but the subsequent introduction of airborne launch control (as well as redundant internetting) eliminated this cheap option. This in turn may explain the Soviet interest in multiple warheads for the SS-9 in order to attack the individual silos. The advantages to be gained by replacing one warhead with three are negligible for attacks on soft targets but are very great for attacks on hard targets; to build enough SS-9s with single RVs to attack every Minuteman silo would be prohibitively expensive.

167

Soviets take their military doctrine is the consistency of the next cycle of decisions on strategic nuclear forces taken in the 1960s, particularly the offensive and defensive systems that would be involved in an engagement with the United States.

Given the relative wealth of data released over the past few years on the Soviet strategic build-up and the lead-times required to develop, produce, and field complex strategic nuclear weapons systems, some inferences may be drawn concerning both the timing and the content of the decision cycle that led to the Soviet strategic forces in being today. The timing appears to be 1961–63, that is, spanning the Cuban crisis and while Khrushchev was still the preeminent political leader. The principal decisions taken during this period appear to be the following.

• To deploy sufficient third-generation ICBM systems so as to match or to exceed the U.S. force of 1,050 ICBMs by 1969–70, and to match the U.S. SLBM force some time in the early to mid-1970s. As far as can be determined, the new ICBMs consist primarily of the well-publicized SS-9 (large payload, relatively accurate) and the SS-11 (small payload, less accurate), at a launcher ratio of approximately 1:3.[29] At this ratio the two programs are probably roughly equal in cost.

[29] The second-generation ICBMs apparently numbered between 200 and 250. The U.S.S.R. now has some 1,200 launchers deployed or in process, of which some 230 are SS-9s. The SS-11s comprise about two thirds of the total force. The SS-9 has been shown repeatedly in parades while the SS-11 has not. The former is judged to be capable of effectively attacking hard targets now and has the payload potential to improve that capability in the future. The latter is assessed to be effective only against soft targets. More recently the Soviets are reported to have begun deployment of a small-payload, solid-fuel ICBM, the SS-13. See *Safeguard Antiballistic Missile System, Hearings before Subcommittees of the Committee on Appropriations* (Washington, D.C.: Government Printing Office, 1969), pp. 8–11.

- To proceed with the ABM system at Moscow and to create an extensive early-warning network which might have some application to national ABM systems beyond Moscow itself.
- To improve and extend Soviet air defenses with the enigmatic Tallinn system and several of the new fighter aircraft shown at the 1961 air show.
- To acquire an ASW (antisubmarine warfare) capability against Polaris submarines some time in the 1970s with some combination of (nuclear) attack submarines and surface vessels. (At least two new Soviet attack submarines are reportedly now entering service,[30] and the two helicopter carriers appear to be part of the surface ASW components.)
- Although not directly related to Soviet strategic doctrine but very much a part of the Soviet strategic image vis-à-vis the United States, the Soviets also decided to pick up the gauntlet on the lunar landing race when President Kennedy announced the U.S. program in 1961.

This is an impressive set of programs that appears to be consistent with the military doctrine of Marshals Malinovsky and Sokolovsky, and with the Soviet leaders' use of nuclear power and space achievements for political ends. In accordance with the doctrine, roughly equal emphasis appears to have been placed on offense and on defense. Reflecting the doctrinal requirement for both retaliatory and damage-limiting forces (to prevent the enemy surprise attack), the SS-11 and the SS-9 appear to have been given equal priority. And the Soviet Union will soon have numerical superiority in operational ICBM launchers—probably next year—while maintaining its overwhelming superiority in I/MRBMs. Hence the Soviets now lag only in their Polaris force, but not for long.

---

[30] Testimony of Vice Admiral H. G. Rickover, *Congressional Record,* April 29, 1969.

Hence the Soviet political leaders are in a relatively much stronger position than was Khrushchev at the height of his missile diplomacy period. Whether they will attempt to make similar use of their growing nuclear power remains to be seen. At the very least, all of this would appear to give them a fairly good bargaining position for disarmament talks.

Neither the forces deployed in 1959–63 nor in the subsequent build-up were obtained cheaply or without economic sacrifice. Instead of staying within the limits provided in the 1959–65 Plan, total national security outlays grew at the rate of at least 7, and more likely 10, percent per annum during the 1959–65 period. The most severe impact was felt in the years 1960–63. Some of the reasons can be discerned in the scale and the characteristics of the weapons systems; others are more speculative. One distinct possibility is that the Soviet planners, like their Western counterparts, underestimated the cost of these new weapons.

The economic consequences were as might have been expected. Not all of the slowdown in the Soviet rate of growth after 1959 was due to the agricultural sector and not all of agriculture's problems were due to bad weather. Most of the higher-than-planned national security costs came out of the supply of the machinery and equipment (the durables component) of investment, and to a lesser extent from consumer durables and from housing construction. As the rate of growth of investment slowed, the share of durables in new additions to capital stock also declined, which in turn reduced the growth of labor productivity and adversely affected the capital-output relationships throughout the economy. Agricultural investment, particularly the supply of new machinery, was especially hard hit during the 1959–63 period. The housing goals of the Seven Year Plan were abandoned.

But the history of the relationship between military programs and Soviet economic growth must be told elsewhere. Suffice to say here that by 1963 Khrushchev may have been ready to shift the priorities back toward economic growth. But by this time he was in serious political trouble for these and other reasons. And despite the heavy burden of military and space outlays, the Soviet GNP still averaged about 5 percent per annum growth during the Seven Year Plan, which is both impressive and sobering.[31]

THE SOVIET STRATEGIC RATIONALE

All of this raises basic questions, such as:

• Why have the Soviets avoided the term "preemption" since 1955, having used it freely prior thereto, when the logic of the formulation on disrupting (or "frustrating") the enemy attack is clearly preemptive in nature?

• If the Soviets, particularly the Soviet civilian leaders, do not really believe in some sort of a war-fighting capability should deterrence fail, why do they place so much emphasis on active and passive defense?

Surely, the Soviet military have not had the power to force the civilian leaders to spend vast sums on what the latter do not

[31] Some resource shifts in favor of economic growth and consumption did occur in 1964–65. Since that time little change in the proportions of national income devoted to investment, consumption, and defense can be detected. There is a widespread impression that under the leadership of Mr. Brezhnev and Mr. Kosygin deployment of ICBMs, and perhaps other weapons, was accelerated. This is possible, but I have been unable to find evidence of significant changes in pace that are explicable in these terms. The economy continues to labor under the burden of military expenditure, and the relatively satisfactory growth of the 1965–68 period appears to be in jeopardy.

171

want, particularly when the economic impact has been so severe.

The following hypothesis is offered in explanation. The Soviets have concluded that there is a fundamental uncertainty as to who will make the first strike in the event of a nuclear war. They want to be able to limit damage to themselves if war appears inevitable, but they cannot confidently count on being able to do so. Hence they wish to maintain as many hedges as possible, to keep their planning as open-ended as possible.

The Soviets are very concerned about a surprise attack on the U.S.S.R. They may overemphasize this concern in public statements, and sometimes use it in internal political polemics, but the concern seems to be very sincere and durable. (After all, they lived through one surprise attack!) They probably think that the attack will come out of a deep crisis, although they worry about attacks launched at the end of what would appear to be a normal training exercise. They also may have some confidence, but at the same time an irreducible uncertainty, that their intelligence net will give them adequate warning of an impending attack. In the face of such fundamental uncertainty, they want to be prepared to strike the first blow in order to destroy as many enemy weapons as possible before launch. At the same time, they must be prepared to survive and to retaliate if the enemy succeeds in striking first. And they want defenses that are capable of blunting a surprise attack to some extent, and that might make the difference between the survival and the destruction of their society in the event they were able to use their offensive forces to reduce the weight of the attack. The objectives of "victory" and "defeat of the enemy" constantly stressed by the military and occasionally endorsed by the civilian leaders mean that the Soviets want to be able to fight a nuclear war and to terminate it on advantageous terms if they have to.

172

In addition, the word "preemption" is avoided because of the planned surprise attack connotation it has acquired in the West. While the Soviets want to make the first move should an attack on them appear inevitable, they do not believe in planning a surprise attack "out of the blue" on their own. So they do not want to use words that would lay them open to this charge.

This hypothesis on the thrust of Soviet military doctrine and the consistency between theory and practice does not fit neatly into such U.S. molds as "finite deterrence," "assured destruction," "sympathetic parallelism," or "surprise attack" designed to take over the world. The Soviets are interested in "deterrence," although they do not use the word. But they do not equate deterrence to "maximum fatalities." Hence their targeting doctrine specifies strikes on military targets, key industries, and command and control centers as the priority objectives. They do seek some degree of damage limiting under any circumstances, so they place much store in both active and passive defenses. They are not resigned to accepting strategic nuclear inferiority with the United States. If national entity survival is the goal of the Soviet Union should mutual deterrence fail for any reason, then a number of things fall into place and appear to make a good deal of sense, at least from the Soviet point of view, namely:

• The Soviet Union is spending at least twice as much for strategic offensive and defensive forces as is the United States.[32]

• While the distribution of these expenditures between offensive and defensive forces has not been made public, there is ample evidence to surmise that the shares have been much

---

[32] Remarks by Secretary of Defense Melvin R. Laird to the Wisconsin Broadcasters' Association, February 25, 1969.

more nearly equal over the years than the rather lopsided U.S. allocations in favor of offense.

• The Soviet Union not only has caught up and surpassed the United States in the number of ICBMs but has bought systems designed to attack both hard and soft targets. Judging from the proportion of SS-9 ICBMs reported in the force, the Soviet Union has probably placed about equal priority on hard and soft target systems. Multiple warheads are being tested on the SS-9, apparently to increase the number of hard targets the force can attack.[33] Meanwhile, Soviet retaliatory forces also are being improved at the rate of some seven to eight new Polaris-type submarines per annum.

• The Soviet Union has taken what seems to be the prudent and logical first step to protect its national command and control center (Moscow) with an ABM. The recent reports of ABM radars oriented toward China and testing of a new missile with loiter capabilities may be harbingers of a national area BMD (similar to Sentinel / Safeguard) in the next few years.

• The Soviet Union is continuing to improve its air defenses with the new interceptors shown at the 1967 air show and by deploying the Tallinn system.

• The reported new classes of nuclear attack submarines, together with the new helicopter carriers, may be the major building blocks in an open ocean ASW program still in the formative stages.

[33] Safeguard Hearings, *op. cit.,* p. 9. Secretary Laird stated the uncertainty concerning these SS-9 tests as follows: "Although we still have no conclusive evidence that these multiple reentry vehicles are independently aimed, the intelligence community considers it likely that the Soviets will go on with the development of MIRVs and install them in a new version of their SS-9 type ICBMs." This suggests that Soviets have not quite arrived as yet, which in turn may be the source of reported disputes within the intelligence community as to the precise objective of the multiple reentry vehicles on the SS-9.

174

• Since the Soviet Civil Defense Program was transferred to the Ministry of Defense in 1960, the Soviets have switched to urban evacuation instead of basement shelters in every new apartment, improved and extended the civil-defense training given to every adult and to high-school students, while apparently continuing to construct shelters at factories and in public buildings.

In sum, what all this amounts to is an attempt to hedge against as many uncertainties as possible rather than to attempt to achieve some narrowly defined goal that may prove to be chimerical. The hedges against the uncertainties are designed to achieve a rational outcome in terms of national entity survival under the worst circumstances and a more favorable outcome under more plausible circumstances. It is a set of programs and a pattern of resource allocations consistent with declaratory strategy and military doctrine. It is the portrait of a regime determined to survive and not likely to enter into a mutual suicide pact à la assured destruction without defenses. It is also a patient and persistent regime that continues to pursue its goals as rapidly as possible, and at considerable economic sacrifice, but not at the price of complete cessation of economic growth and return to a wartime political climate.

Some characteristics of Soviet military planning may also be deduced from the record. Too often the Soviet military planner is assumed to be either a ten-foot-tall giant who is as omniscient as God and as diabolical as Satan, or, conversely, a malignant, mentally retarded midget. I would suggest that the Soviet planner is a more average type, possessing a number of identifiable biases but sincere, diligent, determined, and very persistent. Some noteworthy characteristics of Soviet force posture planning and execution appear to be:

1. The Soviets are systematic and consistent over time in gradually acquiring the forces to fit their

strategy and doctrine. Perhaps reinforced by the momentum of the vast bureaucracy once set in motion and by other institutional forces, Soviet military planning exhibits some of the Anglo-Saxon trait of somehow "muddling through."

2. Their actions may appear somewhat confusing and inconsistent to an outside observer, but there appear to be some obvious reasons for this. First, the Soviets cannot do everything at once because of technological limitations and the competition of military programs with their long-run economic growth aspirations. Secondly, their planning is by no means as prescient as one would expect considering the vast amount of information available on U.S. objectives and weapons systems programs. The Tallinn system, for example, may be a response to the B-58 and the B-70 rather than to Minuteman and Polaris. Thirdly, there are probably plenty of bureaucratic conflicts and institutional rigidities in the Soviet Union.

3. The Soviet Union tends to pursue its own objectives, to exercise the initiative when the Soviet leaders see the opportunity to do so. They do not just react to U.S. initiatives.

4. The observable interaction process is a very mixed one. There is no simple and neat pattern of action-reaction apparent between U.S. and Soviet military programs, beyond the Soviet propensity to build a defense against every U.S. offense. Moreover, to the extent that the Soviets do react to our initiatives, they attempt to fit such reaction into the framework of their own strategic objectives and criteria for force posture planning.

176

5. For good or for ill, the case for convergence of U.S. and Soviet strategic thought cannot be argued much beyond the point of mutual agreement that nuclear war cannot be undertaken to eliminate the other. Both countries prefer mutual deterrence to war. Each country has its individuals and groups who doubt the other's acceptance of this position. But beyond this, the similarities in strategic doctrine are few.

Fear of the U.S. (or NATO) surprise attack appears to be genuine and nearly unanimous among the Soviet elite, while comparable fear of a Soviet surprise attack on the United States appears to be less intense among U.S. elite groups, a significant fraction of which do not appear to believe in the danger of a Soviet, or even Chinese Communist, attack at all. Over the years the United States has shown a growing tendency to rely only upon the threat (second strike) of destruction of Soviet society —usually measured in terms of fatalities—as the basis of U.S. strategic policy. The Soviets, on the other hand, have continued to stress the role of defense and damage limiting rather than moving toward the assured destruction strategy. Soviet strategic doctrine has evolved slowly and in a consistent pattern since the mid-1950s, while our efforts to tutor the Russians in strategy, particularly in the doctrine of assured destruction, have made little, if any impression as yet.

In conclusion, I would like to offer a heretical suggestion. Rather than tutoring the Soviet Union on what strategies it "should" adopt, the United States might be well advised to ask what it can learn from the Soviet view of nuclear strategy. The Soviets evidently believe that a government still has the primary function of preserving the society that created it, of reducing the losses of its population in a war as much as possible, and

177

of limiting damage to property to the extent possible even in the nuclear age. As Mr. Kosygin has said, they do not regard the coin of the realm as the proper measure of the value of defense. This may be a more rational and even a more moral view, by United States value standards, than the assured destruction strategy as it has come to be defined over the past five years. The latter amounts to a mutual suicide pact. It will work very well until one side or the other, for whatever reasons, either decides to invoke the pact or comes to believe that either the will or the command system (or both) of the adversary can be paralyzed. The Soviets probably regard assured destruction as an irrational strategy, now that technology offers some measure of protection should the unthinkable occur. It just may be that they are right.

CHAPTER 7

The Impact of Chinese ICBMs
on Strategic Deterrence*

Harry G. Gelber

Dr. Harry G. Gelber, on leave from Monash University, Melbourne, Australia, is currently at the Center for International Affairs, Harvard University, as an American Council of Learned Societies Fellow. Gelber received an M.A. from Cambridge University, England, and a Ph.D. from Monash University. He is the author of The Australian-American Alliance, *and his forthcoming book,* Problems of Australian Defence and Foreign Policy, *will be published next year by the Oxford University Press.*

The strategic nuclear forces of the United States have been developed almost entirely with a view to the requirements of deterrence of the Soviet Union. It is the various definitions of this central requirement that have primarily guided strategic decisions. Even the possession of nuclear weapons by Britain

---

* This chapter is a preliminary version of an article published in *Orbis*, a quarterly journal of world affairs, published by the Foreign Policy Research Institute, University of Pennsylvania, Vol. XIII, No. 2 (Summer 1969).

and France has brought no fundamental changes in this situation, for the possibility of a British-Soviet or a Franco-Soviet clash which failed to involve the United States has rightly been considered to be extremely remote. The same may not be true of China. China is likely to constitute a unique, and uniquely complicating, factor in the deterrent equations with which other countries have to live. If Clark Clifford is correct,[1] China could possess a modest ICBM force by the mid-1970s, with subsequent refinements for a second-generation force. It is not too early to consider what the implications of this may be.

I

The argument that follows rests upon three propositions. The first is that the Sino-Soviet and the Sino-American disputes will continue in the foreseeable future. While the intensity of both disputes may fluctuate from time to time, neither is likely to abate to the point where an armed clash, including a nuclear confrontation, ceases to be a realistic possibility.

Second, the Chinese government will, in fact, opt for the construction of an ICBM force capable of inflicting damage on the continental United States rather than concentrate on a medium-range missile force to use in relation to the rimlands of Asia.

Third, the strategy in accordance with which Chinese nuclear weapons will be employed will include a wish to deter both the Soviet Union and the United States in some situations. It is important to note that this last proposition does not require an assumption of Chinese aggressiveness in any traditional sense, or the adoption by China of high-risk policies. It is entirely

[1] *The 1970 Defense Budget and Defense Program for Fiscal Years 1970–74,* statement by Secretary of Defense Clark M. Clifford, January 15, 1969, pp. 46, 54.

compatible with the continuance of a Chinese policy that mixes verbal and declaratory violence with practical military caution, and a wish to concentrate upon oblique ways of undermining both the U.S. position in Asia and the Soviet position among communist states and in the Third World.

If these propositions are accepted, several highly important consequences seem to follow. China will be the only nuclear power which might confront the United States or the Soviet Union or both. Furthermore, a clash between any two of these three will not necessarily involve the third. At the time of the Cuban missile crisis, President Kennedy declared that a nuclear strike from Cuba against any nation in the Americas would be regarded by the United States as an action requiring a full retaliatory response against the Soviet Union. It seems certain that a clash with China would not be regarded by the United States in the same light. Nor would a Sino-Soviet clash trigger a Soviet response against the United States. It also seems highly unlikely that the third power—the United States in case of a Sino-Soviet clash or the Soviet Union in case of a Sino-American one—would voluntarily involve itself. It would rather stand aside and reap the fruits of abstention.

The Chinese nuclear posture will thus have some hitherto unique implications. Small nuclear powers, such as Israel might become, would essentially oppose other small powers. The involvement of the United States and the Soviet Union in such a case would be indirect, and probably ultimately avoidable.[2] If Japan or India were to acquire nuclear weapons, it seems unlikely that, under presently foreseeable policies, they

---

[2] Indeed, one would expect both Soviet and American policy planners to react to any acquisition of nuclear weapons by Israel or Egypt by seeking to strengthen the option of mutual abstention from a nuclear clash in the Middle East. Such a prospect might be a more compelling antiproliferation device than the offer of a Non-Proliferation Treaty.

would use them to threaten either the United States or the Soviet Union. As for Britain and France, though the use of their forces against the Soviet Union is conceivable, such use against the United States is not.[3] And the Soviets would not be able to count with any confidence on American noninvolvement in a Soviet clash with either of them.

A further consequence of China's special position is that both the United States and the Soviet Union will, for the first time, be faced with the possibility that a clash with one nuclear-armed opponent will leave them, at the end of the exchange, still face to face with another potential opponent thus armed. And once the possibility is admitted that clashes with these two opponents could be not merely simultaneous but sequential, it follows that the deterrence of one need not necessarily imply deterrence of the other and that both the operational definitions of deterrence and the force structures and deployments of the two great powers will have to be amended to take account of the new situation. So will plans for arms control.

Finally, if a situation were to arise where a clash between any two of these three opponents would not only weaken both in relation to the third but would undermine the subsequent maintenance by either contestant of his deterrence of the third, then each of the three would acquire a much more direct interest in encouraging a nuclear clash between the other two. Fortunately interest here does not imply capacity. But even the suspicion that such an interest was regarded by the other side as exploitable in practice would probably have important adverse consequences for notions of a developing Soviet-American understanding as well as for the prospects for arms limitation agreements.

[3] Some Frenchmen tried to overcome this limitation by suggesting a strategy of *tous azimuts*. But if this was meant to convey that a Franco-U.S. military clash is a possibility, it was difficult to take it seriously.

182

II

It has come to be believed in recent years that the maintenance of deterrent stability between the Soviet Union and the United States depends largely on the ability and perceived willingness of each side to inflict assured retaliatory destruction upon the other.[4] But the new factor, a third nuclear power as a potential enemy to each of the two great opponents, raises fresh possibilities. A clash with China by either opponent could subsequently erode its ability to maintain a credible assured destruction capability against the other. This consideration may be crucial for the development of Chinese nuclear strategy. For while the great powers required forces capable of inflicting unacceptable damage upon each other, the Chinese only need a strategic force which, in the event of a clash—and even its own elimination—would unacceptably weaken the United States or the Soviet Union in its dealings with the other. That capability may be subsequently available to China at a much lower level of effort and expenditure than the acquisition of a full retaliatory force. If so, it will follow that the ability of each of these two powers to continue to deter the other must come to depend on maintaining the same destruction capability (provided, of course, that this continues to be the standard of measurement) following a clash with China[5] as well as a damage-limiting first strike by the major opponent.

[4] The former Assistant Secretary of Defense for Systems Analysis, Dr. Alain C. Enthoven, has explained that "in the case of the Soviet Union, we believe that the ability to kill 20 to 25 percent of its population and to destroy 50 percent of its industrial capacity under any foreseeable circumstances is an effective deterrent." U.S. Congress, Senate, *Hearings* before the Preparedness Investigating Subcommittee of the Committee on Armed Services, 90th Cong., 2d sess., Pt. I, p. 117.

[5] Similar arguments may not hold if a Soviet-American conflict precedes a confrontation by either side with China. The situation which might follow

Current estimates appear to be that the Chinese will have a force of some ten to possibly seventy-five ICBMs by 1975.[6] In the event of a full-scale clash, former Defense Secretary Clifford has estimated that the probable Chinese force could inflict from 11 million to 23 million deaths in the United States. The provision of antimissile defenses could be expected to reduce the total of casualties to one million in the second case and to fewer than one million, with some possibility of no deaths, in the first.

With this first-generation force, the Chinese could theoretically hope for three kinds of damage-inflicting capability against the United States. The first would be the ability to destroy or use up enough American weaponry, including missiles, to leave America with too few deliverable warheads to maintain assured destruction against the Soviet Union. The possibilities here are low. An American first strike against Chinese ICBMs would by 1975 hardly use up enough warheads to produce a significant lowering of capabilities against the Soviets, though the extent of a second strike might be limited by the requirements of maintaining deterrence against the USSR.

The second possibility would be for China to threaten the destruction of vital parts of the American command and control

---

such a conflict is in any case in detail unpredictable, and the very notion of a controlled confrontation with China might cease to have relevance. But it seems quite likely that a first-generation Chinese force will be so limited that the United States, even after an exchange with the Soviet Union, would have enough deliverable warheads left over to give her the technical capability to launch a damage-denying first strike against China. Under what circumstances such a threat could be exercised, and by whom, is of course another matter but one which does not affect the point at issue here.

[6] Defense Secretary Melvin R. Laird, *Non-Proliferation Treaty, Hearings* before the Committee on Foreign Relations, U.S. Senate, 91st Congress, 1st sess., Part II, p. 391. These seem to accord with the median range of the estimates in former Defense Secretary Clifford's statement on the 1970 defense budget, *op. cit.*, p. 54.

system. A measure of survivability has of course already been built into the existing U.S. retaliatory system. But the command and control requirements for the conduct of a counterstrike against the Soviet Union may be of a different order of magnitude and complexity from the requirements for control in the period following a Chinese strike against the United States. These differences would be greatest in the immediate postattack period. Insofar as it seems reasonable to envisage a limited Soviet strike, it would be in the interests of the Soviets themselves to spare much of the American command and control system, including Washington, if only to ensure that the exchange remain limited. In the case of an all-out Soviet attack, on the other hand, all that would be required would be a command system of sufficient capability to operate the mechanics of reprisal. What broader political and command functions would remain to be fulfilled in the postattack phase of such a cataclysm is quite unclear.

The situation after a Chinese strike would be very different. The character of the Soviet-American balance is such that the maintenance of stability would require the survival, even in the immediate postattack phase, of a machinery of control able to perform almost the whole range of functions of a normal government. In the absence of passive, and perhaps active, defenses the Chinese may be able to offer a credible threat to the survival of such a system.

But it is the third category which may be crucial: that of casualties and the associated intangibles of morale. It is, of course, by no means clear what correlation, if any, exists between any specific level of casualties which a Chinese attack might cause and the likelihood of any particular kind of U.S. reaction. Perhaps an exchange with China would break the nuclear taboo and make a subsequent threat to the Soviet Union easier to operate, in spite of the casualties. Perhaps, too, significant casualties would merely lead to a siege mentality and a garrison state. Much also depends on the attack envisaged. No particular level of damage sustained by the United States as the result of a Chinese strike would prevent America from subsequently responding in kind to a direct Soviet attack upon the U.S. But away from such simple scenarios the uncertainties become great. It is difficult to believe that following a disaster such as the loss of 23 million people, any American administration would be able to make the thought of another nuclear confrontation with a different enemy, the Soviet Union, bearable in any circumstances except those of such a direct Soviet nuclear strike against the United States. Even a much lower level of casualties might make the notion of nuclear arms, and all that goes with them, intolerable.

Nevertheless, Peking's capabilities along these lines are comparatively small. The first concern of a Chinese planner would presumably be how to make his first-generation force credible against the massive superiority of the Soviet and American strategic forces. To do that he must be able to dispel or circumvent the assumption that whatever the detailed capabilities of his force, China will be deterred in all likely contingencies from using it. But nuclear deterrence is obviously just an omnibus term for generalizing about a variety of situations which differ in crucial details. The role that nuclear weapons actually play in affecting particular decisions, by particular people, at specific times and places, is at best highly obscure. It is also in most cases incapable of proof. These well-known ambiguities would give Peking room for maneuver, which might be exploited in four ways.[7]

---

[7] The notion of a basically irrational Chinese strategic policy, as distinct from a threat to behave irrationally in a particular situation, seems too unlikely to be worth much discussion. Suggestions along such lines have been made, for example, by the Chief of Staff of the U.S. Air Force, General J. P. McConnell, in the *Hearings on the Status of U.S. Strategic*

In the first place, the Chinese interpretation of deterrence need not be the same as the American one. The U.S. view has usually combined two factors: the desire to deter an opponent from starting a war and the maintenance of an ability to fight a war with relative advantage if deterrence should fail. But these two elements are separable, both in logic and in practice. It would be entirely rational for the Chinese to aim for the first, even if they have no hope of achieving the second. The possibility that any first- or second-generation Chinese missile force could be used to force the United States to withdraw from an established position against its will is quite remote. It would even be difficult to create high confidence that China would respond in a particular situation with a strike against the Soviet Union or the United States. But it would be realistic of Peking to suppose that the mere existence of the Chinese force, and its ability in a bee-sting attack to inflict significant damage upon the United States, would give U.S. leaders pause in a number of situations. It may also on occasion be possible for a nuclear-armed China, by forcing the initiative upon Washington, to compel America to abstain from action that might lead to a Sino-American clash.[8]

In the second place, it is clear that nuclear weapons are not relevant solely to situations of nuclear war. Nuclear-backed deterrence has in the past been highly relevant to assessments of adversary intentions and the various possibilities for response, including irrational response, even in a subnuclear conflict. In central Europe, for example, mutual deterrence works as much

---

Power before the Preparedness Investigating Subcommittee of the Senate Committee on Armed Services, 90th Cong., 2d sess., 1968, p. 205. For a more balanced view, see Alice L. Hsieh, *Communist China's Military Policies, Doctrine, and Strategy* (Rand P–3960, October 1968).

[8] Professor Thomas C. Schelling has discussed this matter of "compellence" in his *Arms and Influence* (New Haven: Yale University Press, 1966), pp. 69ff.

by the implied threat that any low-level military engagement will uncontrollably escalate as it does by any explicit and perhaps less credible threat that the United States is willing to incur the penalties of a Soviet strike against the continental United States for the sake of preventing the nearest Soviet infantry battalion from occupying the town of Helmstedt. In such situations certainty is not required that either side will use nuclear weapons. Any reasonable probability that they might be used is thought to constitute an unacceptable risk. These considerations might apply in a number of situations vis-à-vis China. American assessments of the value of interdiction bombing inside China in case of a renewed conflict in Korea would be different if China had ICBMs than if she did not have them. The conditions for American protection of Taiwan or the offshore islands might also be different. And the Soviet Union would surely be more cautious about retaliating against Chinese border violations and more circumspect about aiding India in case of a renewed Sino-Indian conflict.

Third, China's threat to inflict casualties and damage upon the continental United States would not be based on the idea that the damage was in itself an adequate deterrent to U.S. action against China. It would be aimed at America's unwillingness to risk having that damage, and its social consequences, undermine Moscow's belief in the continuing determination of the United States to operate the deterrent machinery. It is a commonplace of modern strategic studies that in matters of deterrence, possession of hardware is in a sense secondary to the opponent's recognition of one's will to use it. As Henry A. Kissinger has written: "Deterrence depends above all on psychological criteria. It seeks to keep an opponent from a given course by posing unacceptable risks. For purposes of deterrence, the opponent's calculations are decisive. . . . For political purposes, the meaningful measurement of military strength is the

188

assessment of it by the other side."[9] Once America had suffered important damage as the result of a nuclear clash with China, would she find it easy to persuade Soviet decision-makers that her willingness to intervene in marginal situations remained entirely unchanged? What posture would be required to produce such a result? What penalties would be incurred if Moscow were not convinced? Could the impression be readily conveyed that the passions aroused by the clash with China were convertible into political determination against the Soviet Union and, if so, at what rate of exchange? Or would the Soviet leaders be more impressed by possible symptoms of weariness and withdrawal within America? Certainly any substantial chance that opinion might veer in the direction of withdrawal, let alone an abrupt rejection of nuclear arms, is a substantial chance that deterrence against the Soviets would be drastically undermined. It follows that any Chinese force which could credibly command that chance would possess a highly important deterrent capability against the United States. Similar arguments could be made for a Chinese deterrent policy against the Soviet Union, though a variety of other factors would come into play here, including the more indirect relationship between Soviet governmental decision-making and public opinion.

Fourth, there is the presumption that expectations, or even reasonable probabilities, along these lines would cause important changes in the diplomatic alignments of a number of countries. Such expectations would affect the assessment by third parties of America's ability to deter *both* China and the Soviet Union, albeit in somewhat different ways and to somewhat different degrees. They would have an important impact on the confidence with which a variety of America's allies felt able to

[9] "Central Issues of American Foreign Policy," in Kermit Gordon, ed., *Agenda for the Nation* (Washington, D.C.: The Brookings Institution, 1968), pp. 590–91.

189

count on American nuclear, and many forms of nonnuclear, support or protection. This would be likely to cause important changes in the entire worldwide pattern of alliance relationships, fears and hopes which center upon the United States. It also seems likely that these changes would be highly detrimental not merely to the maintenance of anything like America's present world position but to the possibility of securing any necessary changes in the great power balance by means which are controlled rather than uncontrolled and which produce a low level of violence and instability rather than a high one. It is also evident that such uncontrollable changes are likely to be of greater concern to the Soviet Union and the United States, with their global interests and their stake in the present structure of the international system, than to a China whose expectations of advantage are much more clearly geared to instability.

III

It may be objected that an analysis along such lines overestimates the rationality and predictability of the political process. The Chinese, for example, could not reasonably bank on U.S. responses in the direction of moderation. No Chinese planner could altogether dismiss the possibility that the United States might, instead, respond to these dangers by lashing out. Even more uncertain would be the consequences within the United States of any Sino-American nuclear exchange. Neither an expectation of American war-weariness nor even the opposite assumption could safely be adopted by Moscow as a planning factor. There is, of course, some truth in this. There can be no guarantee that a particular response will be made, or even that the strategies of the contending parties will be determined by rational categories. Nevertheless, it would be dangerous to dismiss the possibility that the Chinese can achieve an effective measure of deterrence against the United States, even without adopting unduly high-risk policies. In fact, those who assume that China will adopt high-risk policies are more apt to be deterred than those who do not. Surely the Chinese government would be on safe ground in assuming that the United States was most unlikely to react against the mere creation of a Chinese threat capability. Even beyond that, the historical evidence is persuasive for saying that the major thrust of U.S. policy in nuclear matters over the last twenty years has been not only to try to make irrationality less effective but to ensure that nuclear weapons are not used at all. The U.S. reaction to the Soviet Union's acquisition of nuclear weapons, American reactions in various Berlin crises, the self-imposed limitations in Korea, Vietnam, and Cuba, the whole logic of the strategy of flexible response—all these have been part of a continuing American disposition to avoid the use or immediate threat of nuclear weapons.[10] A lashing out would be highly uncharacteristic as well as politically most expensive. Indeed, if the Chinese leadership fails to come to some such conclusion about the United States, this is more likely to be because of its own ideological preconceptions about aggressive capitalism than because of the genuinely unpredictable elements in American policy formulation.

One more suggestion can be made with some confidence. At the conclusion of every major conflict in this century, the American mood has been to seek a settlement that would permit an American withdrawal and make a renewal of war unlikely or impossible. In no case, not even following the stalemate in Korea, was there a disposition to turn and rend others in unpre-

---

[10] The idea that a tradition of the nonuse of nuclear weapons increases the opponent's freedom of maneuver has of course been much discussed. For a notable contribution, see Bernard Brodie, *Escalation and the Nuclear Option* (Princeton: Princeton University Press, 1966).

dictable ways. Here, too, therefore, the Soviets might be tempted to assume that a Sino-American exchange would be followed, in the absence of deliberate and direct provocation from them, by an American search for reconciliation and a machinery to ensure peace, rather than any fresh confrontation.

In any case, it must be stressed that the central strand of the suggested Chinese strategy would be an attack not upon American forces, or American people, but upon American morale, and the influencing of the prior expectations of others as to likely change in that morale. Such an attack, if made, cannot be met by mere superiority of weaponry and certainty of retaliatory damage. It is not yet possible, of course, to predict accurately the lines of approach that Chinese planners will actually adopt in nuclear strategic matters. But it may be pertinent to see in these suggestions some distinct compatibilities with Maoist strategic doctrine. The emphasis on ways in which a weaker force can defeat a stronger one, and particularly the emphasis on morale factors, both the maintenance of one's own and the undermining of one's enemy, are standard Maoist doctrines. In this limited sense the considerations here merely transfer to the nuclear field some of the recognized principles of revolutionary warfare, designed as these are to be undercut and render ineffective the opponent's material superiority.

IV

Three principal methods are available to counter such tactics. The first would obviously be to seek a general political understanding with China of a kind that would devalue, and perhaps one day eliminate, the fears that must underlie a Chinese policy of deterrence. For the long term, this may be the only objective likely to rally serious support within the United States. The vision of an eventual reconciliation is powerful and morally persuasive. None of America's positive aims is furthered by the prospective deaths of several million Chinese or Russians. For the Soviets, too, reconciliation would offer major attractions.

Nevertheless, the practical difficulties remain. The Maoist segments of Chinese opinion believe in a revolutionary posture which itself predetermines hostility to both the United States and the Soviet Union. China's presently dominant perception of the requirements of her own revolution, as of her place in the world, implies a belief in revolutionary struggle as a verity in its own right.[11] Any abandonment of this struggle in favor of accommodation with either capitalists or revisionists would constitute an intolerable betrayal of the Chinese revolutionary state. Hostility to both America and the Soviet Union is confirmed by a number of other considerations, ranging from America's support for the Taiwan regime, the war in Vietnam, and border conflicts with the Soviets in Siberia, to the consciousness of a century of foreign intrusion in China. It may well be that these attitudes are not all-pervasive. It is also quite possible that they will soften in time. But the timing and direction of any decline from these extreme positions is quite uncertain, and in the meantime all Chinese attitudes toward the outside world are likely to be formulated in terms compatible with them. The Maoist core of these views is quite unlikely to be susceptible of modification by anything the Soviet Union or America can do. On the contrary. The important point is that it lies in the logic of Maoism that attempts by American capitalists or Soviet revisionists to promote politically significant understandings will be interpreted as efforts to encourage revisionism within China. The proper reply to such counterrevolutionary subversion can

---

[11] See an interesting discussion of these matters in Robert Jay Lifton's *Revolutionary Immortality; Mao Tse-tung and the Chinese Cultural Revolution* (New York: Vintage Books, 1968).

only be redoubled vigilance and struggle. It follows that, while negotiations on comparatively minor matters, and mutually beneficial bargains, are always possible, a major initiative to secure a rapprochement is likely to be viewed as a hostile act and therefore to be directly counterproductive. Genuine progress toward a political understanding will surely take a long time. If the Laird-Clifford estimates about the appearance of a Chinese ICBM force within five years are correct, what happens in the interval? [12]

The second possibility would be to declare a first-strike policy designed to convince Peking and, equally importantly, third parties, that China would be unable to get its first-generation missiles into the air before they were hit by a preemptive strike. The length of time needed to prepare for launching what will probably be unhardened and liquid-fueled missiles may make this possible. But important difficulties remain. It is not clear that an American first-strike posture vis-à-vis China could fail to imply a move away from America's second-strike posture of a sort which the Soviets would find highly alarming. Similar considerations may hold for an American response to a partial Soviet first-strike deployment. Such mutual alarm would have the gravest consequences for the Soviet-American balance, as well as possible arms limitation agreements. Beyond that, there remain the well-known general objections that any first-strike posture is inherently incompatible with deterrent stability, that it accentuates the dangers of constant tension, accident, or miscalculation. These dangers could easily become greater than the dangers against which the posture was designed to guard.

Furthermore, the mere adoption of such a position would

[12] In his testimony before the House Appropriations Committee on May 22, 1969, Secretary of Defense Laird said that "the Chinese Communists seem to have all of the major elements required for the production and deployment of ICBMs." See Chapter 3.

involve enormous political costs. Open American preparations to threaten a nuclear strike against a poor Asian nation, in circumstances where the need for action could not be proved beforehand in the court of public opinion (as President Kennedy was able to do in the Cuban missile crisis), would be certain to arouse the strongest opposition. The Soviet Union, too, would find the costs of such a policy toward another socialist country extremely heavy. It is far from certain that the strategy would be politically practicable in either case.

Finally, such a posture would be quite incompatible with the notion of reconciliation with China, even as a long-term aim. Its adoption could only make existing hatreds more enduring and appear to China as the proof of the worst that Maoists had ever said about American wickedness or Soviet treachery. In all, while a first-strike position might have to be declared as a measure of last resort, every effort should be made, and be seen to be made, to avoid it.

There remains the third possibility: active defense. Most importantly, this should mean a system giving high confidence of containing damage from a Chinese strike to some very low figure. Proposals for such a system, code-named Sentinel, were put forward by the Johnson Administration. President Nixon has adopted a revised version named Safeguard. It has been stated that virtually all the anti-Chinese area cover originally proposed for Sentinel could also be accomplished by the Safeguard system. Defense Secretary Laird, former Secretary Clifford, former Deputy Secretary of Defense Paul Nitze, and Dr. John Foster, the Defense Department's Director of Defense Research and Engineering, have at various times suggested that Sentinel and Safeguard would have something close to a damage-denial capability against China. Both Clifford and Nitze have indicated that this capability could be prolonged until the mid-1980s. Melvin Laird made a sympathetic review of the Sentinel system upon assuming office.[13] It seems likely, too, that once Safeguard's operational development had begun, the lead-time for an extension of its area cover capability would be less than the lead-time for China's missile deployment. If this can indeed be done, the advantages would be very great. It would deprive the Chinese force of that part of its rationale which consists of deterrence of the United States, and the Chinese leadership of an important potential tool for destabilizing the Soviet-American nuclear balance. It would do so in ways that were visibly nonaggressive toward China and to that extent politically acceptable within America and reassuring to her allies.[14]

Though any American measure to fend off a Chinese threat would cause alarm and frustration in Peking, a U.S. ABM system would be less alarming than, say, a first-strike posture. Indeed, it would be, and would be seen by others to be, evidence that America could afford not to act preemptively against China in a variety of situations. Yet its existence would reassure other nations, especially in Asia, that the United States would not be deterred from supporting them against China. It would therefore powerfully support current efforts to inhibit the proliferation of nuclear weapons: it would reassure allies that they

[13] Secretary Laird, *Safeguard Anti-Ballistic Missile System, Hearings* before the Subcommittee of the Committee on Appropriations, House of Representatives, 91st Congress, 1st sess., pp. 17, 28; also *The New York Times,* February 9, 1969, pp. 1, 64, and February 14, 1969, pp. 1, 10; Clifford, *op. cit.,* pp. 54–55; Foster, *Hearings on the Department of Defense Appropriations for 1969* before a Subcommittee on Appropriations, House of Representatives, 90th Cong., 2d sess., Pt. II, April 24, 1968, p. 455; Nitze, *Scope, Magnitude and Implications of the US Antiballistic Missile Program, Hearings* before the Subcommittee on Military Applications of the Joint Committee on Atomic Energy, 90th Cong., 1st sess., November 6–7, 1967, p. 2.

[14] The suggestion here is not that a technical distinction between aggressive and defensive weaponry is possible. It is rather that an area defense capability will probably be perceived at the level of public opinion as essentially defensive with respect to China and judged accordingly.

did not need nuclear weapons of their own and persuade others that nuclear weapons in the hands of a secondary power did not necessarily confer political leverage against the United States. It would allow a defense whether against China or the Soviet Union, to absorb an accidental or demonstration shot, or one fired following some breakdown in command or discipline. Such a defense could therefore add importantly to deterrent stability.

In any of the more likely forms of deployment, Safeguard would also seriously complicate Soviet targeting against the United States and to that extent add to the strength of deterrence against the Soviet Union. It could therefore increase the pressures on the Soviet Union to pursue arms limitation talks with Washington, whether for straightforward arms control reasons or a hard-headed desire to prevent the United States from increasing or exploiting its technological lead.[15]

Finally, it would open the way to further technical developments. In constructing it, production lines would have been established that would shorten the lead-time for any subsequent elaborations of the system, either qualitative or quantitative, against the Soviet Union or China. As with other weaponry, the operation and running of such systems would give the United States technical and engineering experience of the greatest value. It would also train key operating personnel.

In addition to the advantages, there would be penalties incurred by abandoning such a program after President Nixon had committed himself to it. An outright rejection of Safeguard would give away a major diplomatic and military prize to the Soviets and Chinese. It would add to the difficulties of adopting any subsequent BMD plans, even of a much more sophisticated kind. And though the Safeguard proposals have aroused strong opposition, any administration that now rejected them might

---

[15] The alternative would be an increased Soviet force buildup. But one would expect Moscow to explore ways by which this additional expense and effort might be avoided.

make itself more dangerously vulnerable later on to charges that it had opted against the means of preserving the deterrent or of saving millions of American lives in a war whose avoidance could not be guaranteed. It is highly important to note that many, if not most, of these reasons for mounting an anti-Chinese area cover system would be equally valid for the Soviet Union. Indeed, it seems most unlikely that Moscow, faced by a Chinese threat, would agree to opt out of all forms of BMD deployment.

V

Four kinds of objections have been raised against this sort of reasoning: that a BMD system would not work; that it would be too expensive; that it would be incompatible with other American obligations, notably those under the nuclear Non-Proliferation Treaty; and that it would trigger a fresh arms race with the Soviets which would bring a net decrease in the security of all concerned, as well as counter past and present arms control efforts. The first three of these objections can be dealt with briefly.

It has been argued that a weapons system as complex as BMD, which cannot be fully tested in peacetime, would prove a complete failure in practice. The Chinese could and would equip their missile force with penetration aids to overcome Safeguard. And the system would have to operate with an improbably high degree of efficiency if it was to hold casualties down to an insignificant level.[16] Some of these objections are

---

[16] See, for example, Richard L. Garwin and Hans A. Bethe, "Anti-Ballistic Missile Systems," *Scientific American,* March 1968, pp. 21–31, reprinted in *Survival,* August 1968, pp. 259–68; George W. Rathjens, *The Future of the Strategic Arms Race: Options for the 1970's* (New York: Carnegie Endowment for International Peace, 1969), especially Appendix, pp. 41–44; Abram Chayes and Jerome B. Wiesner, eds., *ABM: An Evaluation of the Decision to Deploy an Anti-Ballistic Missile System* (New York: Signet Books, 1969).

technically of great weight. But the point is not that Safeguard is invulnerable, or that the Chinese cannot devise penetration aids, or that Safeguard is certain to function with impeccable efficiency. It is merely that the creation and subsequent refinement of an operational Chinese ICBM capability is likely to lag behind America's capability to deploy operational systems capable of coping, with a high degree of confidence, with the Chinese systems which are actually operational at that time. If, in order to ensure penetration of America's 1975 BMD system, China needs equipment that will not be operational before 1980, then BMD will "work." In the meantime, low-confidence penetrability for a Chinese force is relatively useless for the strategic purposes here outlined. For the notion of Chinese deterrence of the United States must imply the creation of a degree of doubt about America's damage denial capability which, given the small number of launchers in the initial Chinese force, only high-confidence penetration aids could give.

Then there is the cost. The initial estimate of some $6.6–7.1 billion is admittedly likely to prove too low. DOD costs in the range of $10 billion to $12 billion seem a more probable total if the effects of inflation and technical refinements are taken into account. Whether expenditures of this order are justified is essentially a matter for political and social judgment. But it is worth noting that these sums are between 12 and 14 percent of the FY 1970 defense budget alone. Or, in different terms, the United States has spent $46.2 billion on its strategic forces (excluding R & D) in the six years from FY 1965 to FY 1970.[17] The suggested sums for Safeguard would mean spending between 21 and 26 percent of the original investment, spread over several years, to maintain the viability of the system against a new threat. Or, in different terms again, the total cost of Safeguard as estimated here is equivalent to less than six months'

[17] Clifford, *op. cit.*, Table I, p. 157.

expenditure on the Vietnam war. If and when it becomes possible to wind up that war, it would be feasible to build a BMD system, as well as a variety of other needed strategic weapons, and *still* reduce the defense budget as a proportion of a growing American GNP and perhaps even in terms of dollars spent. It might be argued that once Safeguard is built, it will inevitably be expanded. But the system is due for annual review, and in any case initial deployment is not the same issue as preventing subsequent expansion.

It has been said that Safeguard is incompatible with that part of the Non-Proliferation Treaty (Article VI) that calls on the great powers to seek negotiations on effective measures to end the arms race. But that is a general measure of arms control. It would be difficult to construe the obligation in terms that necessarily require the abandonment of any one particular weapons system. Moreover, the treaty does not stand by itself. It must be read in conjunction with the proposals about great power guarantees to nonnuclear powers who agree to remain nonnuclear. These smaller nonnuclear states therefore face a choice. They can agree to American measures that would make the maintenance of an American nuclear guarantee against China more credible. Or else they can interpret the American obligation to pursue disarmament not just in the general sense in which it is spelled out in the treaty but in terms of a need to avoid this particular system. They cannot have both, though they will doubtless try.

In many ways the most important criticism is that the installation of a BMD system would trigger a fresh round of the arms race with the Soviets. No presently foreseeable system would be an adequate defense against a heavy Soviet strike. Nevertheless, the Soviets would be compelled to react on the assumption that the system might operate with high efficiency. They would also have to treat any light screen as a potential building block in the construction of a heavy system. Their reaction would probably include increases in both numbers and penetrability of Soviet warheads targeted on the United States. Such increases would be perceived by the United States as endangering the maintenance of the U.S. assured destruction capability against the Soviet Union and therefore as requiring a further counter. At the end of this action-reaction process both sides would, at great expense, merely reestablish the previously existing balance between them, possibly with some diminution to their real security.

Nor does ABM stand alone. The United States and the Soviet Union are also far along the road to introducing multiple individually targetable reentry vehicles (MIRV). With each U.S. and Soviet launcher carrying several warheads (figures of more than ten have been mentioned) the number of warheads that U.S. ICBMs and SLBMs could deliver against an opponent would multiply by about six. From Moscow's point of view, U.S. MIRVs would raise the specter of a successful American preemptive strike. The Soviet reaction might include further increases in their ICBM and SLBM deployments and the accelerated development of their own MIRVs.[18] This would cause important changes in the ratio of deliverable Soviet warheads to American land-based launchers, which would in turn be interpreted in Washington as a dangerous degrading of America's assured destruction capability.

The danger of destabilization would be greatest if the development of both systems were to proceed simultaneously. For the Soviets would then face the possibility that while MIRV had given the United States a real preemptive strike capability against Soviet land-based ICBMs, the U.S. BMD and air defense systems could give Washington confidence in the absorption of

[18] Secretary Laird has stated that the Soviets have already tested some kind of multiple warheads. See Chapter 3.

the retaliatory blow by any remaining Soviet SLBMs and aircraft. Even in the absence of an actual damage-denial capability the American calculation, as seen by Moscow, could be that damage suffered in such an exchange would be much less than that suffered by permitting the opponent to strike first. This would be a powerful incentive to launch an American first strike in time of crisis.

A growing assumption of danger from America may in any case fit in with the broader Soviet assessments of current U.S. policy. There are grounds for believing that Moscow sees itself as reacting in an essentially defensive way against a forward, not to say aggressive, American foreign policy. The hypothesis of American forward ambitions is supported, in Moscow's view, by a series of events from Vietnam to U.S. support for Israel. The policy of détente in Europe has been to the Soviet Union's disadvantage. The German policy of openings to the East was seen as a policy of peaceful penetration by Western and pro-American influence, likely to undermine both the cohesion and the pro-Soviet attitudes of the Eastern European nations.

VI

If this is a fair sketch of Soviet attitudes, what American response can combine the need to maintain the strategic balance with the avoidance of an uncontrolled and open-ended arms race? There are clearly important areas of Soviet-American common interest. Each side has an interest in convincing the other that its aims are both limited and nonprovocative. Each side has an interest in avoiding actions that push the other in the direction of destabilizing forms of arms escalation. Each side also has an interest in preventing third parties, especially China, from using the disagreements between them for its own benefit. The maintenance or restoration of a Soviet-American balance at a higher level of armaments, in a way which insulates that balance from destabilizing activities by a smaller nuclear power, might carry benefits of a very high order. In the light of such consider-ations, and leaving aside the possibility of yet other weapons systems, four categories of action are presumably open to the United States: to proceed with both BMD and MIRV; to pro-ceed with BMD but not with MIRV; to proceed with MIRV but not with BMD; or to proceed with neither.

It is not clear that the second or fourth of these is possible. The cancellation of the Poseidon and Minuteman III programs, with their implications for multiple warheads, is hardly now practicable. And the lines of division between ordinary MIRVs and highly accurate MIRVs are so fine that no American MIRV halt announcement, and perhaps not even an agreement con-fined to MIRVs, could satisfy either side that the other was not deploying refined and accurate weapons. Nor is there any evi-dence for supposing that, in the absence of a far-reaching agree-ment which included adequate verification provisions, the Soviets would be content to accept any particular force level as a desir-able upper limit for their own strategic forces. All this is quite apart from the fact that a rigid limitation on American and Soviet armaments could only make the balance between them vulnerable to a China which had not subscribed to any limitation agreements.

To proceed with MIRV but not with Safeguard also raises problems. Abandoning the BMD program would not resolve those Soviet anxieties connected with Poseidon or Minuteman III. Indeed, it seems likely that U.S. MIRVs would constitute a much greater danger to the Soviet assured destruction capability against America than would Safeguard. The Soviets are there-fore much more likely to be worried about MIRV than about Safeguard.[19] Prime Minister Kosygin is indeed on record as being quite relaxed about BMD systems, on the ground of their

[19] Chapter 8, "The Case for Missile Defense" by D. G. Brennan, also sup-ports this line of reasoning.

essentially defensive character.[20] The way in which the U.S. public debate has concentrated on BMDs is thus quite likely to be regarded by Moscow as a crude attempt to divert attention from the more important area of MIRVs. Similarly, arguments in the United States about the acceptability of "parity" in strategic missiles are likely to be interpreted as a deliberate disguise for a situation in which America, while accepting approximate parity in land-based launchers, moves back to a posture of massive superiority under the more realistic heading of deliverable warheads. Moreover, if either side has doubts about the other's multiple warhead development, a BMD system becomes more important as a hedge against dangerous uncertainties.

A solution may therefore lie in limited deployments in both fields. It may be possible to agree on BMD systems for *both* the United States and the Soviet Union which provide a shield for each against China, yet are sufficiently limited to avoid serious danger to each other's assured destruction capability. This may have to be accompanied by an acceptance, on each side, of some multiple warhead developments by the other, partly limited by agreements on the numbers and throw-weight of launchers. The basic American strategic requirement has been changed. If assured destruction is to be maintained, its interpretation must be based on the proportion between the number of the opponent's *warheads* which can be expected to penetrate one's own BMD screen in a sudden first strike, and the number of one's own *launchers* which must survive such a strike to ensure that enough warheads are sent in reply to guarantee the penetration of a number large enough to inflict the desired degree of destruction.

The problem, of course, is how to assure each side that the other's developments, both of BMD and warheads, will stay

20 See Kosygin's London news conference of February 9, 1967, reported in the *Times,* February 10, 1967.

limited. A probe for solutions along such lines would have to include a variety of elements. It should be possible to persuade both sides that even if inspection agreements are not yet negotiable, it is in their interests to concentrate on weapons systems that are capable of inspection or surveillance rather than on those that are not. If this principle were accepted, it could result in important self-imposed limitations upon multiple warhead developments, whose policing would present the greatest difficulty.[21] It should also be possible to emphasize those aspects of a U.S. BMD that have a specifically anti-Chinese damage-denial connotation.

A fully workable solution to this major problem is not in sight. It is, indeed, not clear that any particular probe need be successful. The United States would have to carry its allies with it, including those allies whose own nuclear forces would be devalued by the parallel development of Soviet and U.S. armaments. The Soviets would not wish to furnish open proof of Chinese charges that Moscow was ganging up with imperialist America against socialist China. But the greater dangers surely lie in trying to cut off arms developments arbitrarily, especially in the absence of a clear and verifiable agreement with the Soviet Union.

Even if this line of approach is accepted, however, it is no substitute for an attempt to establish lines of communication and mutually understood signaling arrangements with China leading, eventually, to a *modus vivendi*. On the contrary. Long-term stability must imply at least the ability to understand each other's language, intentions, and modes of behavior. And even if BMD will suffice against a first-generation Chinese strategic force, it is not certain that damage denial can be maintained

---

[21] It may be extremely sensible actually to tell the opponent how many warheads one's MIRVs contain. But this is unlikely to be a politically acceptable proposition.

against Chinese penetration aids and other capabilities after, say, 1985. And if it can not, then BMD may have done no more, but also no less, than to provide the time needed to replace the concept of a bipolar nuclear balance with a tripolar one. What this will look like in practice cannot now be predicted. If the three powers remain mutually hostile, and if the conviction gains hold that conflict between any two of them can only result in a victory for the third, it may even prove to be quite stable. But the achievement of such a balance, like the notion of its stability, crucially depends on a degree of understanding on nuclear matters between Peking and the other two, which is comparable at least to that which now exists between Washington and Moscow. Clearly this does not yet exist. To bring China into the international debate on politics and strategy, including ways of communicating intentions reliably to opponents, is a matter of considerable urgency.

CHAPTER 8

The Case
for Population Defense*

D. G. Brennan

Don G. Brennan, a mathematician and a student of national security problems, is a senior member of the professional staff (and former president) of Hudson Institute. He is a frequent contributor to strategic literature and was the editor of the well-known anthology Arms Control, Disarmament, and National Security *and is the editor of the new international journal* Arms Control and National Security. *He has served as consultant to several government agencies.*

* This article is republished with the permission of the author and Pergamon Press. This paper appears as Chapter 5 in the volume *Why ABM? Policy Issues in the Missile Defense Controversy,* edited by Johan J. Holst and William Schneider, Jr. (Pergamon Press, 1969). It is based partly on the author's article "The Case for Missile Defense" in the April 1969 issue of *Foreign Affairs* and partly on "Post-Deployment Policy Issues in Ballistic Missile Defence" in D. G. Brennan and Johan J. Holst, *Ballistic Missile Defence: Two Views,* Adelphi Paper No. 43 (London: The Institute for Strategic Studies, November 1967). We are grateful to *Foreign Affairs* and The Institute for Strategic Studies for permission to include this material. Nothing in this document can properly be attributed to the Hudson Institute.

EDITOR'S NOTE: *While President Nixon's Safeguard decision specifically precludes population defense, this article is included to round out the debate and to show the value of BMD to potential strategic arms limitations.*

The subject of defense against ballistic missiles occupies, in terms of the debate about it, a unique position among strategic issues of the nuclear era. Missile defenses have been more intensely debated in the United States than any other weapons system selected for development, such as the air defense system or the Polaris and Minuteman offensive missile systems, or any arms control measure adopted to date, including the ban on nuclear tests. In fact, the decision to deploy defenses may well be more important than any other single decision made to date concerning our strategic nuclear forces.

But the published literature of this debate has been one-sided. With few exceptions, and those few mainly confined to journals not noted for their opposition to any weapons system whatever, most of the articles and editorials relating to ballistic missile defense (BMD for short—sometimes, but not here, denoted ABM) published before the spring of 1969 have opposed U.S. deployment of missile defense. For example, there have been three articles in *Foreign Affairs* prior to the April 1969 issue concerned in whole or in part with BMD, and all three opposed U.S. deployment.[1] In view of the facts that the U.S. administration clearly supports American deployment of BMD and that most of the senior American academic strategists and many prominent students or advocates of arms control favor deployment at least under some conditions, it is odd that so much of the early published material was single-mindedly in opposition to BMD.[2] The present article is an attempt to clarify for a

[1] J. I. Coffey, "The Anti-Ballistic Missile Debate," April 1967; Robert L. Rothstein, "The ABM, Proliferation and International Stability," April 1968; and Carl Kaysen, "Keeping the Strategic Balance," July 1968.

[2] An important exception is Charles M. Herzfeld, "Ballistic Missile Defense and National Security," *Annals of the New York Academy of Sciences,* Vol. 134 (November 22, 1965), pp. 119–25. Beginning in the spring of 1969, substantial material favorable to BMD began appearing in various sources.

larger audience some of the reasons why many analysts think it entirely reasonable to favor American deployment.

Missile defenses can have either or both of two major applications: for the protection of people and resources and for the protection of strategic offensive forces. The Safeguard program announced by President Nixon on March 14, 1969, has important elements of both kinds. The defense of strategic forces has been discussed elsewhere,[3] and I shall concentrate mainly on the protection of people and resources.

I shall discuss several considerations relating to a U.S. BMD system intended to have substantial effectiveness against major Soviet attacks, rather than discuss only a so-called light or thin system intended to be effective only against Chinese or other marginal attacks. Much of the support (both inside and outside the government) for the original deployment decision for the former Sentinel system came from quarters that believed that the system would eventually have significant capability against large Soviet attacks. It seems possible that whatever system finally emerges will eventually have such a capability, and therefore it seems appropriate to provide some discussion here of the policy issues this prospect presents. However, I shall also mention a number of points that relate equally to a "light" defense of cities.

In the first section I shall take up the technical-effectiveness issues and state several positive reasons favoring a BMD. The next section provides an examination of certain fundamental problems of deterrence and attempts to show that some of the

---

[3] See especially Albert J. Wohlstetter, Statement before the Senate Armed Services Committee, April 23, 1969 (in Chapter 11), and supplementary statements submitted by Wohlstetter for the record of those hearings. This material also appears as Chapter 6, "The Case for Strategic Force Protection," in the volume *Why ABM? Policy Issues in the Missile Defense Controversy*, edited by Johan J. Holst and William Schneider, Jr.

arguments about deterrence made by some critics of BMD are unsound. Arms control issues are taken up in the final section, where it is argued that BMD can contribute positively to traditional objectives of arms control and, in particular, need not lead to a new arms race.

SOME TECHNICAL ESTIMATES

In an important sense, the key issues in the debate about BMD are not technical. The sense is as follows. There are certain estimates generally believed within the community of people who have carried out the U.S. BMD development to characterize the plausible range of technical and economic effectiveness of systems achievable in the near future. These estimates are subject to some controversy. The sense involved is that even if the uncertainty and controversy concerning the prevailing estimates were wholly removed, most of the articulate critics of BMD deployment would remain critical: their objections are rooted in other concerns, which I shall discuss below.

On the other hand, there is an important sense in which technical issues are vital to the debate, namely that most of the support for BMD deployment, at least within those quarters in which such opinion is subject to change, depends on the fact that the prevailing estimates indicate that a defense of substantial effectiveness is feasible. Indeed, I myself was shifted from being a mild opponent to something of a proponent in part by a substantial shift in the estimates of effectiveness prevailing in the 1963–65 era. (The other major reason for my own shift stemmed from an improved understanding of Soviet perceptions of these matters, which will be taken up later.)

With this perspective on their role in the debate, let us consider briefly some of the prevailing technical estimates. The main published sources of such information are the unclassified "posture statements" issued annually in recent years by the Secretary of Defense, especially those issued by McNamara in 1967 and 1968, although some supplementary information has been contained in government hearings and speeches.

A useful way of characterizing the effect of a substantial BMD system is to estimate the number of lives it might save in various specified circumstances. In a table of such estimates given in McNamara's 1968 posture statement, it was indicated that there could be 120 million American fatalities in certain possible wars of the mid-1970s if no significant BMD were deployed in the United States. Against the same Soviet forces and attacks, it was indicated that BMD systems costing from $10 billion to $20 billion could reduce expectable fatalities to between 10 and 40 million Americans, depending on the level of the defense and the details of the war. Damage to production and transportation resources would, of course, be similarly reduced, a result not achievable with economically feasible civil-defense shelter programs. Thus, such a defense might change the postwar U.S. situation from one in which over half the population was gone and recovery in any time period would be problematical to one in which perhaps 90 percent survived and economic recovery might be complete within five to ten years. This difference would be enormous.

It is this possible difference that constitutes the major motivation for deploying effective defenses, at least in the minds of many analysts, myself included. In effect, procuring such defenses is like buying "insurance" that would limit the consequences of a war; the outcome would still be a disaster, but probably one very different from the result of having the same offensive forces expended in a war with no defenses. The immediate survivors of the war would certainly notice this difference; indeed, it would probably make all the difference in their own long-term prospects for survival and economic recovery.

It is possible that a BMD system might perform in an actual war less effectively than expected because of some unforeseen technical failure; it is, however, about equally likely that the opposing offensive forces will perform against the defense much less well than expected, which is to say that the defenses may perform much better than expected. (Critics of BMD are prone to emphasize the first of these points much more than the second.) And, as I shall indicate later, the deployment of defenses may result in saving many millions of lives in a war even if they fail altogether in the war itself.

Of course, the U.S. defense might have to face a Soviet offensive force larger than the one that would have existed it the U.S. defense did not exist. In other words, the Soviets could increase their offensive force so as to nullify, partly or wholly, the U.S. defense. I shall later discuss whether it seems likely that the Soviets would do this; let us here consider how difficult it would be for them to do it. This is one of the important technical characteristics of offense-defense interactions.

A useful way of characterizing the degree of difficulty is with a parameter called the cost exchange ratio, defined as follows. The United States might deploy a particular defense system at a particular cost. It would generally be feasible for the Soviets to add an increment to their strategic offensive forces that would offset or nullify the opposing defense, and this increment of offense would also have a particular cost. The ratio (cost of the offsetting increment of offense)/(cost of the defense) is called the cost exchange ratio. Thus, relatively ineffective defenses would have a relatively low cost exchange ratio, while a defense system that would be relatively difficult to penetrate would have a relatively high ratio.

Several years ago it was widely believed that missile defenses were easy to penetrate, so easy that offensive increments costing only one or a few percent of the opposing defense would serve to nullify it. In recent years, however, it has become apparent that cheap forms of decoys and other penetration aids cannot be relied upon to nullify modern defense techniques. A good defense can be overcome, but it is extremely difficult. This is reflected in the fact that cost exchange ratios for a good defense are in the region of $1:1$, *i,e.,* unity. Thus, *it is about as expensive to nullify a good defense as to build it.*

Some specific examples were provided in the 1967 posture statement. Two postulated defense systems were considered, one costing $10 billion and the other $20 billion. Under the conditions of a hypothetical war in which U.S. fatalities were estimated to be 100 million without any missile defenses, these BMD systems reduced the fatalities to 30 million and 20 million, respectively, if the Soviets did not change their offensive forces in reaction to the defenses. If the Soviets added an increment to their offensive forces costing one-quarter as much as the BMD, they could raise American fatalities to 40 million; if they spent one-half the cost of the defenses, they could raise the level to 60 million; and if they spent as much as the full cost of the defense, the fatalities would rise to 90 million. To raise the level of fatalities back up to the undefended level (100 million)—the usual criterion of offsetting a defense—would require an incremental Soviet expenditure on their offensive forces that would exceed the cost of the defense. These calculations assumed that the Soviets had advanced technology for their offensive forces and made effective use of it.

It is worth pointing out that these estimates were published by McNamara, who was an intense critic of missile defenses. It is therefore in no way to be expected that these estimates are biased in favor of missile defenses.

Although McNamara published information showing that exchange ratios were about unity as far back as January 1967, and although information to this effect was known in the gov-

213

ernment for perhaps two or three years before that, many critics of missile defenses continue to assert that it is cheaper to offset defenses than to build them. For example, Kaysen, in his July 1968 article in *Foreign Affairs,* said: "Were we to deploy much stronger and more costly defenses [than the initial Sentinel program] it would remain within the Soviet capability to counter them by corresponding increases in the size of their offensive deployments—*which could probably be made at significantly less cost than that of our increased defenses.*" (Emphasis added.) If "counter" means "wholly or largely offset," as is usual and as Kaysen's context suggests, there is no objective basis for the italicized statement, and there has not been for some few years. As additional examples of peculiar reporting of this matter, an unambiguous misstatement of fact concerning exchange ratios was contained in a much-cited article by Garwin and Bethe,[4] and a very misleading statement was made by Wiesner.[5]

Some remarks on these estimates of effectiveness and cost are in order. To begin with the matter of cost, the two deployments considered above were estimated to cost $10 billion and $20 billion. McNamara, in speaking about the latter program, several times referred to the fact that many weapons systems proved

[4] "[McNamara] finds invariably [in the 1968 posture statement] that the offense, by spending considerably less money than the defense, can restore casualties and destruction to the original level before defenses were installed." Richard L. Garwin and Hans A. Bethe, "Anti-Ballistic-Missile Systems," *Scientific American,* March 1968, pp. 21–31. (Quotation at p. 31.)

[5] "Secretary McNamara . . . concede[s] that an anti-Soviet ABM defense would not be worth the huge expense, because the Russians could nullify its effectiveness at considerably lower cost to themselves." Jerome B. Wiesner, "The Case Against an Antiballistic Missile System," *Look,* November 28, 1967, pp. 25–27. (Quotation at p. 26.) The Secretary had perhaps quoted such estimates in earlier years, but ten months preceding Wiesner's article he had published a posture statement including unity cost exchange ratios.

to cost twice as much as originally estimated, as indeed they have, and suggested that this program would more likely cost $40 billion when completed.[6] Some journalists and others have in turn doubled McNamara's estimate once again, and one can find articles and newspaper editorials referring to BMD systems alleged to cost $80 billion to $100 billion. It is difficult to escape the feeling that these latter estimates are made purely for their political effect and have no significant basis in reality. Missile defense systems had been much more extensively studied at the time these estimates were worked out than was true of many of the weapons systems whose early cost estimates proved much too low. Moreover, it is possible for the Secretary of Defense to decide to spend no more than a certain sum, say $15 billion, on investment cost in missile defense, and to instruct the services to produce the best possible defense within that budget, rather than to commit himself to a deployment specified in quantities and characteristics of equipment of possibly uncertain cost.

Obviously the relationship between cost and performance of a system as large and complex as those considered here cannot be specified in advance with anything like precision. This should not obscure the fact that the range receiving major consideration or advocacy is, say, $8 billion to $20 billion.

For some perspective on this range of costs, it is instructive to consider that the United States has spent perhaps $50 billion on air defense since World War II.[7] We are currently still spending almost $2 billion per year on air defense. And while estimates of the impact of the air defense system on U.S. casualties from

---

[6] The Polaris program, with a total hardware cost of about $14 billion through fiscal year 1969, is an example of a major program in which the actual costs were very close to the estimated costs.

[7] Herbert Roback, Staff Administrator of the Military Operations Subcommittee, U.S. House of Representatives, in E. P. Wigner, ed., *Who Speaks for Civil Defense?* (New York: Scribner's, 1968), p. 95.

215

Soviet bomber attacks are not available, it is a good bet that the current air defense system is and has been less important as insurance for the country than the major proposed BMD systems would be.

It would be fair to ask how stable these estimates of effectiveness are likely to prove in the future. That is, while it now appears that a U.S. BMD system could reduce American fatalities from 100 or 120 million to perhaps 10 to 40 million in possible wars of the mid-1970s if the Soviets do not substantially increase their offensive forces in reaction, and that the cost to the Soviets to substantially nullify the defense would be at least comparable to the cost of the defense, is it likely that these estimates will still seem reasonable when we get to the mid-1970s?

A question of this form does not admit an unequivocal answer; one cannot say with confidence whether inventions not yet invented or developments not yet realized will more favor offense or defense, although there are some reasons for thinking the trend will continue to favor the defense. But a parallel may be useful. In the United States we have had fairly high confidence for over a decade that the Polaris submarine force is a reasonably secure component of our strategic offensive forces. The main reason for this confidence resides in the fact that we have conducted a major research and development program— on the order of one-half billion dollars per year—in antisubmarine warfare for many years, and no cheap and reliable way of attacking such submarines has been found. A similar statement is beginning to be true in relation to BMD: We have conducted a major research and development program—on the order of one-third billion dollars per year—in means of penetrating missile defenses for several years, and no cheap and reliable way of penetrating a good defense has been found. This does not guarantee that one cannot be found, and it does not say that expensive ways of penetrating are not known, as are expensive ways of attacking Polaris submarines. But it does not suggest that the technical prospects for missile offense-defense interactions, while not yet as stable as the submarine-antisubmarine situation, are likely to prove acceptably stable, and in particular should be a great deal better than the early estimates of air defense proved.

It is worth noting that a BMD system may possibly have important effects even if it later failed to perform as expected in a war. If the Soviets were to react to a U.S. defense by retrofitting their existing missile force with decoys and other penetration aids, without a major increase in the number of rockets, they would reduce the total payload available for warheads and thereby reduce the potential damage the United States might incur in a war even if the defense failed utterly. This effect, which is known in the trade as "virtual attrition" and is often encountered in defensive systems of other kinds, is likely to be quite modest. A more important possibility could arise through retargeting of the Soviet offensive force because of a U.S. defense; the Soviets might concentrate most or all of their offensive missiles (apart from those used for missile bases or other military targets) on the largest cities to be sure of destroying them and leave unattacked many medium and small cities. Or they might attack only undefended areas and leave aside most or all the largest (defended) cities. In either case, the mere presence of the defense could result in saving many millions of lives no matter whether it "worked" or not. Freeman Dyson has summarized this possibility with the amusing observation that BMD is very good at protecting cities that are not attacked; the real point, of course, is that it may sharply reduce the number of significant cities that are attacked.

Let us mention briefly here three other positive reasons favoring U.S. BMD deployment. First, the time may soon arrive, if it is not already here, where there will be some possibility of attacks of anonymous or disguised origin. Since these would not be subject to standard threats of deterrence, active defenses may be the primary protection against such attacks. Second, the possibility of a purely accidental launch of some part of the Soviet force is probably very remote, but the possibility of an unauthorized launch, especially during an intense crisis, may not be so remote and should be protected against. Even a modest defense might be very effective against such an attack; this has been one of the arguments used—rightly, I believe—in support of the current Safeguard program. Third, missile defenses (even light defenses) considerably complicate the planning of an attacker who would penetrate them; this phenomenon seems likely to serve as an additional "firebreak" to the initiation of a strategic nuclear war.

It may be useful to expand briefly upon one of these points, namely, the possibility of a disguised attack, or what is sometimes called a "catalytic" attack—an attempt by some third country to trigger a war between two countries by attacking one in such a way that it will be thought to have been done by the other. Some strategists have been skeptical of the possibility that such an attack could or would be carried out. While it does seem unlikely that disguised attacks would be a serious threat in periods of low international tension, the possibility could be very real— and correspondingly dangerous—in a period of acute crisis.

Consider, for example, the Cuban missile crisis. At the onset of that crisis, President Kennedy said: "It shall be the policy of this nation to regard any nuclear missile launched from Cuba against any nation in the Western hemisphere as an attack by the Soviet Union on the United States requiring a full retaliatory response upon the Soviet Union." If the Chinese had had a missile-launching submarine near Cuba at that time, they might well have been tempted by what would have appeared, as a consequence of that statement, to be a possibility of eliminating both of their major opponents with one stroke. And if they *had* been tempted, the stratagem, as a consequence of the intense tension within the U.S. government at that time, might have worked.

It is not possible to protect against threats of this kind by ordinary deterrence; indeed, the major hazard of a catalytic attack arises out of, and is motivated and made possible by, an existing posture of deterrence. The potential role of active defense against such attacks is twofold. First, since such an attack would be relatively "small" (perhaps a few tens of missiles might be plausible in some circumstances), there is a good chance that even a light defense would completely or almost completely eliminate the damage the attack would have produced in the absence of any defense. Second, eliminating or greatly reducing the possible damage the attack might cause would greatly reduce the likelihood that the attack would trigger a near-reflex catastrophic —and catastrophically mistaken—response.

It should be noted that there are still other possibilities of undeterrable attacks, apart from the disguised variety, but construction of the relevant scenarios would take us too far from the main path.

PROBLEMS OF DETERRENCE

One of the main areas of concern to critics of missile defense has to do with the impact of missile defense on fundamentals of deterrence. While it is certainly natural that this concern should arise, I believe that any specific justification for the concern largely evaporates on examination. Let us consider this area.

The problem has often been related to what McNamara termed the assured destruction mission of the U.S. strategic forces, identified by him in his 1968 posture statement to mean "an ability to inflict at all times and under all foreseeable conditions an unacceptable degree of damage upon any single aggres-

219

sor, or combination of aggressors—even after absorbing a surprise attack" (p. 47). McNamara recognized that what constituted "an unacceptable degree of damage" was not subject to precise specification, and in spelling out this requirement, he said (p. 50): "In the case of the Soviet Union, I would judge that a capability on our part to destroy, say one fifth to one fourth of her population [*i.e.,* about 50 million Russians] and one half of her industrial capacity would serve as an effective deterrent." [8]

Let us note here that in this and in every other context in which McNamara discussed this issue, he defined the assured destruction requirement *without any reference to the nature or scale of the Soviet threat.* I shall come back to this fact.[9]

Because McNamara came to regard the ability to destroy 50 million Russians as the keystone of Western security, he viewed Soviet deployment of BMD as a potential threat to that security, and intended to nullify any Soviet defenses with added U.S. offensive forces. He also appeared to believe, and frequently asserted, that the Soviets had a similar requirement for an assured destruction capacity, and that any U.S. interference with this requirement would in all likelihood only cause the Soviets to increase their offensive forces. It appears that this perception was at the core of McNamara's opposition to BMD deployment, as it was for many other opponents of missile defenses. The U.S. strategic posture that has evolved from this perception in recent years has been aptly dubbed a posture of assured vulnerability

[8] However, in his table on p. 57 of Soviet population and industry destroyed at various levels of attack, McNamara underlined the entries for 74 million fatalities and 76 percent industrial capacity destroyed.

[9] It will appear throughout that I am highly critical of McNamara's handling of BMD—as, indeed, I am. I should like to add that, in spite of this fact, I still believe he was the greatest Secretary of Defense the United States had had, at least until 1964 or 1965.

by Steuart Pittman.[10] I shall later discuss the evidence concerning Soviet views on this matter; let us first review the origin and nature of the alleged American requirement for a fixed large number of Russian hostages.

The United States first became involved in the business of strategic nuclear deterrence in the very late 1940s and the early 1950s, say up through 1953. The Soviets had no major ability to attack the United States directly in this period and the primary perceived requirement of the American strategic forces was to deter a Soviet assault on Western Europe. This requirement (among others) was articulated by John Foster Dulles in his famous "massive retaliation" policy early in 1954. The U.S. offensive forces that were intended to provide the deterring threat were changing in this period, but the U.S. threat may be roughly summarized as a few hundred bombers armed with pure fission (not thermonuclear) bombs with a yield of a few tens of kilotons, for a total deliverable threat of a few tens of megatons. It is doubtful if the Soviet fatalities that this force would have produced were accurately estimated in that period, and they certainly were not publicized, but it is most unlikely that they would have exceeded a few million, at least until quite late in the period.

Now, there were many criticisms made of the "massive retaliation" policy when it was first publicized, but there were few if any criticisms to the effect that the U.S. threat was inadequately deterring. It is therefore instructive to recall the perceived Soviet threat of that period: It was the Soviet Union of Stalin, believed to have a six-million-man army, a Soviet Union which had only recently subjugated Eastern Europe, and which was believed to have instigated or at least approved the Korean war. Not even

[10] Steuart Pittman, former Assistant Secretary of Defense for Civil Defense, "Government and Civil Defense," in Wigner, *op. cit.*

221

the recent Czech invasion makes the Soviet Union of today seem nearly as threatening. And this was the threat that was widely judged to be adequately deterred by a few tens of megatons.[11]

Beginning in about 1954, two important changes occurred. The first of these was what can fairly be called a technological accident, namely, it was found that thermonuclear bombs could be made to work. This made it possible to increase the explosive yield acheivable in a given weight of bomb by factors such as 20 or 50 or 100. The other (and more important) change was that the advent of a Soviet long-range bomber force armed with substantial numbers of nuclear weapons presented the threat of a direct strategic attack on the United States.

In the period when the Soviets could not mount a major attack on the United States, an implicit part of the U.S. threat to protect Europe was the fact that even if the Soviets overran Europe at a time when U.S. strategic forces could not have put an immediate full stop to the Soviet production and military establishments, the Soviets would have been unable to prevent the continuation of the United States as a fighting society and the continuation of U.S. attacks against Soviet facilities and forces. The Soviets could scarcely have counted on any net gain from an attack on Europe in this situation and could not have eliminated their principal opponent.

When major direct Soviet attacks on the United States became possible, the structure of the situation changed considerably. It might then have become possible for the Soviets to have eliminated the United States as a fighting society and thereby to secure Europe and eliminate their principal opponent at one blow.

---

[11] As McNamara and others have rightly pointed out, the total yield in megatons does not adequately reflect the total effect of a force. We have, however, no better measure readily available with which to make these comparisons, and the comparisons in these terms will at least not be grossly misleading.

Thus, many strategists judged that there were two reinforcing reasons why it was appropriate to react to this possibility with a large strategic threat to deter it: On the one hand, this possibility might in some crisis have loomed as extremely valuable to the Soviets, a possibility for which they might have been prepared to pay large costs, such as a few million fatalities; on the other hand, if such a possibility came to pass, it would have been essentially and promptly lethal for the whole of the West—in a political sense, in a literal physical sense for many millions, and in an economic sense for the survivors.

The Soviets might in some circumstance have badly wanted to do it, and we certainly wanted badly that they should not do it. Moreover, there appeared to be no technical defense in sight that would have substantially reduced the possible Soviet motivation to do it, or our motivation to deter it. This was the fundamental driving force behind the evolution in the later 1950s and early 1960s of a U.S. strategic threat measured in thousands of megations—a deterrent threat for which "assured destruction" was indeed the correct phrase. It was the result of designing a force that would assure the Soviets that they could not mount a lethal attack against the West without encountering lethal retaliation.

It is clear from the origin of this perfectly reasonable logic that to the extent the maximum possible Soviet motivation for such an attack might have been reduced, the scale of the retaliatory threat might have been reduced in some corresponding degree. It is this linkage that appears to have been wholly absent from McNamara's thinking about strategic forces in recent years. So far as can be seen from the record, at least when missile defense was under consideration, McNamara was determined to be able to kill 50 million Russians *no matter what* the maximum Soviet threat.

If a maximal Soviet strategic attack were capable of destroy-

223

ing, say, 10 million Americans and 15 percent of our industry, they would no doubt be more deterred by the threat of losing 50 million Russians and 50 percent of their industry than if our retaliatory threat were "only" 15 million Russians and 20 percent of their industry, other things being equal. There is therefore a certain attractiveness in trying to forget about any linkage between threat and retaliation, and fixing once and for all some intended level of assured destruction which is believed capable of deterring the Soviets from any actions whatever that might bring this force into play. Among other things, this would spare the necessity of thinking through some difficult issues (though it brings in some new ones of its own, notably the question of how much assured destruction is "enough"). But there are a number of problems resulting from such a posture, of which the most immediate for our purposes is that it tends to make it difficult for us to limit damage to *ourselves*—that is, it tends to force *us* into a posture of assured vulnerability.

In particular, a determination to maintain a large fixed level of assured destruction capability against the Soviets led McNamara to respond to incipient Soviet missile defenses by increasing U.S. offensive-force capabilities, and the theory that the Soviets would do likewise led McNamara to oppose the deployment by the United States of an anti-Soviet BMD system. In view of the effectiveness of modern defense, we might better have used the U.S. resources committed to increasing our offensives forces to increase our defenses instead. By thus reducing the Soviet threat, rather than increasing our own, we should have reduced both the extent to which the Soviets might gain by attacking us and the extent to which we are intensely motivated to deter the attack.

It is easy to understand the effects involved here in a simplified case. Consider a situation in which Soviet and American offensive forces are fixed at similar unchanging levels on each side,

224

and in which both the U.S. and the Soviet Union are building comparable levels of defenses. If the American and Soviet defenses are both "light," then our BMD would not much diminish Soviet ability to destroy us, but then Soviet BMD would not much reduce the effectiveness of our assured destruction forces either; if both American and Soviet defenses are "heavy," then our assured destruction forces would be significantly degraded, but so too would be the capability of the Soviets to eliminate the United States as a fighting society.

This points to the following formulation of a reasonable basic requirement for a conservative American strategic posture:

> Following any plausibly feasible strategic attack by the Soviet Union, the United States should have the capacity to inflict as much or more total damage (of similar kind) on the Soviet Union as the Soviets had inflicted and could still inflict on the United States.[12]

In short, we should have a reliable capability to do at least as badly unto the Soviets as they had done or could do unto us. This would imply that if the Soviets started a strategic war with us, they would be guaranteed to come out worse—a powerful deterrent to starting such a war. The Soviets could not achieve a significant military advantage by a strategic attack, and an irrational, coercive, or punitive attack—whether large or small— would risk bringing as much or more destruction on the Soviets as they could or did bring on us. This would make the initiation of nuclear blackmail unattractive to any reasonable decision-maker at any effective level of strategic forces.

Let us note explicitly that this posture does not imply that a

---

[12] This principle implies that the strategic offensive forces must be quite well protected, which appears to be feasible.

U.S. capability to destroy 50 or 74 or 100 million Russians is a fundamental requirement of nature, without regard to the circumstances. It indicates that both the United States and the Soviet Union might reasonably engage in some measures to limit the possible damage of a war without necessarily impairing U.S. security in the process. Such measures might include, for instance, direct reduction of strategic offensive forces by agreement—or deployment of defenses with or without explicit agreement.

It is interesting that the United States has, in fact, proposed direct reductions in strategic offensive forces. For several years, we have had a proposal before the Geneva disarmament negotiations to reduce such forces by cutting a substantial percentage from each side in each of two stages.[13] It is obvious that this proposal must have been evaluated with regard to some criterion for a strategic posture similar to the one discussed just above; one cannot carry out unlimited reductions in offensive forces and still be able to guarantee the capability to kill 74 million Russians, or whatever such number is selected. Now, if certain necessary requirements are met, as they can be, a symmetric increase in active defenses deployed by each of the superpowers would have approximately the same kind of potential impact on possible war outcomes that percentage cuts in offensive forces would have. It seems odd that McNamara (among others) never appeared willing even to consider possibilities of missile defense in the light of the strategic criteria he applied to percentage cuts in offensive forces.

One may ask: If BMD deployed by both superpowers would have roughly the same effect on possible war outcomes as direct reductions on both sides in offensive forces, why not simply reduce the latter, and save the money and trouble of the BMD?

[13] U.S. Draft Treaty of April 29, 1965.

226

The answer is that in some circumstances one might, but the circumstances are not those now prevailing. To reduce U.S. and Soviet offensive forces to a level where the possible casualties on each side (without defenses) did not exceed, say, 20 million would likely be acceptable to the United States only with a degree of inspection that is most unlikely to be acceptable to the Soviets. In other words, there appears to be no current political feasibility of offensive-force cuts on such a scale, while there seems to be ample feasibility of suitable BMD deployment—which, rather than increasing U.S. needs for inspection of Soviet offensive forces, might actually *reduce* our sensitivity to such information. This effect, indeed, would facilitate later direct reductions in offensive forces. (There are other motives for BMD, such as protection against Chinese or anonymous attacks, that would not be affected by Soviet-American reductions. These motives, however, might be satisfied by a light defense.)

From the mid-1950s to the mid-1960s, the strategic postures of the superpowers were dominated by the logic that, since we could not defend, we had to deter. This position, for which there was originally ample justification, now seems to be interpreted in some minds—chiefly certain American ones—to mean that, since we must deter, we cannot defend. This should count as the *non sequitur* of the decade.

ARMS RACES AND ARMS CONTROLS

The final major area of concern to critics of missile defenses is that of arms races, and correlated arms control problems. The kind of arms race involved here is what is called an offense-defense race. The usual image of this is that if, say, the United States procures some missile defenses, the Soviet Union will feel obliged to respond by increasing its offensive forces sufficiently to nullify the defense. This increase in Soviet offense capability

227

might in turn motivate the United States to increase its defense capability still further, and so on. For example, McNamara said (in his 1967 posture statement, p. 53): *"It is the virtual certainty that the Soviets will act to maintain their deterrent which casts such grave doubts on the advisability of our deploying the Nike-X system for the protection of our cities against the kind of heavy, sophisticated missile attack they could launch in the 1970s. In all probability, all we would accomplish would be to increase greatly both their defense expenditures and ours without any gain in real security to either side."* (The entire passage is underscored in the original.)

If arms race responses of this kind occur, they will not be because of some fundamental law of nature, but will result from interactions of achievable technology with prevailing attitudes and budgets. Each of these factors is of importance.

It is useful to discuss this problem in terms of the concept of cost exchange ratios. If cost exchange ratios were as low as .01, or one percent, there would be little doubt that within the present political environment a defense system deployed by one superpower would be nullified by the other. For example, if the Soviets built, say, a $20 billion system, and if it would cost the United States only $200 million to neutralize it, there would scarcely be any debate about the matter within the U.S. bureaucracy, the Congress, or the public: the Defense Department would simply go ahead and neutralize the Soviet defense. In this world, the technology (as linked to budgets) would surely dominate the attitudes, and deterrence would reign supreme; defense would have at most a marginal role, at least as between the superpowers. There would be very slight motivation in either country to build defenses against the other, and most likely they would not be built.

On the other hand, if cost exchange ratios were in the neighborhood of 100 or more, there would again be little debate, but in this world, defense would reign supreme, and deterrence would rest on very different threats and counterthreats than those that loom as dominant today. In this case, to nullify a $20 billion Soviet defense would cost the United States $2,000 billion. The expenditure of such a sum within foreseeable budgets is not, of course, a realistic possibility, and the United States would instead be building its own defense—about which there would be little controversy, and which the Soviets could not offset either. Again, the technology would dominate prevailing attitudes.[14]

In the actual world that is upon us of cost exchange ratios near unity, perhaps one-half or three but not one-tenth or ten, the attitudes prevailing are not driven by the technology toward either deterrence or defense, but may (and do) go in either direction. It is much more a matter of preference and conscious decision whether we and the Soviets wish to spend our strategic-force budgets chiefly to increase the level of "hostages" on the other side, or to decrease our own. Thus, whether we are to have an offense-defense arms race or not depends in the first instance on whether Soviet and American attitudes are lined up the same way or not. If both governments are willing to accept a high level of hostages on each side, with modest or no defenses, there will be no great pressures for an offense-defense race; similarly if both are willing to live with substantial defenses and relatively low levels of hostages, with modest or no attempts on either side to offset the defense of the other. But if one side attempts to reduce its own hostages below the level demanded by the other, or attempts to increase the hostages of the other above a level the other considers acceptable in the circumstances, and especially if both happen together in any combination, the resulting

---

[14] Experts may recognize that this discussion is simplified. The principle illustrated, however, remains valid when the complications are taken into account.

pressures for an arms race might well be limited mainly by budgetary forces.

The fact that these issues are importantly influenced by attitudes is not always clearly recognized. There is, however, something of a "fashion" in some circles against interfering with the so-called requirements for assured destruction capabilities on either side, especially when (almost only when) the interference comes from missile defense. But, as I have argued earlier, maintaining very high levels of possible Soviet damage does not seem to be a requirement of U.S. security in circumstances where we can correspondingly limit damage to ourselves, and indeed it is in some degree antithetical to the objective of limiting our own possible damage. Still less, of coure, is it a requirement of U.S. security to maintain high levels of U.S. hostages on behalf of the Soviets. Outside of the group who have been actively opposing defenses, I believe that these facts are generally recognized among people concerned with national defense. Assured vulnerability has characterized the trend of our strategic posture in recent years because of the views of McNamara and a few others, not because of the defense community as a whole, most of which has opposed the trend. Therefore, while the kind of fashion mentioned above has and has had important adherents, it seems unlikely to prove dominant in the U.S. policy process in the future. American attitudes in this regard are mixed, but there is at least a fair chance that views favoring more emphasis on defense, views which are in fact rather widely held, will prove important in the evolution of the U.S. strategic posture.

Soviet attitudes concerning hostage lavels seem much less mixed, so far as can be seen; they are much more friendly to the deployment of defenses. In particular, contrary to many statements made by American critics of U.S. BMD, it appears that the Soviets are not substantially antagonized by the prospect of U.S. BMD. I shall mention some of the evidence for this.

230

Let us begin with the passage of McNamara's quoted above, in which he implied that it was a "virtual certainty" that the Soviets "will act to maintain their deterrent," that is, will act to nullify any U.S. defense by increasing their offense. Now, if the Soviets were in fact committed to a response of the sort McNamara said they were, which would at least cost them substantial money, the first ones we should expect to hear making such statements would be, not McNamara but the Soviets themselves. So far as can be seen, the Soviets have never been bashful about making political and diplomatic statements designed to deter publicly known U.S. programs they did not like, or to embarrass the U.S. over programs that at least were not advantageous to them. For example, they have repeatedly made public statements opposing the operation of U.S. Polaris submarines in the Mediterranean and the operation of nuclear-armed air-alert bomber forces.

In the light of past Soviet political offensives against unwanted U.S. programs, it would be remarkable in the extreme if the Soviets had the attitudes attributed to them by McNamara and yet did absolutely nothing to discourage U.S. defenses. The fact is, however, that there seems to be no reliable report of any Soviet attempts to deter our BMD by such statements—either public or private, official or unofficial.

There is a great deal of additional evidence, beyond this negative but persuasive fact, indicating that Soviet attitudes have not been at all in McNamara's direction. There have, for instance, been many statements by individual Russians at both official and unofficial levels, both impromptu and carefully considered. In a press conference in London on February 9, 1967, Premier Kosygin was asked: "Do you believe it is possible to agree on the moratorium on the [deployment] of an antimissile defense system [a then-current American proposal] and if possible on what conditions?" He replied in part: "I believe that defensive sys-

231

tems, which prevent attack, are not the cause of the arms race, but constitute a factor preventing the death of people. Some argue like this: What is cheaper, to have offensive weapons which can destroy towns and whole states or to have defensive weapons which can prevent this destruction? At present the theory is current somewhere that the system which is cheaper should be developed. Such so-called theoreticians argue as to the cost of killing a man—$500,000 or $100,000. Maybe an anti-missile system is more expensive than an offensive system, but it is designed not to kill people but to preserve human lives. I understand that I do not reply to the question I was asked, but you can draw yourselves the appropriate conclusions." Indeed, one can.

A detailed rebuttal to the standard arguments against BMD was given by the late Soviet military publicist Major General N. I. Talensky in the quasi-official Soviet journal *International Affairs* in October 1964. It may be interesting to note that the Talensky article, though not so identified, was at least partly a response to a paper presented to Talensky and other Russians earlier in 1964 by a group of Americans that included the present writer, a paper opposing defenses written by Jeremy Stone but which I had a good deal to do with. I have, of course, since changed my views, although Stone has not.[15] Many other contacts with Russians at official and unofficial levels, including several meetings I personally have had the chance to observe, illustrate that the attitude exemplified by the Kosygin quotation above is very widely held in the Soviet Unon, while the attitude held by American critics of BMD such as McNamara or Kaysen

[15] Stone's paper was later published, with modifications, in his book. See J. J. Stone, *Containing the Arms Race* (Cambridge, Mass.: The M.I.T. Press, 1966), especially Chapter 1, "Antiballistic Missiles and Arms Control."

toward the alleged importance of maintaining high hostage levels seems not to be held at all. Soviet strategic literature also does not reflect a McNamara-like view. So far as can be seen, the Soviets simply do not adhere to such a model of deterrence.

The main criticisms of BMD that have been expressed by any Russians, so far as I am aware, have come from a few scientists who have been skeptical of the effectiveness of defenses and therefore regarded them as wasteful of resources. It is probably significant that these scientists seem not closely associated with current Soviet weapons programs; I believe it likely that they are following the lead of some of their Western friends and counterparts, except that even these Russian critics seem not to share in the theoretical opposition to BMD. One major Russian scientist who *is* closely associated with the Soviet missile program has said (to Americans) that effective missile defense is on the whole probably realizable. Other Soviet criticisms, arising out of the March 1969 Safeguard decision, have been political (rather than strategic) in character.[16]

One additional bit of evidence is worth mentioning. After McNamara announced the decision to deploy the Sentinel BMD system in September 1967, the United States came under attack from several of our allies and neutral friends, especially from several countries participating in the Eighteen-Nation Disarmament Committee then meeting in Geneva, who complained that the American deployment decision would be bad for the incipient Non-Proliferation Treaty and would only heighten the arms race. There was one country that came to our assistance in that context, holding that the decision would not harm the prospects

[16] See Johan J. Holst, Hudson Institute Paper HI–1200–P, which also appears as Chapter 7, "Missile Defense, the Soviet Union, and the Arms Race" in the volume *Why ABM? Policy Issues in the Missile Defense Controversy,* edited by Johan J. Holst and William Schneider, Jr.

for the Non-Proliferation Treaty: that country was the Soviet Union.[17] So far as I am aware, this is the only case on record in which the Soviet Union has defended us diplomatically against our friends and allies. This is all the more remarkable in view of the fact that the Soviets did not, then or since, believe that the Sentinel system was intended only for Chinese attacks. (In some sense, as will be evident from this article, their skepticism was well placed.)

The fact that the Soviets apparently do not share the view of McNamara and some of his associates toward deterrence and assured destruction requirements does not, of course, mean that they are disinterested in military matters. It appears that Soviet strategists generally emphasize the importance of maintaining a good position in relation to the United States, but seem not to understand this to mean that they must maintain some large fixed number of American hostages without regard to the circircumstances. The sharp increase in Soviet offensive forces that has taken place in the recent past is evidence that they did not wish to remain in a position inferior to the United States in such forces; it provides no evidence whatever that they have come to hold the assured destruction dogma that has held sway here.

Some American critics of BMD have described these Soviet attitudes as "unsophisticated" and argued that the Soviets will "get over it" and come to respond to an American defense as McNamara predicted even if they are not yet committed to it. It is true that strenuous efforts to "educate" the Soviets have been made by McNamara and others, and one cannot say with certainty that these efforts will fail; it would not be the first time that the Soviets lost their senses over some issue just as we were coming to ours. But their views in the past should not be deni-

---

[17] See Thomas J. Hamilton, "U.S. Says Nike Will Spur Atom Pact," *The New York Times,* September 20, 1967.

grated; it seems to me, and to many other Western strategists, that the defense-oriented philosophy exhibited by the Soviets makes good sense. As to matters of fundamental approach to deterrence and defense, I should say that we in the United States might better acquire some "education" from the Soviets.

In view of the fact that Soviet attitudes already seem to favor defenses, and that American attitudes, while currently mixed, *ought* to favor defenses, the obvious way of trying to improve prevailing strategic postures through arms control arrangements is to limit offensive forces primarily, and to limit defenses only secondarily, if at all. This is exactly the reverse of the order of priorities frequently suggested in the United States in the past few years. It is, however, more in keeping with the traditional aims of arms control. The primary objectives of arms control have often been stated to be reducing the likelihood of war or mitigating its consequences if it occurs.[18] In view of the arguments of the preceding sections, it seems to me highly probable that deployment of missile defenses will contribute to both of these objectives, while abstaining from defenses will likely contribute to neither. If the deployments are managed with at least modest intelligence in both the United States and the Soviet Union, there need not even be arms race responses that would further add to prevailing arms expenditures.

This is not the place for detailed examination of technical issues, but I should remark that a suitable way of limiting offensive forces in such a context might well be to have an understanding between the United States and the Soviet Union, preferably an informal and flexible one, that the total weight of all offensive forces on each side—missiles, planes, and tankers—

---

[18] See my introductory chapter, "Setting and Goals of Arms Control," in D. G. Brennan, ed., *Arms Control, Disarmament, and National Security* (New York: Braziller, 1961). The definitions given there have been widely used.

should be held within some ceiling. This ceiling should be the same for each side and set high enough, at least initially, to include forces on hand or already in procurement. In that case, it would impose no new inspection requirements, that is, beyond those we already try to satisfy in the present world. My personal inclination would be to exempt defensive forces from controls altogether, except perhaps for interceptor missiles that were large enough to serve as offensive missiles, but if there were a suitable consensus that some mild limitation was desirable, such as limiting the rate of deployment to (say) one thousand interceptors per year, I should not oppose it.

Many opponents of BMD have agreed that an arms control program of this form seemed fundamentally preferable to a posture of abstaining from defenses and leaving the offensive forces unconstrained; they argue that a program of the type suggested here will not prove feasible because it will not prove acceptable to the U.S. military "establishment." [19] This assertion is subject to investigation, and considerable investigation suggests it is incorrect. Many senior military officers, in the U.S. Air Force as well as in other services, are favorably disposed to a suitable ceiling on offensive forces (at prevailing levels), providing it is possible to deploy defenses.

A more important objection to postures with a heavy component of defense that is sometimes encountered is the following. The Soviets might, it is argued, find some way of attacking our offensive forces with sufficient effectiveness so that their defenses could intercept most or all of our remaining offensive forces. By thus initiating the first strike, they might escape relatively unscathed—which, if true, could motivate the initiation of the strike in an intense crisis. It should be noted that the major studies of BMD performance do not show a dramatic dependence

---

[19] For instance, this seems to be the main point of difference between J. B. Wiesner and myself.

236

on who attacks first, so this concern has no current substantial basis; it is rather an apprehension about some future possible vulnerability that might occur.

Obviously no one could give an absolute guarantee that such a weakness could not occur. It requires, however, a vulnerability in our offensive forces of the kind that people have been trying to prevent for years; only the degree of vulnerability that would be significant would be changed by a heavy Soviet defense. If the United States were to provide added protection of its offensive forces by BMD, there would seem to be no reason whatever for believing that postures with heavy defense in both the United States and the Soviet Union would leave us more vulnerable to this type of problem than we are at present.

In fact, such vulnerabilities might be reduced. It is important in considering problems of this type to evaluate the risks of proposed postures in comparison to realistic alternatives, which are not without some risks themselves. In particular, our offensive forces of the present and recent past may well have had important vulnerabilities, including the possibility of undetected ones. For example, Senator Henry Jackson, in a Senate speech of September 25, 1968, discussed electromagnetic-pulse phenomena from nuclear bursts in terms that suggest these phenomena are a continuing source of concern for the security of our offensive forces. A potential vulnerability of a different type might have threatened the fixed component of our offensive forces if the Soviets had developed multiple, independently guided reentry vehicles (MIRV) before we had understood the concept ourselves. There is nothing in the public record that suggests that these have been the only vulnerabilities of major or potentially major concern in our strategic postures of the past. In view of this, it is not at all obvious, to say the least, that a posture of pure deterrence, based wholly on offensive forces, would be more secure against unpleasant surprises (such as a suddenly discovered extreme vulnerability to a first strike) than postures with heavy emphasis on defense. Even if there were some added risk associated with the defensive posture, this would have to be weighed against the possibility that the defense might save 50 or 80 million Americans in the event of a major war and make possible much more rapid economic recovery.

It will be clear that I believe an arms control program giving first priority to constraints on offensive forces, and second priority to limitations on defensive forces, is in the national interest of the United States; in particular, it would sharply reduce any remaining pressures for an offense-defense arms race. It is no contradiction that I believe such a program would also be in the interest of the Soviet Union, and therefore in our common interest. Moreover, as recently as September 1968, I have heard senior Russians suggesting unofficially exactly this order of priorities. There is thus some reason to believe that U.S.-Soviet discussions about stabilizing strategic forces may prove fruitful.

This discussion has mainly concerned near-term limitations on strategic forces. In the longer term, it may prove possible to bring about major disarmament of the offensive forces. I mentioned before that suitable BMD deployment, by reducing our sensitivity to inspection information, would facilitate direct reductions in offensive forces. Indeed, I believe the only possible routes to major reductions in offensive forces—that is, to a degree that would make a large difference in the scale of possible damage—that could prove feasible in the next decade or so all involve substantial defenses.

It may be useful to illustrate the effect involved with numerical examples. At 1969 levels of offensive forces, an uncertainty of, say, one hundred missiles in the number of Soviet missiles deployed would be of relatively little consequence for the United States. However, if it were decided to reduce offensive forces by agreement to a level that could not cause more than, say, 20 million fatalities, then the allowed forces themselves would have to be limited to something like one hundred missiles on each side, if there were no defenses. At *this* level of offensive forces, a clandestine stock of one hundred missiles could be of great—indeed, literally overwhelming—significance, again if there were no defenses.

Now, an inspection system that would reliably detect as few as one hundred clandestine missiles does not seem likely to be politically feasible within the next decade or more. On the other hand, a BMD system that would reliably intercept all or almost all of one hundred or two hundred missiles is highly feasible, and, if deployed, would substantially reduce or wholly eliminate the threat a modest clandestine force could constitute. (A large clandestine force could probably be detected by inspection.) Thus, defenses would make possible major disarmament of the offensive forces, as well as reducing the possible impact of forces in being when the defenses were deployed.

In contrast, I do not believe that any of the critics of BMD have even the beginnings of a plausible program for achieving major disarmament of the offensive forces by, say, 1980. Many of them seem committed to support forever a strategic posture that appears to favor dead Russians over live Americans. I believe that this choice is just as bizarre as it appears; we should rather prefer live Americans to dead Russians, and we should not choose deliberately to live forever under a nuclear sword of Damocles.

Quite apart from offense-defense races, a different mechanism that might lead to an arms race—perhaps a defense-defense race, or simply a one-sided race of escalating requirements—is sometimes said to reside in the possibility of generalized public pressures for "more." This line of argument is sometimes sum-

239

marized by saying that, in matters of defense, one cannot be "a little bit pregnant." Our experience in both air defense and civil defense is so much against this idea that it should be dismissed without further discussion. Similarly, it is sometimes said that the American public would not tolerate any inequalities in local defense effectiveness.[20] We have had a major air defense system with substantial inequalities in local defense effectiveness for perhaps fifteen years, and scarcely anyone other than experts associated with the system is even sure of whether his own home city even *has* a local defense, much less how it compares to other cities. The degree of awareness of these matters that has prevailed in the past in the general public is reflected in a public-opinion poll conducted in 1964, which found that two thirds of the U.S. public believed we had a BMD system all deployed and ready for action!

CONCLUSION

Space has not permitted here a discussion of several other problem areas sometimes associated with missile defense, such as the implications of U.S. BMD for the Western Alliance, or the frequently repeated assertion (which I believe is false) that BMD would require as a prerequisite a major expansion of civil-defense programs. Several scholars have, however, studied these problems, and I believe it is fair to say that on examination they seem even less likely to prove troublesome than the problems already considered.

It seems to me there is little doubt about which way the policy

[20] A good design objective for a BMD planner is to make all targets equally unattractive for the opposing offense. This requires that large cities be more heavily defended than smaller ones, but has the effect of protecting everyone equally in a suitable sense. Actual BMD deployments can approximate this objective, so the alleged problem is of limited relevance even in its own terms.

process in the United States ought to evolve in relation to BMD. The American body politic is unlikely to judge that pursuit of assured vulnerability is a proper objective of the Department of Defense.

The defense rests.

CHAPTER 9

The Safeguard BMD and Arms
Control Prospects for the 1970s[1]

Richard B. Foster

Richard B. Foster, director, Strategic Studies Center of the Stanford Research Institute (the "Rand of SRI"), during the past fifteen years, one of the pioneer systems analysts, has made a major contribution to many techniques and methods in the cost-effectiveness field of operations research, including the offense-defense cost exhange ratio formula. He specializes in analyses of the contribution of ballistic missile defense to deterrence of nuclear war. He pioneered early research on arms control aspects of strategic nuclear deterrent forces.

[1] This paper is an extension of some ideas presented in the Third International Arms Control Symposium in Philadelphia in 1966, in a paper entitled "The Impact of Ballistic Missile Defense on Arms Control Prospects." In it I analyzed the arguments of the opponents of U.S. BMD deployments that *any* U.S. BMD system deployed for *any* purpose would have a deleterious effect upon our efforts to negotiate arms control agreements with the Soviet Union. The paper appeared in the proceedings of the symposium, published in the book *Arms Control for the Late Sixties* (Princeton: Van Nostrand, 1967), and as a Stanford Research Institute Research Memorandum (RM–SRI–1), dated June 1966.

Three studies (Threat Analysis Study of 1964, DEPEX Study of 1966, and X-66) were undertaken by the Strategic Studies Center at the direction of former Secretary of Defense Robert S. McNamara, who praised the professional competence of these studies even if he did not agree with all of the findings. The SRI Center as a group, and Mr. Foster as an individual, lay few if any claims to certainty on the findings of its research, in accord with the best liberal intellectual tradition. But the center has striven to gain the best possible insight into complex problems and to arrive at what appear to be the more likely approximations, with the assumptions and methods stated as clearly as possible. Accordingly, this document does not constitute an official report of Stanford Research Institute.

THE SAFEGUARD PROPOSAL AS AN "ARMS CONTROL DEPLOYMENT" OF BMD

It is the thesis of this paper that certain U.S. ballistic missile defense (BMD) deployments will enhance rather than disrupt the chances of reaching significantly useful arms control agreements with the Soviet Union in the 1970s.

The Safeguard deployment of certain components of the Nike-X system announced by President Nixon on March 14, 1969, is just such a U.S. "arms control deployment" of BMD. As a unilateral U.S. arms control measure, I believe it will add to U.S. security and restabilize the strategic balance for the following reasons:

• In the face of the increasing Soviet strategic threat, the hard-site defense of Minuteman silos is preferable to doing nothing and risk inviting the Soviet development and deployment of

243

a MIRV capability in their SS-9 force, or proliferating the number of Minuteman silos and/or Polaris/Poseidon submarines.

• Some area defense protection over the entire United States using Spartan missiles against accidental, unauthorized, or "psychotic commander" attacks on the United States from the Soviet Union significantly reduces the risks of nuclear war arising from any of these causes.

• Safeguard will help dissuade Nth countries from developing strategic nuclear forces to coerce the United States, and in the case of Communist China, it provides the President other options than retaliation against Chinese cities in the event of a Communist Chinese attack on the United States.

• Some defense of Washington, D.C., as the seat of federal government, the center of our national command and control system and of the continuity of the nation's civil government, is a vital necessity against any kind of an attack from any source, particularly a desperation attack by an Nth power which might seek to initiate a catalytic war between the United States and the Soviet Union.

Most of the opponents of any U.S. BMD grant that the offensive planners in both the United States and the Soviet Union are forced to estimate that both the United States and the Soviet BMD systems *will* work in the future, and, therefore, must use high-confidence offensive tactics and penetration systems to overcome one another's ballistic missile defenses.

With Safeguard we are after all dealing with deterrence, not with actual war fighting capabilities against the Soviet Union. Deterrence, as defined in Webster's Dictionary, is "the restraint and discouragement by . . . fear." The deterrent equation has been defined as a product of *forces* in being, times the *value* at stake, times the *will* to order the forces used. Safeguard helps stabilize mutual deterrence: for example, the protection of

244

stabilize mutual deterrence: for example, the protection of Washington, D.C., as the national command center, helps to communicate our *will* to the Soviet Union or any attacker to selectively retaliate in response to an attack.

Former Chief of Staff of the Army, General Harold K. Johnson, defined deterrence in this way:

> The principal objective of U.S. military strategy is the deterrence of aggression at any level. . . . Deterrence is a state of mind and it is conditioned by perceptions as well as actualities of force effectiveness and judgment as to the willingness to employ those forces. . . . Deterrence is not so much what we believe as what the other person believes. There are risks and uncertainties in selecting various levels of military force. The requirement for both strategic offensive and strategic defensive forces is necessary to both deterrence of general nuclear war and is a means of insuring the survival of the United States as a national entity, should deterrence fail.[2]

Throughout the next decade of strategic arms limitation talks, arms control negotiations, and possible agreements with the Soviet Union, both we and the Soviets will have as a single overriding objective the minimization of the risk of nuclear war from any cause—mutual deterrence must continue to work throughout the negotiations. Soviet miscalculation of U.S. intent and overestimation of its own nuclear capabilities—both offensive and defensive—relative to those of the United States will, in my opinion, be the single greatest threat to mutual deterrence. Anything the United States can do to reduce the chance of a

[2] U.S., Congress, Senate, Preparedness Investigating Subcommittee of the Committee on Armed Services, *Status of U.S. Strategic Power,* 90th Cong., 2d Sess., Pt. II, 1968, pp. 245–46.

Soviet miscalculation in a crisis, or to reduce the temptation of any Nth country to attack the United States or the Soviet Union is an arms control measure, and the Safeguard BMD is precisely designed to meet those objectives.

Ensuing sections of this paper will discuss some of the major factors affecting the relationship of BMD and arms control prospects for the 1970s, including:

• The nature of the arms race between the United States and the Soviet Union

• The current setting for U.S. and Soviet arms control negotiations and the value of U.S. BMD at the bargaining table

• A new perspective on arms control

• Elements of strategic stability and BMD

• Enhancing the prospects of arms control in the 1970s with BMD.

THE NATURE OF THE ARMS RACE BETWEEN THE UNITED STATES AND THE SOVIET UNION

The Soviet Union is engaged in an arms race with the United States. They are trying to overtake the U.S. technological and production leads over their strategic offensive forces, and the U.S. technological lead over their MIRV and BMD programs. It is not, however, the kind of "action-reaction" race which involves a tendency by each of the two powers to respond to any expansions of or new additions to the opponent's forces by expanding its own. If the response of a second power to an initiative by the first power were followed by a larger response in kind by the first power, this would be a continuing arms race, increasing exponentially, until one or both powers reached the limits of economic capacity.

In the past there has been only a vaguely discernible correlation between changes in the U.S. and Soviet defense expenditures and allocations within the annual military budgets. This was especially true for supposed changes in components of Soviet defense budget in relation to changes in corresponding parts of the U.S. budget. Some new defense expenditures on specific items by one power have provoked little reaction from the other power—as is the case for the Soviet I/MRBM force arrayed against NATO-Europe. The United States, by cancellation of its MMRBM (Mobile MRBM) program, yielded local strategic missile superiority in Europe to the Soviet Union.

In 1967 the Washington *Post* reported that the Soviet Union had spent up to that time more on ABM deployment and development than the United States.[3] It was estimated that Russia expended from $4 billion to $5 billion on the Moscow ABM system and possibly some in other locations. The account further noted that these expenditures had begun in the late 1950s. Neither this early ABM expenditure nor the even heavier Soviet expenditures on air defenses triggered a counter U.S. outlay as the strategic "action-reaction" process would imply. Other outlays have provoked quite irrelevant reactions—not a direct counter to the adversary's move, but an imitation of it. For example, the U.S. bought more B-52s—not more active defense or even more protection for the B-52s it already had— after a Soviet display of heavy jets and turboprops in a May Day parade.

It would appear that the choices of offensive weapons by the United States and defensive weapons by the Soviet Union reflect national institutional biases, rather than a mirror-image "action-reaction" phenomenon.

Neither the United States nor the Soviet Union has permitted

---

[3] Hendrick Smith, "Soviet Spending on Antimissiles Put at $4 Billion," January 28, 1967.

military expenditures to reach the full level that its economy is capable of supporting, nor is the trend in that direction. However, in the Soviet Union, persons who have argued for increased nonmilitary investment seem now to have yielded to those who would increase military investment at the expense of other programs. The Soviet build-up to twelve hundred ICBMs in the past few years does not appear to be the result of a crash program, although the high cost of new weaponry and their space program has undoubtably retarded the growth rate of their GNP.[4] Currently the total national security[5] expenditures of the Soviet Union exceed those of the United States if Vietnam costs are excluded, and seem to be increasing these expenditures to somewhere between 4 and 6 percent per year. The Soviets are spending at least twice the annual U.S. expenditure rate for strategic offensive and defensive forces, and are still increasing these expenditures with no upper ceiling in sight. Soviet expenditures cannot be related to a "reaction" to U.S. outlays, except for the possibility that the sharply *increasing* Soviet expenditures for strategic forces (now about $16 billion to $18 billion per year) are a "reaction" to *decreasing* U.S. expenditures for the same programs (now $8 billion to $9 billion per year, compared to the peak of over $11 billion in 1962).

The Soviet Union has shown serious interest in developing and deploying its present BMD systems around Moscow. Delays in further deployment of Soviet BMD seem more attributable to technical difficulties than to a decision to defer action to await U.S. moves or to reduce annual military budgets. The Soviets are investing heavily in military RDT&E (research and development, testing and engineering) of modern weapons sys-

[4] See Chapter 6 of this book.
[5] "National security' 'includes the U.S. equivalent of combined DOD, NASA, and AEC budgets.

248

tems—particularly in strategic forces and in space. Russian research and development expenditures for national security in 1970 will be about $17 billion to $20 billion compared with the probable U.S. expenditure of about $13 billion to $15 billion. Thus the character of the arms race between the United States and the Soviet Union is increasingly becoming a scientific-technological contest.

The political aims and military objectives that inspire Soviet decisions are important factors in analyzing the character of the arms race. Soviet strategic doctrine sets a goal of strategic superiority over the United States.[6] The main elements of the Soviet strategic force posture development and design concept to support Soviet military doctrine are summarized in previous chapters. The element of Soviet strategic doctrine that causes the most concern in the United States is that part of their doctrine which calls for the capability to deliver a counterforce strike on the adversary's missiles before they are launched.[7]

The current high rate of development and deployment of Soviet ICBMs—particularly the large, accurate SS-9 with a

---

[6] See particularly Chapters 2 and 6 and Appendix A, "Soviet Views of the ABM and Soviet Strategy," particularly excerpts from the third edition of Sokolovsky's *Military Strategy*, and Chapter 11 (Wigner on Soviet civil defenses). I am indebted to Albert Ferri, Jr., and Harriet Fast Scott for their research in Soviet military doctrine and strategy.

[7] The third edition of Sokolovsky's *Military Strategy* contains this passage (p. 337) which defines the Soviet doctrine of strategic preemption:

"Possibilities of averting surprise attack are constantly growing. Present means of reconnaissance detection and surveillance can opportunely disclose a significant portion of the measures of direct preparation of a nuclear attack by the enemy and in the very first minutes locate the mass launch of missiles and the take-off of aircraft belonging to the aggressor and, at the right time, warn the political leadership of the country about the impending danger. Thus, possibilities exist not to allow a surprise attack by an aggressor; to deliver nuclear strikes on him at the right time."

potential MIRV capability—is at the heart of the Safeguard decision to make the initial BMD deployment around two Minuteman fields. When this estimate of Soviet capabilities is combined with the Soviet statements concerning their intentions[8] to achieve a preemptive posture, the *rate* of deployment of their ICBM force is the factor of most concern today in the U.S. view of the arms race. This factor will, I am sure, be high on the agenda in the forthcoming SALT discussions.

We can see that the complexity of factors in defense analyses do not allow any easy operational definition of the "arms race." The "race" is a compound of numbers (for example, ICBMs, SLBMs, megatons, deliverable warheads, annual expenditures), of values and outcomes (national and ideological values, will, population fatalities, damage to industry), of quality (RDT&E budgets and allocations, scientific manpower allocations), of strategic doctrine (balance of forces, relationship of forces, preemptive attack capabilities), and perceptions of the adversary's intentions.

All of these factors must be considered, and they provide no simplistic model, as I shall point out in the next section, for negotiations with the Soviet Union.

To treat ballistic missile defense as if all deployments and all rates of deployment were equally undesirable is to ignore the full range of actual decision options open to U.S. planners and to the President as a result of rapid advances in defense technology. A simplistic treatment of ballistic missile defense is an easy way to avoid thought about the real issues of stability of mutual deterrence and prospects for arms control discussions and strategic arms limitations agreements.

---

[8] I am using "intentions" in the broadest sense, in the manner that W. T. Lee presents in Chapter 6 of this book—namely, that the current strategic doctrine of the Soviet Union is to achieve both a deterrent and a preemptive posture.

THE CURRENT SETTING FOR U.S. AND SOVIET ARMS CONTROL NEGOTIATIONS

In recent years the United States has tended to devalue its qualitative and quantitative superiority over the Soviet Union in strategic nuclear forces. Some U.S. officials have argued that no usable political power can be gained from any form of strategic superiority in the era of mutual deterrence: ". . . it has never been possible to develop a clear concept for translating nuclear superiority into political power or international advantage once the other side has an assured destruction capability against us."[9]

Opponents of any U.S. BMD deployments—first Sentinel, now Safeguard—have argued that any BMD deployment, even a hard-site defense of Minuteman, against a Soviet threat would have, at best, zero strategic utility, and at worst, catastrophic effects on prospects for U.S.-Soviet arms control agreements. BMD would, in their opinion, accelerate the arms race, upset strategic stability, and decrease U.S. national security.[10]

To obtain a truer picture of the political value and strategic utility of U.S. BMD in the conduct of negotiations with the Soviet Union, it is necessary to distinguish between the projected and present value of future U.S. BMD deployments. The projected value can be illustrated by considering what contribution the Safeguard BMD may make to deterrence of Soviet aggression in the mid-seventies. The present worth might be illustrated by considering what value the United States should place on the Safeguard system, which, although scheduled for

[9] U.S., Congress, Senate, *Status of U.S. Strategic Power,* Pt II, p. 126.

[10] See Jerome Wiesner's May 14, 1969, statement to a Senate subcommittee, Chapter 11, for example, and the Chayes-Wiesner book, *ABM* (New York: Harper & Row, 1969).

deployment in the mid-seventies, can still influence possible strategic weapons negotiations with the Soviet Union in 1969. However, in order to do this, we should have a model of the U.S.-Soviet "strategic interaction process."

This strategic interaction process between U.S.-Soviet decision-making is not well understood and has not been extensively studied. Usually a mirror image approach toward the other side is taken by Americans. In this approach the values currently accepted by some U.S. decision-makers are assumed to apply with equal validity to the entire Soviet leadership. As a result, the United States tends to undervalue new strategic defense systems, particularly BMD, through U.S. eyes and biases, including the American strategic bias toward the "inherent superiority" of offense. In evaluating the U.S. BMD, the most advanced U.S., rather than Soviet, offensive penetration technologies are postulated for Soviet ICBMs in the 1970s by the opponents of U.S. BMD. These typically include a U.S.-style penetration MIRV, small thermonuclear warheads with good yield-to-weight ratios and high-speed reentry vehicles. Yet none of these advanced technologies is estimated to be in the current ICBM or SLBM development inventory of the Soviet Union; they do not seem to have either a Minuteman III or a Poseidon penetration system under development.

In a curious loss of logic, the same U.S. BMD opponents who postulate these highly advanced technologies for Soviet ICBM penetration systems to defeat U.S. BMD also argue that the Soviets could not achieve a much simpler MRV * technology in the same time-frame to attack our Minuteman silos.

The Moscow BMD system is probably at least eight years

---

* The Soviet MRV is a primitive kind of multiple independent reentry vehicle (MIRV) in that individual reentry vehicles can be aimed at an individual Minuteman silo.—Ed.

behind the technology of the U.S. Nike-X components of Safeguard. Dr. John S. Foster recently stated:

> They have, however, deployed a ballistic missile defense
> system, and deployed it before the United States; and the
> system they have deployed is very similar to the system
> that the United States decided not to deploy in the period
> of 1958 to 1961. But the system they have deployed is
> far inferior to the system we plan to deploy. I believe that
> is simply a mark of superiority we have in planning and
> instrumentation, manufacture, quality control, and so on.[11]

Although they are not proven, U.S. advanced penetration systems now in design and development are believed to surpass
the present Soviet BMD system. The multiple warheads on a
Polaris, for instance, are intended to exhaust a defense. This
means that the United States does not need to value more highly
the present Soviet BMD since we have already paid the price to
overcome it.

The components of the Safeguard BMD system, therefore,
should not be bargained against the Soviet BMD system, but
rather should be recognized as having much higher potential
and value, because there is no evidence that the Soviets have
paid the price to overcome it. There need not be a one-to-one
correlation in bargaining. If U.S. negotiators start by placing
a very high value on the proposed Safeguard BMD—that is,
that it is nonnegotiable—and then listen to Soviet views of urban
BMD deployments,[12] our negotiators would soon find out how
seriously the Soviet leadership values its current Moscow BMD

[11] U.S., Congress, Senate, *Status of U.S. Strategic Power,* Pt I, p. 113.
[12] As suggested by W. T. Lee in Chapter 6, and in Appendix A, "Soviet
Views of the ABM and Soviet Strategy."

and possible future urban BMD deployments in the 1970s and the consequent present worth it imputes to these deployments. Such reasoning also leads to a possible new perspective on the nature of arms control.

A NEW PERSPECTIVE ON ARMS CONTROL

Additional insight into the potential strategic value of the Safeguard BMD deployment against the Soviet and Chinese Communist threats of the 1970s can be gained by examining an alternate perspective on arms control, which meets U.S. objectives but proceeds from assumptions radically different from those currently held. This perspective offers the means to critique, and possibly improve upon, three often expressed assumptions: (1) that strategic nuclear weapons probably have only negative strategic utility or political value, (2) that they are only useful for deterrence of direct attack, and (3) that the direct danger flowing from an undefined arms race is greater than that from Soviet military aggressions resulting from miscalculations of U.S. intent or of Soviet misestimates of the balance of forces in strategic weapons, which could result in a nuclear war in a crisis. Under the assumption of negative utility, the objective of the current U.S. arms control policy is to work toward the reduction and elimination of nuclear weapons.

Alternatively, the premise that nuclear weapons may actually have positive strategic utilities and political values should be examined. This examination must begin with the history of the first twenty-five years of the nuclear age. So far, there has been no World War III, and no nuclear weapons have been used since Hiroshima and Nagasaki. Nuclear weapons apparently induce caution, if not wisdom, in those nations who possess them by limiting the temptations to use war—nuclear or conventional, however limited—as an instrument of policy or to

254

serve aggressive imperialist aims. By dampening the dangerous aspects of nationalism and sovereignty, nuclear weapons may make nonviolent adjustments of international disputes a more achievable and enduring goal.

The new perspective developed from the position that nuclear weapons—including certain BMD systems and deployments—have positive strategic utility and political value permits different approaches concerning arms limitation measures. This change in approach does not necessarily imply change in the fundamental U.S. objectives of arms control as stated by ACDA: "The Arms Control and Disarmament Agency [ACDA] seeks to determine a strategic balance among various groups of opposing powers which best contributes to the prevention of nuclear warfare, minimizes the destructiveness of war should it occur, and dampens the strategic arms race."[13]

Several significant reasons for examining this alternative perspective on arms control are:

1. The continuation and acceleration of the strategic arms race by the Soviet Union and the presence of conventional arms races, exemplified by the Soviets arming the Arab states and to a lesser extent the United States and its allies arming Israel.
2. The seeming invalidity of the technological plateau thesis, particularly for strategic nuclear offensive and defensive weapons systems.
3. The vitality and persistence of scientific discovery and technological growth in both the United States and the Soviet Union, as well as in many technologically and economically advanced third powers.

[13] U.S. Arms Control Disarmament Agency Letter, on "Strategic Utility of Nuclear Weapons," December 7, 1967.

4. The possible failure to reach enforceable agreements with the Soviet Union in the 1970s as to what would constitute a safe balance approaching strategic equality or parity.[14]

These reasons begin to point the direction for and provide the dimensions of an alternative U.S. arms control policy. Consideration must be given to nuclear weapons utilities which relate this alternative arms control policy to the strategic arms limitation talks (SALT) with the Soviet Union. These utilities are erected upon the following assumptions:

1. That nuclear weapons will continue to exist and may proliferate regardless of the Non-Proliferation Treaty.
2. That nuclear weapons might be used, thus requiring intrawar deterrence, war-termination capabilities, and defensive systems and control systems which would provide a capability to limit damage and prevent escalation to all-out general nuclear war.
3. That the broad interest of civilization, as well as the more narrow interests of the United States and the Soviet Union may be furthered by learning to utilize the presence of nuclear weapons, as an active component of deterrence to influence the behavior of antagonistic states, and using mixes of strategic nuclear systems to serve objectives beyond deterrence.

U.S. arms control policy is one part of the total U.S. basic national security policy and strategy vis-à-vis the Soviet Union

[14] Strategic parity as a basis for a stable balance of nuclear power is impossible to define.

and all other powers. It is assumed that the Soviets view their arms control policy similarly. Therefore, the underlying problem is to discern the influence of the various national policies and strategic concepts on the development of strategic offensive and defensive weapons. Viewed in this light, the controlling factors in any analysis of the strategic utility or political value of nuclear weapons are the more enduring policy goals and national values of both the United States and the Soviet Union. From the moment both the United States and the Soviet Union acquired nuclear weapons, neither side has abruptly changed its value systems, foreign policy goals, alliance system commitments, or nuclear policies.

There are seven additional controlling factors which I have examined in both past and current studies. These factors affect the formulation of a sound basis for both proposing and evaluating arms control measures within the framework of the foregoing reasoning. This list is by no means exhaustive, but it does suggest some of the complexities facing us in any arms control discussions and negotiations with the Soviet Union. I will treat only one of these—strategic stability—in this paper. It is listed last for editorial convenience, although it has first priority of all factors in any consideration of strategic force design. These factors are:

1. The impact of scientific and technical innovations, particularly those that would affect the relative cost-effectiveness of strategic offensive and defensive weapons and measures.

2. Development of tactical nuclear weapons, command and control systems and arrangements, and tactical and strategic doctrines that would limit nuclear exchanges to something less than all-out war.

3. Perceptions on the part of both the United States and the Soviet Union of the other's primary political and military objectives and concerns with regard to strategic nuclear deterrent forces and their potential differences as to the strategic utilities or political values of strategic weapons.

4. Lack of consensus among U.S. political leaders about the long-term Soviet objectives, intentions, estimates of capability, behavior, and strategic thinking.

5. U.S. perceptions of the nature and danger of the arms race contrasted with the U.S. perceptions of the nature and danger of a possible Soviet challenge to U.S. strategic superiority.

6. The changing number of Nth country nuclear guarantees, operational consequences of such political instruments as the Non-Proliferation Treaty, and the ability of one or both superpowers to "manage" crises created by third parties.

7. Finally, the most important factor to be considered: the conditions surrounding strategic stability.

ELEMENTS OF STRATEGIC STABILITY AND BMD

Strategic stability is a complex phenomenon. In this brief space it will be possible only to outline the differences between the U.S. and the Soviet views of strategic stability. Within this framework, we can examine some of the more significant elements that affect stability in order to show that BMD, if deployed as suggested by a Safeguard-type concept by either or both the United States or the Soviet Union, need not be destabilizing; and in fact, is more probably stabilizing and can act as a major "restabilizing" factor in the 1970s.

The concept of strategic stability, as it has been applied until now, refers mainly to the relationship of mutual deterrence between the United States and the Soviet Union. Mutual deterrence is derived from the present military situation between the major powers. The U.S. view is that both powers are capable of inflicting unacceptable damage in retaliation following any plausible and feasible strategic attack by either power. Any nuclear war would be short and would achieve no valid military objectives nor serve any political aims. This conception makes nuclear blackmail unattractive to any reasonable decision-maker, according to the assumptions that underlie this U.S. view. Some of these assumptions bear closer examination.

First, it is evident that strategic stability cannot be bought at the price of relinquishing all political and strategic initiatives to the antagonist in the conduct of foreign policy. Throughout the 1970s both the United States and the Soviet Union will probably attempt to meet their current worldwide commitments and to defend their currently perceived interests. Stability of mutual deterrence cannot be bought by the United States by giving up all alliance commitments, by unilateral arms limitations, by giving up sufficiency as the design goal of strategic forces, or by permanently yielding the strategic and technical initiative to the Soviet Union. This political fact of life has been made abundantly clear to the possible detriment of U.S. security by recent abrupt changes in Soviet rates of strategic offensive force deployments and of expenditures for production and RDT&E. How did we get into this situation?

The United States made some critical assumptions about U.S.-Soviet arms control policies and strategic interactions in the mid-sixties. The most important was the assumption of "sympathetic parallelism": if the United States held down or reduced expenditures for strategic nuclear forces, the Soviets would follow our lead. If we were to stop at one thousand

259

ICBMs, forty-one Polaris boats, *not* proceed with a new heavy bomber development, an advanced manned interceptor, or a new surface-to-air missile system to replace Nike-Hercules in defense of the continental United States, and if we further deliberately refrained from deploying a "heavy" BMD system around our largest cities, but rather, deliberately placed our cities in hostage to the Soviet Union to show our intent *not* to achieve any semblance of a nuclear war fighting capability, then it was as-sumed—or hoped, perhaps—the Soviets would follow us down the same path. We hoped that they would hold down their expenditures for strategic forces, would stop deploying ICBMs when they reached numbers like eight hundred or nine hundred or one thousand, would not deploy BMD, would slow down their R & D programs, would give up their "long-war" and preemptive first-strike doctrines, and so forth. None of these hopes has materialized. It appears that the Soviets have regarded the U.S. unilateral initiative in holding down expenditures for strategic forces as presenting them with an historic opportunity to achieve strategic superiority. This Soviet response, if con-tinued, will have the effect of destabilizing mutual deterrence between the United States and the Soviet Union in the 1970s. It is also evident that the Soviets hold a different view of the conditions of strategic stability than the United States.

It is now evident that neither the Soviet Communist party leadership nor the military establishment has given up the notion that the Soviet Union could survive a thermonuclear war, even if it received massive damage to its industry and suffered enormous loss of life. From a global strategic point of view, the Soviets probably believe that they would have a geopolitical advantage over the United States in such a war. Thus, the Soviets could exercise their regional strategic nuclear superiority over NATO forces in Western Europe where they have the capability and proper balance of forces to disarm, seize, and occupy a relatively intact territory. They could then convert the European economy to a producer goods economy to restore the damaged Soviet industrial base. They would probably consider this as giving them an advantage in postattack recovery capability, since the United States has no equivalent human and industrial resources in the Americas upon which to draw. They have held on to the long-war view of a strategic exchange.

All the available evidence suggests that the Soviet leaders believe they may have to fight a nuclear war with the United States and that, if they do, they will use their forces to achieve valid military objectives in support of their postwar political aims. Soviet military doctrine, strategic weapon development and deployment programs, the mission and organization of naval and ground forces, the Civil Defense Program, all appear to be derived from the objectives of survival of the Communist party and the Soviet State, with Russia emerging with a political and military advantage over all comers—Communist China, the United States, and NATO-Europe—from such a war. Their policies, programs, training, and doctrine derive from the expectation that such a war may be unavoidable.

The Soviet view of strategic stability derives directly from their concept of the dialectical nature of military conflict. The condition for stability of mutual deterrence is that of a balance of strategic offensive and defensive forces and measures.[15]

Their views of air and missile defense derive directly from this basic conclusion. Consequently, Soviet attitudes toward BMD appear much less mixed than our own: missile defense has been an accepted fact of the Soviet strategic environment since at least as early as 1963. The favorable attitude toward a BMD also follows logically from the Soviet Union's traditional "insti-

[15] See the quotations from Talensky, Kosygin, *et al.*, in Chapter 6 and Appendix A.

tutional bias" toward defense. This background has provided the Russians with ample theoretical basis for developing and deploying their missile defense systems.

In the 1963 edition of Sokolovsky's *Military Strategy,* the statement of the logical development of defensive strategic systems is presented: ". . . as surely as an offensive weapon is created, a defensive one will be too." The book continued this line by stating that in a future war the role of the PVO (air defense) and PRO (antimissile defense) will increase significantly. Protection of the rear of the country from nuclear strikes remains a cardinal objective in Soviet strategic planning.

Now almost ten years after the BMD question was raised in the first edition of *Military Strategy,* the utility of ballistic missile defense according to Soviet perceptions has not diminished; rather, it has increased as we can see in the new third edition of Sokolovsky's book.

Thus from the Soviet point of view, a U.S. BMD deployment will probably not necessarily lead into an exponential "arms race" any more than have the past interactions between the two powers. Premier Kosygin did not believe such a deployment should lead to such a race. In fact, Talensky's statement that the creation of an effective antimissile defense merely serves to build up the security of peaceloving states and would increase the stability of mutual deterrence, seems to reflect more precisely Soviet strategic thinking. And faced with the problem of arms expansion in other areas the General poses the question: "Which is preferable for security as a result of the arms race, a harmonious combination of active means of deterrence and defense systems or the means of attack alone?"[16]

The foregoing perception of Soviet objectives, values, and views of BMD is based upon the evidence of what they have

[16] Major General N. Talensky, "Anti-Missile Systems and Disarmament," reprinted in *Bulletin of the Atomic Scientists,* February 1965.

done, what they are doing, the explicit and inferred motivations for their actions, and their writings on strategy. Many of the opponents of any type of U.S. BMD argue from a perception of what the Soviets "should" do, and inevitably "will" do, no matter how contrary this assumed future course of Soviet behavior is to the observed Soviet actions, policies, and strategic doctrine. But even if the former perception is nearer the mark, what are the Soviet prospects for achieving the kind of strategic force posture relative to that of the United States required to fulfill their strategic doctrine—that is, victory in a nuclear war, with a preemptive strike capability built into their strategic force posture?

We have examined some of the evidence of the Soviet drive to "catch up" with the United States militarily. The U.S. view is that the United States and the Soviet Union are reaching a rough parity of effective strategic forces. If the Soviets regard the U.S. concept of strategic parity as a transient state, do they conclude that the opportunity to achieve strategic superiority over the United States is opening to them in the 1970s? To answer this question the Soviet leaders must make an analysis of the "relationship of forces" between the United States and the Soviet Union. There are six critical areas influencing a Soviet estimate of the current and projected relationship between U.S. and Soviet strategic forces. These are:

1. The Soviet Union has caught up with the United States and will soon be ahead in the number of ICBMs and has undertaken a major SLBM program. In terms of deliverable nuclear warheads, however, the Soviets may still face several years of numerical inferiority extending well into the 1970s because of the U.S. MIRV program, which to the Soviets may appear as a counterforce threat. The Soviets need time to catch up technologically with the United States in order to achieve qualitative parity with the United States and perhaps numerical superiority

263

in the number of deliverable warheads, to acquire an accurate MIRV capability against hard targets, and to develop a high-confidence penetration capability against U.S. BMD systems.

2. The Moscow BMD, the Galosh missile system, is comparable to the old Nike-Zeus missile, although the radars are apparently sophisticated phased-array high-capacity systems. Thus, the Galosh may never be deployed nationally for reasons comparable to those that led the United States to move on to the Nike-X. The Soviet Union is apparently in no position to match the current U.S. Nike-X system qualitatively, and there is considerable doubt about the growth potential of the Tallinn system as a BMD. The Soviet Union may have to continue research and development for several years before they can make the choice of going ahead with a national BMD or limiting the deterrent to ICBMs and air defense, although the Soviets are apparently testing a new "area" missile that can "loiter" in the atmosphere, according to Secretary Laird.

3. If the United States were to proceed with Nike-X deployments to defend cities beyond Safeguard in the 1970s, it would probably be perceived by the Soviets as a new and perhaps decisive dimension of U.S. strategic superiority in the 1970s. They may, of course, already have assumed such an eventuality and planned for it. Even if the Soviet Union followed the same pattern as in the ICBM case—that is, tried to catch up several years later—technological changes in defensive systems in the interim (the defense equivalent of the MIRV) could maintain the U.S. advantage and nullify the Soviet effort. On the other hand, should the Soviet Union succeed in developing an effective BMD in the next few years, while the United States refrained from deploying BMD against the Soviets, the margin of U.S. strategic offensive force superiority provided by the programmed U.S. strategic offensive forces—both ICBM and SLBM—to enforce the U.S. concept of parity may well disappear. Under such

circumstances, the Soviet leaders could well estimate that the balance of strategic missile forces was in their favor and adjust their policies accordingly.

4. While the performance of the SA-2s in Vietnam suggests that Soviet air defenses may leave much to be desired, they appear to be pouring money into improvements. A new generation of manned interceptor aircraft is evidently about to enter service, and the Tallinn system, if not a BMD, represents a major addition to SAM coverage.

5. While a comprehensive view of the Soviet antisubmarine warfare (ASW) program is not yet possible, some of the candidate elements reported to date are new classes of hunter-killer submarines, new classes of surface ships (frigate types), and two helicopter carriers.

6. As part of the rounded Soviet strategic defensive force posture, their civil-defense program also has some pertinent implications for the future strategic balance between the United States and the Soviet Union.[17]

From the foregoing estimate, the Soviet leadership may welcome SALT-type "talks" and negotiations with the United States that may extend over the entire decade of the 1970s. If research and development were not severely limited by agreement during this period, a moratorium on deployment of BMD and advanced MIRV systems would provide the Soviet planners with an opportunity to overtake the United States in the quality of its BMD and MIRV weapons. Meanwhile, their civil-defense program affords them a last-ditch back-up in the event of a nuclear war even without an effective nationwide BMD to carry out their strategic doctrine of the long war.

So far, in crises that have occurred since the Soviet Union

---

[17] See Chapter 11, statement by Dr. E. Wigner, for more information on the extensive Soviet civil-defense program.

acquired a significant nuclear strike capability—but one that is not yet equal to that of the U.S.—it has been possible to re-stabilize the situation before deterrence failed. However, with a "state of parity" rapidly approaching, a new setting for crises arises. Brzezinski writes:

Until now peace was safeguarded through asymmetrical deterrence. . . . That system worked for twenty years. It is being replaced by a novel state of symmetrical deterrence. . . . Perhaps that, too, will suffice to promote restraint, but the fact is that until now deterrence was unbalanced and the United States never had to face a crisis with the Soviet Union in the setting of parity."[18]

One of the most thoughtful analyses of the effect of Soviet BMD deployments around their cities on U.S. perceptions of strategic stability comes from Dr. Freeman Dyson of Princeton:

By [strategic] stability is meant a situation in which neither side is tempted to an unprovoked attack on the other by hopes of a cheap victory. Among American civilian strategists and, in particular, among experts on arms control, the notion of stability has come to be identified with the notion of the supremacy of the offensive. It has become a dogma that the maintenance of stability demands the existence of invulnerable and irresistible retaliatory offensive forces. . . . This dogma, equating stability with mutual vulnerability, has the consequence that deterrence and defense are regarded as incompatible. . . .

The incompatibility of deterrence and defense is, however, only valid if U.S. short-war doctrines are accepted.

---

[18] Zbigniew Brzezinski, "Peace and Power," *Encounter*, November 1968.

. . . Soviet experts who accept the long-war doctrine find no incompatibility between this kind of deterrence and a reliance on the most modern defensive weapon system, including BMD.[19]

Correlative to the question of a Soviet heavy BMD around cities is the decision of whether or not the United States will deploy BMD around its own cities. This question, I would guess, is largely out of U.S. hands and depends on Soviet decisions to defend their cities with a "heavy" BMD.[20]

Maintaining strategic stability will become increasingly difficult as allies of the major powers seek to attain an increasingly independent posture in the international arena, and as the involvement of both the major powers in the unrest in underdeveloped areas increases.

If nuclear proliferation continues, additional nations will seek increasingly to influence stability. And even if nuclear proliferation goes no further, Communist China and France will—as their atomic capabilities grow—be able to exert more impact on strategic stability than they have in the past.

Strategic stability, then, is not a static phenomenon. Every day, events occur which serve to alter strategic relationships temporarily or permanently. But these events do not necessarily include the gradual modernization and build-up of certain portions of the strategic offensive and defensive forces of the United States and the Soviet Union. Both powers have engaged in such acts, but until recent years their efforts have not been destabilizing with respect to the U.S.-Soviet balance of power. Yet the possibility arises that the Soviet Union might achieve

[19] Freeman J. Dyson, "Defense Against Ballistic Missiles," quoted in the *American Enterprise Institute Special Analysis: The SAFEGUARD ABM System*, pp. 57–58.

[20] See Chapters 6 and 8.

what it would consider to be a politically usable margin of strategic superiority in the early 1970s. Since a Safeguard-type BMD is a logical evolution from the U.S. strategic force structures currently in being, and since the Soviets view the buildup of defensive systems as a necessary and nonprovocative act, it is difficult to see how Safeguard could be destabilizing. It would be, instead, part of the evolutionary conditions for strategic stability to take into account the increasing ability of the lesser powers—particularly China—to engage in destabilizing moves.

Related to this is the problem of Nth power attacks that might destroy the national command and control system of either or both the United States and the Soviet Union. A BMD system deployed around both Moscow and Washington, D.C., is vital to effective "strategic conversation" with other nations, to ensure that the United States and the Soviet Union are functioning at all times during a crisis to prevent a breakdown of communication that has been an influencing factor in bringing about unwanted wars during previous periods of hostility between states. If a strike from an Nth power damaged considerably or destroyed the national command and control system of the United States (or of the Soviet Union, for that matter), such a situation would create an environment of grave uncertainty fraught with the worst possible effects. Safeguard insures against this hazard.

BMD could also introduce a certain amount of additional stability under certain other types of arms control arrangements when these might be agreed upon. Consider, for example, the proposal for a freeze on strategic nuclear delivery vehicles. Assuming that both sides pursue current policies and strategies up to the time that an agreement for a freeze goes into effect, the agreement would start with either the United States or the Soviet Union having numerical superiority in the inventory of

strategic offensive forces. If the Soviets continue to deploy ICBMs and SLBMs at current rates for just two or three years, they would enjoy a large quantitative margin over the United States. In all probability the United States will insist on altering this arrangement to permit parity, if not in the initial stages, then certainly at some later stage in the implementation of the agreement—just as the Soviet Union was unwilling to start talks until it had overtaken the U.S. missile lead. This alteration of the status quo—that is, the continued deployment of missiles by the Soviet Union while the United States stands still—could be potentially destabilizing. Unless, meanwhile, a strategic first strike had been made more complicated, even under conditions of numerical parity, by the addition of BMD, there would be a risk that the dimensions of deterrence would change. Furthermore, as Brezezinski brings out in his essay, "Peace and Power":
". . . since formally contrived parity appears unlikely, it is to be expected that the Soviet Union will seek to undo what remains of U.S. strategic superiority, and, in the process, whatever the Kremlin's actual calculations, will inevitably appear to be seeking superiority. . . ."[21]

Under such conditions it is doubtful whether any amount of inspection would insure that all cheating could be prevented. If the levels of strategic nuclear delivery vehicles retained in the inventory were progressively reduced under arms control agreement, it would require fewer and fewer additional hidden missiles in the absence of BMD to destabilize the balance. By increasing the aggressor's force requirements for threatening effective damage to a potential victim, BMD would considerably increase the number of additional missiles that would have to be obtained or retained through cheating. Large missile requirements for such action, to be certain of penetrating BMD would also increase

[21] Brezezinski, *loc. cit.*, p. 393.

the risks of detection of the would-be aggressor's missile stockpiling.[22]

Stability at the low force levels accompanying any significant arms control agreement would seem, therefore, to presuppose the existence of some active defense. This would be true not only of the proposed freeze on the strategic nuclear delivery vehicles but of all other proposals envisaging the reduction by stages of present arms levels. What many analysts overlook is that any changes in the status quo in the absence of retaining an active defense could be destabilizing at any stage before general or complete disarmament (GCD) was achieved. A small force of purely offensive vehicles of the kind that figures in minimum deterrence doctrines has deficiencies that flow precisely from its simplicity. Such an uncomplicated force may become vulnerable, if not as a result of violations of the agreement, then as the result of changes in the technological state of the art permissible under the agreement.

For all force sizes, but particularly for small strategic offensive forces, a mixture of offense and defense is less calculable and therefore more uncertain as to prediction of war outcomes. This introduction of significant uncertainties into the opponent's calculations (or large costs) presents greater risks for a potential arms control violator. Thus, while the attacker might believe that a BMD system can be penetrated, neither defender nor attacker can be sure of this. In addition to this, the reduction by the great powers of offensive forces without any existent defense would offer temptations to ambitious Nth countries. The lower the force levels of the major powers, the more feasible it then is for smaller powers to play a destabilizing role in the international environment. In this situation the existence of a defense

[22] Dr. Albert Wohlstetter has done extensive research and analysis of this problem, and I am indebted to him for much of the logic and many of the conclusions which appear in the balance of this discussion.

force by the great powers tends to keep smaller powers out-classed. This point must also be considered when evaluating the stability of multilateral agreements. Such agreements are threatened, not only by alterations in the status of great power forces that are subject to these agreements, but also by the destabilizing potential from smaller powers, both those that are party to any agreements and those that are not.

The greatest threat to stability is the Soviet attempt to gain strategic nuclear superiority—particularly in strategic offensive missiles—by the mid-seventies. The two entirely differing U.S. and Soviet views of the conditions of strategic stability—views that will ultimately have to be reconciled in order to achieve any lasting agreement on strategic weapons limitations—can in part be reconciled by agreement on certain roles for defense.

ENHANCING THE PROSPECTS OF ARMS CONTROL WITH BMD

What role can BMD play in meeting the two apparently contradictory U.S. objectives of restabilizing the deterrent with-out fueling the arms race while at the same time encouraging arms control negotiations with the Soviet Union in the 1970s? These two apparently contradictory U.S. objectives may well be met by a Safeguard-type arms control deployment of BMD.

Any agreement for a freeze or reduction of strategic nuclear delivery vehicles connected with BMD "arms control" or "sta-bilizing deployments" would in many ways be more complex, more momentous, and more wide ranging than the sum total of all past agreements with the Soviet Union. It would involve for both sides difficult calculations of its effect on the relative strategic balance: for the United States, vital concerns about inspection, verification, and sanctions; for the Soviet Union, grave issues of intelligence and the loosening political control,

271

a further exposure of Soviet society to outside influences. While it is possible that these issues can be responsibly settled to the mutual satisfaction of both groups, the working out of these negotiations will be spread over a period of time—some say ten years at least—if they will be successful at all. When present international factors such as the schisms plaguing the Soviet bloc and the international communist movement (perhaps movements is more accurate) are inserted into the discussions and contemporary Soviet politics are taken into account, the requirements of "opening up" the Soviet Union even slightly, do not seem presently promising. Finally, Soviet negotiators have shown little interest in a freeze; instead they have argued for a most drastic reduction of nuclear delivery vehicles in accordance with their declaratory policy of general and complete disarmament.

The Soviets do not accept the idea that all BMD deployments are destabilizing. Since the Soviets have already deployed some BMD, the United States would be faced with the additional difficult task of inducing the Soviet Union to dismantle its present BMD and whatever BMD it may have at the time of an agreement to freeze offensive forces. This situation would complicate the negotiations over a freeze on nuclear delivery vehicles with ones of BMD force reductions. We would not be dealing with simple equal reductions (such as the percentage reduction envisaged in another of our disarmament proposals), but with a trade of their BMD dismantling against another type of reduction on our side.

One of the most intricate problems of arms control talks and possible subsequent agreements to freeze, limit, or reduce strategic weapons is the reflection any such activity will have in the international strategic environment. What political, military, strategic, and technological ramifications will any or all arms control measures have for the United States vis-à-vis the Soviet

272

Union, China, our allies, and the neutral Third World? What type of action can be taken to insure against the widest possible range of disadvantageous situations that may result in the 1970s and beyond? Both questions point to the paramount importance of BMD as a part of a balanced strategic offense-defense posture that has the required elasticity for unforeseeable "scenarios" that may occur in the 1970s.

All arms agreements have to start somewhere. A likely way to start is with a freeze on further deployments of weapons. If we freeze only offensive delivery vehicles (and prohibit also the testing of such vehicles—including advances in technology, such as MIRV—except in some critical amount necessary to maintain an operational capability), the advances by one side in the development or sophistication of the defense might upset the balance aimed at in the agreement. In that case, the other side might increase its research and development expenditures on defense to restore the balance—and so we return to an "arms race", one restricted, however, to a competition on active defense. Alternatively, the other side would be tempted to abrogate the offensive agreement by increasing its penetration capabilities through a test program for penetration aids based on advanced technologies, such as MIRV, in violation of the agreement. Thus, from the viewpoint of long-term arms control objectives, a freeze (and later reduction) of strategic delivery vehicles that permitted no BMD at all would be less desirable than a freeze that permitted a certain level of BMD, at least of the Safeguard type of coverage.

As has been pointed out already, a combination of offense and active defense is more complex to analyze than a posture that involves only controlled and inspected offensive forces. Hence, a violator of the arms control agreement who wanted to plan an attack would be confronted with greater uncertainties if the remaining "mix" included defensive forces than if there

273

were only offensive forces left. This uncertainty would strengthen the deterrent and make the intended violator of the agreement more cautious.

Secondly, active defenses—and especially BMD—can facilitate U.S.-Soviet disarmament agreements on strategic delivery vehicles by reducing the obstacle that the presence of ambitious independent nuclear powers (such as China) would otherwise present. It is hard to see how China could be induced to accept an agreement to freeze strategic delivery vehicles unless she had already acquired—or was permitted to acquire—a strategic capability of her own that was not insignificant in relation to either the U.S. or the Soviet capability. But given such a Communist Chinese capability, an agreement without active defenses would seem highly unstable. From the Soviet point of view, an agreement that left Great Britain, Communist China, and/or France free to upset stability might be equally risky. The problem will be compounded if nuclear proliferation continues.

Thirdly, if one envisages a progressive reduction of strategic offensive forces, periods of instability may occur as these forces are reduced. Without active defenses, periods of acute instability may occur as the remaining offensive forces reach the lower levels. At lower levels of offensive armament active defenses might be restabilizing because they would reduce the incentives to violate the agreement.

Retention of active defensive forces, including BMD, might enhance the stability of arms control agreements, and hence, improve chances of reaching such agreements. To envisage such agreements solely in terms of controlling the offensive forces of the two sides is an oversimplification of the problem. More attention must be given to the role of active defense in the strategic postures of the two sides. As long as this role exists—and technological trends indicate that it will increase and not decrease in the future—the defensive systems including BMD must be taken as fully into account in arms control proposals as now are offensive systems. In fact, BMD seems to hold promise of rendering otherwise risky and potentially destabilizing arms control arrangements far more stable and far less risky.

Many of the concerns over the dangers of the nuclear arms race expressed by some U.S. leaders flow from considerations for human life and other humanitarian values. However important, these do not give sufficient guidance either for the design of the U.S. strategic force posture for the seventies or for the conduct of arms control negotiations with the Soviet Union. Any evaluation of U.S. alternative nuclear strategies and policies for the seventies vis-à-vis the Soviet Union must take other values into account—particularly political and ideological values. In this regard, it may be instructive to read a formulation of the problem by Henry L. Roberts:

> In what sense does the possibility of extending obliteration from the individual, or even the society or the nation, to the whole of humanity make a difference? . . . *To affirm, without any qualification, that the human race must go on is to accept, if it proved to be necessary for the race's survival, the obliteration of one's own nation, community, family, or self.* The human individual can make such an affirmation for himself. The statesman or citizen cannot, at least not without denying the state he is serving or the society of which he is a member. As a political act it would mean an absolute, unconditional surrender. This not only would be the last political act but would of course make nonsense of all policy, since the opponent, if he so willed, could safely impale all proposals, negotiations, or bluffs on this ultimate renunciation.[23]

[23] Henry L. Roberts, *Russia and America: Dangers and Prospects* (New York: New American Library, 1956), pp. 39–40. Emphasis added.

275

We cannot afford to let the Soviets unilaterally achieve a balanced strategic offensive and defensive posture with a capability to defend their cities against U.S. retaliatory attacks. Independent of U.S. estimates of Soviet BMD effectiveness, the Soviets could—and probably would—increase the tempo of their political initiatives. Arms control prospects would disappear in the Soviet conviction that they had "won"—that their political values and strategic concepts were inherently superior to those of the United States.

The lead-times for high-confidence intelligence are too short to allow a delay in beginning procurement and deployment of the principal elements of the Safeguard system after we are certain that the Soviets have developed and deployed a MRV capability and after the Chinese Communists have test-flown an operational ICBM. The Sprint and Spartan missile, the PAR and MSR radar, the associated computer and automatic data processing equipment, the intricate communications and switching equipment that nets the various radars and the missile sites, and the cadre of trained men who will maintain the early deployed systems can be carried in development inventory just so long—and at a certain point, operational deployment is necessary to prove the system and to deny the Soviets an opportunity to blackmail the United States.

The Safeguard-type "arms control deployments" of BMD in defense of Minuteman silos, SAC air bases, a light area defense of the entire country against light attacks from any source, and the combined area and local defense of Washington, D.C., should be regarded as the minimum U.S. defensive elements of any arms control agreement with the Soviet Union. The Safeguard-type system will also contribute to a considerable degree in restabilizing strategic deterrence by preventing the Soviets from gaining an effective first-strike capability against our Minuteman force and our SAC bomber bases. For these reasons I

276

do not believe that the Safeguard system is or should be negotiable. I believe that a decision to deploy Safeguard is a necessary prelude to successful arms control talks with the Soviets. I would expect the Soviet leadership to regard their ABM deployment in the Soviet Union in the same way.

CHAPTER 10

Why a Senator
Is in Favor of Safeguard

Senator Howard H. Baker, Jr.

Senator Howard H. Baker, Jr., a son of former Congressman Howard H. Baker and former Congresswoman Irene Baker, is the first Republican to be elected to the Senate by the people of Tennessee. After doing undergraduate work in Electrical Engineering at Tulane University and receiving a Doctor of Jurisprudence degree from the University of Tennessee, he engaged in private law practice in Knoxville prior to his election to the Senate in 1966. Because he grew up in a family involved in public affairs and partly because of his technological education and his long association with scientists at the Oak Ridge Laboratory, Senator Baker developed a sustained interest in the rationale of defensive missile systems—heightened by President Johnson's decision to deploy the Sentinel ABM system in 1967. He closely follows the latest technological intelligence-information concerning matters of national security. He has often conferred with scientists and diplomats, some of whom have supported the deployment of an ABM and others who have not. He has have not. He has addressed the Senate several times on the ABM question and supported the Safeguard system when it was announced by President Nixon on March 14, 1969.

For many Americans, the antiballistic missile is no longer part of a specific weapons system; it has become the symbol of an increasing public concern about the goals of this nation's foreign policy and the wisdom of those who make and administer it. It is seen as the most recent and most politically vulnerable example of the way an unholy though natural alliance of military and industrial leaders can promote for its own purposes an expensive weapon of dubious need and technical efficacy. In a time of serious domestic crisis, it is viewed as evidence that the political and economic establishment is either unwilling or unable to respond to growing public demand for a major shift in funding priorities, from defense spending to social programs.

There is much that is healthy in this public interest and participation in the examination of a major weapons system. In a speech at the Air Force Academy on June 4, 1969, a speech for which he was vigorously criticized in some quarters, President Nixon acknowledged the value of "those responsible critics who reveal waste and inefficiency in our defense establishment, who demand clear answers on procurement policies, who want to make sure that a new weapons system will truly add to our defense."

That there has been such waste and inefficiency is beyond doubt. Recent and widely publicized experience with such projects as the F-111 or TFX and cost overruns on the C-5A and Minuteman II has inspired overdue demands for greater congressional and administrative control in the authorization and procedures under which major contracts are awarded. One highly salutary effect of this new public interest in defense

279

spending has been recognition by the Congress of how ill-equipped it is itself to evaluate adequately the merits of complex military hardware.

Steps are already under way to remedy this deficiency, and it is difficult to imagine that any future major military proposal will be approved without the most exhaustive and critical Congressional examination. A concomitant development is the virtual certainty that no President will ever again send to Congress a major system or project without being satisfied that it can be well defended against anticipated public and congressional scrutiny.

Thus, much good has come from new, critical public interest in defense expenditures. However, there lies in this same public interest a grave danger; the formulation and execution of a genuinely responsible foreign policy and defense strategy may be impeded or even rendered impossible by an *uncritical and categorical public opposition to anything military.*

I do not believe, as some profess to do, that a significant segment of the American public would advocate unilateral disarmament by the United States. It appears that there are a growing number of Americans who feel that international realities now permit the formulation of an effective foreign policy that would not include a strong defense posture. There is a great difference between a demand that defense expenditures be efficiently administered and the view that the maintenance of American military strength is unwarranted and even immoral. There is cause for serious concern if there is, or is about to be, a significant number of American citizens who feel that any military proposal, simply because it *is* a military proposal, is evil and should be prevented.

Currently appearing in magazines and newspapers around the country is an advertisement by one of several groups opposing deployment of the ABM that shows a quite cleverly drawn

280

cartoon of a group of frenzied and addled generals gloating around a mock-up of a Spartan missile. The cartoon bears the legend: "From the people who brought you the War in Vietnam —the anti-ballistic missile." A respected publishing company asks the readers of another advertisement to respond "yes" or "no" to the statement: "I really believe that my family and I will be safe [not "safer," it will be noted] once we proceed with the Safeguard ABM." *The New Yorker* includes a parody of how the Defense Department justifies the ABM. It features, among other things, two faceless military officers holding keys to the launch mechanism as well as a chart simultaneously comparing the output of dairy products in the Soviet Union and in the United States and the first- and second-strike capabilities of both nations.

All this suggests that public debate on the Safeguard system has lost sight of the system itself. Whether the system has merit has become largely irrelevant. I do not mean to imply that the large and symbolic issues that pertain to the system are not important. They clearly are. But I am deeply concerned that the factors that *should* control the decision of whether to deploy the Safeguard system may have little to do with that decision. I find myself possessed of the curious and ironic fear that a military system I believe to be needed by this country may be sacrificed to broad national concerns and commitments in which I also believe and which would, I think, be advanced and protected by the Safeguard ABM system.

It is important that a serious effort be made by responsible proponents and opponents alike to restore some degree of perspective to the public debate on the ABM deployment. Almost as important as the authorization is the manner in which that decision is reached. There are ominous implications for the political processes of this country if such important issues are settled in an emotional and reckless atmosphere. Bertrand Russell has observed, "The essence of the Liberal outlook lies not in *what* opinions are held, but in *how* they are held." In the ABM debate, emotional and specious appeals by either side are equally reprehensible and destructive to the deliberative process, whether they are to arrogant and adolescent self-righteousness or to irrational fear of a Communist menace and nuclear annihilation.

I find that the arguments of Safeguard opponents can be summarized in the following way: (1) the system is at best unnecessary and at worst will severely limit the prospects for productive arms talks with the Soviet Union; (2) it is technologically unreliable and could be easily overwhelmed or neutralized by the Soviet Union; (3) it represents a dangerous and immoral commitment to an expanded arms race at a time when there exists a unique historical opportunity for the United States to exercise restraint, which is consistent with its national ideals and its desire for peace; and (4) it diverts to military purposes public resources critically needed for social progress at home.

It is my carefully reached and strongly held conviction that, on the contrary, deployment of the Safeguard antiballistic missile system: (1) is necessary for national security and will greatly enhance the possibility of meaningful arms agreements with the Soviet Union; (2) is technologically adequate for the restricted functions that it is designed to fulfill; (3) will not provoke escalation of the offensive arms race and is, in fact, far more moral than the alternatives available to us; and (4) is not properly viewed as an alternative to domestic spending but is influenced by considerations of a wholly different nature.

How can informed and conscientious men and women reach entirely different conclusions based on the same information? It must be confusing to the American public to find the U.S. Senate so divided on this issue. Hopefully, we are all reasonably intelligent and responsible men whose chief loyalty is to the public interest. We all have access to the same technical information about the ABM and the same intelligence estimates of Soviet and Chinese capabilities and intentions. Senators from the same state with the same constituencies part on the issue. The debate has been remarkably free from partisan political considerations, and the leadership of neither party has seriously tried to make of the Safeguard ABM a test of party loyalty. The Senate has heard more expert testimony from a divided scientific community than it has on any other weapons system previously proposed. How, then, do we explain the fact that roughly half of us vigorously oppose the Safeguard system and the other half support it with equal conviction?

Although many subtle factors of personality and circumstance go into each individual decision, perhaps the most important cause of the divergence of views in the Senate on this issue is a tendency to confuse the Safeguard system proposed by President Nixon on March 14, 1969, with the Sentinel system proposed by President Johnson on September 18, 1967. Although much of the hardware is the same, the purposes of the two systems are vastly different. It is precisely in the differing purposes that the great value of Safeguard lies. The systems reflect a fundamental and all-important difference in presidential philosophy, and that disparity can tell us a great deal about the different conclusions the two men have drawn about the future of the arms race and the prospects for genuine international détente.

Much is made by the opponents of the system of the fact that it has been presented to the Congress and to the people in so many successive disguises—first as a defense of the cities against a future Chinese threat, which no one seemed to take seriously, then as the first step in a large system to protect the population against a determined Soviet attack, and now as protection for America's retaliatory deterrent. The President is widely criticized for having made an unprincipled and wholly

283

political decision to simply repackage the Sentinel system. He is said to have realized that, after the public agitation at Boston, Chicago, and Seattle, installations near major population centers were unacceptable to local residents. Thus, his avowed intent to strengthen the deterrent is said to have been arrived at as the only justification for deployment that might prove palatable to Congress and the American public.

What this argument overlooks is the fact that while several presidential justifications have been offered for the ABM, only one justification has been offered by President Nixon. As he reviewed the Sentinel decision of his predecessor—a decision already authorized by Congress—in the light of his own view of international realities and within the context of a full-scale reassessment of defense priorities, he concluded that the Sentinel system and the purposes for which it had been authorized were not consonant with what he saw happening in the Communist world and with the avenue that he perceived prospects of a significant deescalation of world tensions and the arms race.

What are the differences between Sentinel and Safeguard, and why do they seem so significant? With a few minor changes and presumed improvements, the physical configuration and components of the two systems are about the same: the long-range Spartan missile, the short-range high-acceleration Sprint missile, the long-range Perimeter Acquisition Radar (PAR), and the highly complex time-share computer system that is in essence the "brains" of the system as a whole. The principal distinction between Sentinel and Safeguard is that whereas the former was to be configured and deployed to provide an area defense of population centers against a determined attack, Safeguard rejects such a purpose. Although it is true that, fully deployed, Safeguard might provide some degree of population defense against the kind of attack Communist China is likely to be able

284

to mount within the 1970s, this is strictly a secondary advantage and one that responds to a highly uncertain threat. As it did with respect to the Soviet Union in the early years of its nuclear build-up, the United States will continue to rely on its retaliatory capacity to deter attack by the Communist Chinese.

The primary justification offered for the Safeguard system—increased protection of our land-based retaliatory forces against a direct attack by the Soviet Union—has three important implications when contrasted with the objective of population defense advanced for Sentinel but rejected by President Nixon.* Those implications are that: (1) the acknowledged technical limitations of the system are much less bothersome; (2) it represents for the first time a response to an increasing Soviet offensive capacity, not in kind, but in a way that threatens the life of no Soviet citizen; and (3) it cannot be viewed by the Soviet Union as provocative, as Sentinel might well have been.

To meet its stated objective, a population defense system such as Sentinel must be highly reliable. Any serious question about its reliability is cause for grave concern. Each offensive warhead that penetrates a population defense system represents thousands and perhaps millions of human casualties. Add to this the fact that an offensive missile need not be delivered with great accuracy to inflict unacceptable damage and it will be understood that, to be of significant value, population defense must be virtually perfect. Such a system is not yet possible. "Although every instinct motivates me to provide the American people with complete protection against a major nuclear attack," President Nixon said on March 14, "it is not now within our power to do so." It is not likely that it ever will be. It is virtually axiomatic that any population defense can be overwhelmed or

* This opinion is not shared by all contributors. For another view see Donald Brennan, Chapter 8.

at least penetrated to an unacceptable degree if the potential attacker is willing to divert the necessary resources to that task. It would be folly to expend in the neighborhood of $100 billion on such a "thick" system. However, a hard-point defense, such as Safeguard, requires substantially less reliability. To begin with, an offensive missile launched by the Soviet Union against a hardened Minuteman silo in the remote plains of Montana and North Dakota would have to be targeted with extraordinary accuracy. Secondly, penetration by such an accurately targeted warhead and a direct hit would mean the loss of only a single American ICBM, not the massive loss of human life. Thirdly, Soviet military planners would be required to impute to our defensive system a far greater reliability than it might actually possess. In fact, plans for a Soviet first strike would have to assume a high degree of reliability for Safeguard in order to ensure destruction of the American retaliatory capability.

The opponents of Safeguard have enlisted the testimony of a number of distinguished scientists to the effect that its radars and computers could be easily confused and neutralized by decoys, chaff, nuclear blackout, and electronic countermeasures. But Soviet planners could never have any certain confidence in such countermeasures, even though they might in fact be totally effective. As Chayes, Wiesner, Rathjens, and Weinberg note in their introduction to the book resulting from the study undertaken for Senator Edward Kennedy, "In an attack on a hard-point target, such as a missile silo or command center, the usefulness of decoys is limited. The defender can wait before deciding to commit an intercepting missile until the incoming objects reach very low altitudes, where the atmosphere will have filtered out most of the decoys. Moreover, the object may be disregarded completely by the defense unless it is going to land within a very short distance of the point to be defended." All these factors indicate that questions about the reliability of Safeguard are not nearly so important as they were in the case of the Sentinel system.

It is useful at this point to question how real the Soviet threat is. Opponents of the system delight in pointing out the seeming discrepancy between the assertion by Secretary of Defense Laird that the Soviet Union is "going for" a first-strike capability and a subsequent statement by Secretary of State Rogers that, in his view, there was no "intention" on the part of the Soviets to launch a first strike against the United States. The two statements are in no way inconsistent; they simply draw attention to the difference between "capability" and "intention." As President Nixon has said, "I believe that defensive decisions must be made on the hard realities of the offensive capabilities of our adversaries, and not on our fervent hopes about their intentions."

In the past two years, the Soviet missile force has tripled to more than 1,000 ICBMs including the giant SS-9, and continues that rate of deployment. It has in being or under construction more ICBM launchers than the 1,054 possessed by the United States. The Soviets are also producing ballistic missile submarines at the rate of 8 per year. They are thought to have done advanced work on the so-called fractional orbital bombardment system (FOBS), a weapon whose low trajectory greatly reduces the time in which the attacked target can prepare for its own defense or launch a retaliatory strike. The Soviet Union is also, of course, the only power with an ABM system in place.

All this does not prove that the Soviet Union is "going for" or "intends" to launch a first strike against the United States. There is much to be said for the view that this offensive build-up is directed more toward the Communist Chinese than at our own country. Statements by party chief Leonid Brezhnev at the Moscow summit in early June revealed serious apprehension within the Kremlin about the Chinese threat. But the difficulty is that, barring any response by the United States, the "hawkish"

287

faction in the Russian leadership might begin to believe that the threat of a first strike could become credible. As President Eisenhower noted during the same farewell address in which he warned of a military-industrial complex, "Our arms must be mighty, ready for instant action, so that no potential aggressor may be tempted to risk his own destruction."

The real differences between the Soviet Union and the United States are not military but political and ideological. A reduction of nuclear stockpiles, while highly desirable, would ease but not resolve tension. Each country maintains an apostolic fervor about its own value system. In spite of encouraging signs in recent years that the gulf between the two nations has narrowed, the invasion of Czechoslovakia and the enunciation of the Brezhnev "Sovereignty Doctrine" should have convinced the most sanguine among us that it is still wide. President Nixon has said that "the adversaries in the world today are not in conflict because they are armed. They are armed because they are in conflict and have not yet learned peaceful ways to resolve their conflicting national interests."

By rejecting the deployment of a population defense ABM system in favor of Safeguard, the United States will respond to increased Soviet offensive activity not by adding to its own offensive arsenal and thus contributing to an offensive spiral, but by deploying a system with no offensive capacity whatsoever and thus achieving the same incremental increase in the strength of its deterrent force that could otherwise be achieved only by additional offensive weapons. This is an enormously important departure from precedent and marks, in my view, the watershed of the arms race. The Soviet Galosh ABM around Moscow did not mark the same kind of qualitative departure because it is a population defense system and could thus become part of an aggressive strategy. Although the Safeguard system in no way lessens the United States reliance upon its retaliatory strike capacity to deter nuclear aggression by any enemy, those who oppose Safeguard would have us rely solely on the deterrent and would do nothing to provide an alternative response. Without Safeguard, in the event of a minor, accidental, or unauthorized attack the United States would have no alternative to unleashing the full fury of its deterrent against the country believed to be the origin of attack. This would happen under the most confusing and terrifying conditions and would depend on ideal communications and an awesome presidential decision. I grow somewhat weary of those who oppose deployment of the Safeguard system on the grounds that it is somehow immoral. Is it not more moral to provide an alternative to all-out use of our enormous deterrent that would incinerate millions of Soviet citizens than to simply continue adding to that deterrent? Is it not more moral to strengthen our defensive posture with a system incapable of inflicting harm on anyone beyond this hemisphere than to build greater and more powerful machines of human devastation?

I believe that, although the rapid Soviet build-up of offensive weapons should be of serious concern, deployment of a limited, phased system such as Safeguard would be more than justified if the Soviet threat were even less real than it now appears. The most important aspect of Safeguard is that it gives us a degree of flexibility in our defense, a new kind of non-militant, wholly defensive tool with which to work toward peace. It marks the first shift from an offensive posture to a defensive posture. It does not add fuel to the arms race; it throws water on it.

This brings us to the third important implication of President Nixon's decision to deploy a hard-point defense rather than a population defense, and that is that the deployment of Safeguard will clearly not be viewed by the Soviet Union as provocative. Because it is designed for and capable only of defending land-based ICBMs against a first strike, the only circumstances under which it could conceivably provoke a further build-up of offensive weapons would be those under which the Soviet Union indeed sought to attain a first-strike capability.

On the other hand, deployment of a population defense system by the United States might well provoke an offensive response by the Soviet Union. This is because any nation, including the United States, that had in place a "thick" population defense system in which it had a high degree of confidence could be seriously tempted to develop and even utilize a first-strike capability. In spite of all our disavowals of aggressive intentions, Soviet military planners would have to respond to the deployment of a "thick" population defense system by the United States as if it were evidence of a potential first-strike capability. In fact, the United States reacted to the deployment of the Soviet population defense system, the Galosh, in precisely this way. We began work on the multiple independently targetable reentry vehicles (MIRV). Although there are, perhaps, some Pentagon strategists and certainly some eminent civilian scientists who would prefer the deployment of a population defense system by the United States, I am vigorously opposed to such a system, not only because it would provoke an escalation of the offensive arms race, but also because such a system could never be wholly effective and could thus only reduce but not eliminate civilian casualties in the event of nuclear war.

Some argue that deployment of Safeguard will make later expansion into a population defense system a great deal more probable. It is my hope and belief that an agreement limiting defensive systems would be high on the agenda of the imminent arms talks with the Soviet Union. Chayes, Wiesner, Rathjens, and Weinberg in the study mentioned above note that the shift in site locations from the Sentinel system to the Safeguard system "makes it somewhat more expensive, but by no means impossible, to alter the system at a later date in an attempt to provide defense of population against heavy attack." It is clear that the President has emphatically rejected this objective for Safeguard. As he said on March 14, "the Sentinel system had the disadvantage that it could be misinterpreted as the first step toward the construction of a heavy system." He went on to say that the Safeguard "program is not provocative. The Soviet retaliatory capability is not affected by our decision. The capability for surprise attack against our strategic forces is reduced. In other words, our program provides an incentive for a responsible Soviet weapons policy and for the avoidance of spiraling U.S. and Soviet strategic arms budgets."

The public and private Soviet reaction to the President's announcement certainly seems to support his contention that the system would not be provocative. The eagerness of the Soviet Union to proceed with arms talks has not abated. In fact, even the Sentinel system, which could far more easily have been expanded into a "thick" and thus threatening system, did not provoke the Soviets. It cannot be coincidental that Soviet Foreign Minister Andrei Gromyko announced publicly for the first time the readiness of the Soviet Union to participate in arms talks only three days after the Senate had voted appropriations for Sentinel in June, 1968. Shortly thereafter, a prestigious Soviet scientific journal offered to publish a speech by the director of the Oak Ridge National Laboratory, the thesis of which is that defensive systems can be deployed in such a way as to decelerate the offensive arms race.

Defensive systems are among the easiest kind to monitor with existing satellite reconnaissance systems. An agreement on the deployment of defensive systems, which might allow some degree of population defense—particularly important to the Soviet Union—against the Chinese threat, could be efficiently policed.

The "phased" deployment of Safeguard as proposed by President Nixon contemplates the kind of flexibility necessary in order to comply with such an agreement.

However, it is not enough to say that Safeguard will not provoke an offensive escalation by the Soviet Union. It must be shown that deployment of the system will positively enhance the prospects for meaningful and effective arms limitation agreements with the Russians. It would do this in a number of ways.

In the first place, congressional rejection of the Safeguard system would severely handicap U.S. negotiators at the forthcoming talks. As Secretary of State Rogers has publicly stated, the ABM would be regarded by the United States as negotiable at such talks. Quite apart from our estimates of the value of the Soviet Galosh ABM system now deployed around Moscow, if it were to be offered as a concession by the Soviets, U.S. negotiators would be required to offer in return a concession of an entirely different qualitative order.

Secondly, we must take into account the knowledge and experience gained about defensive systems by the Soviet Union as a result of having deployed a system, regardless of its imperfections. Practical knowledge of the capacity and limitations of a defensive system that can be gained only through deployment will significantly strengthen the hand of the Soviet negotiators, for they will have a far better grasp than we of what concessions in the area of defensive weapons might mean qualitatively. As Dr. Edward Teller testified before the Senate Subcommittee on International Organization and Disarmament Affairs, "Today's arms race is qualitative rather than quantitative." He went on to say that there is only one "group of people which probably has reliable estimates" of the effectiveness of defensive systems. "They are the Russian experts who have practiced the deployment of defense for many years. . . . If we are going to negotiate an agreement on arms limitations we are going to face experts who have actual experience in the deployment of missile defense. We shall be at a disadvantage unless we gain some experience of our own."

A third way in which phased deployment of the Safeguard system would enhance the likelihood of an effective agreement on the limitation of offensive weapons has been eloquently advanced by, among others, Dr. Alvin M. Weinberg, director of the Oak Ridge National Laboratory. In a speech delivered on the occasion of his receiving the Atoms for Peace award in November, 1967, Weinberg posed these questions: "Does anyone really believe, in the kind of hard, untrusting world we live in, and shall have to live in during the next several decades, that either side will agree to a disarmed world unless it feels secure in its defensive systems? Can we realistically contemplate disarmament, with the possibility of clandestine sequestering of a few missiles without being reasonably certain that our defenses can handle sporadic and secret attacks?" Although I feel strongly that each nation should agree not to deploy the kind of "thick" population defense system provocative of an offensive reaction by the other, I am greatly persuaded by Weinberg's thesis that the prospects for significantly limiting and even reducing offensive weapons are greatly improved by the deployment of a limited or "thin" missile defense system.

Lastly, the cost-exchange ratio is now such that the cost of the added Soviet offensive power required to overcome the Safeguard system exceeds the cost of the system itself. In other words, the Soviet Union would be required to allocate more of its own resources to offsetting the protection afforded by Safeguard than Safeguard would cost the American people. It is considerably more expensive to overcome a hard-point defense than a population defense because the requisite accuracy of the delivered warhead is much greater and because virtually all the targets must be destroyed. This prospect of greatly increased

293

costs to the Soviet Union, which faces the same growing demand for domestic expenditures that we do, should provide added incentive for Soviet leaders to participate conscientiously in arms limitations talks.

Finally, I would like to say something about the contention of those who see in President Nixon's decision a callous insensitivity to domestic priorities. This argument posits, I think, an entirely false choice. It would hold only if the President felt that the Safeguard system was not really required for the national security but that he would rather spend public funds on an unnecessary military project than on pressing domestic needs. This would be criminal, indeed.

President Nixon is painfully aware of the many problems confronting our country. Yet, as President and Commander-in-Chief, he must abide by a single overriding commandment: The security of the United States of America must be preserved. Much of the public discussion of the anti-ballistic missile issue in the United States has ignored this fundamental fact. The freedoms and liberties enjoyed by our citizens exist because our country has always provided for our common defense. The arguments advanced that there is direct trade-off relationship between domestic programs and defense programs are fallacious. Without a secure nation there would be no need, indeed no opportunity, for the introduction and expansion of domestic programs.

The yardsticks by which we measure the presumed effectiveness of our forces, including the Safeguard system, are not yardsticks at all because they cannot be fixed nor definitive. Rather, the measuring devices are human judgments, subject to human error, and subject to the influence of rapidly changing circumstances. What additional means are necessary to assure the preservation of the United States? This is the question that now confronts the President. Because of today's rapidly changing technology, there is a marked increase in the uncertainties concerning issues about which a high degree of certainty is desirable before decisions can be made.

The Safeguard system will help deter war by adding to the credibility of the striking power of the United States. Safeguard will improve the assurance or degree of certainty that some level of striking force is available to the Commander-in-Chief if the security of the United States demands that a striking force be employed. The responsibility of the Commander-in-Chief defies description; but it is a responsibility that accompanies the highest office to which a citizen can be elected by his peers. After a careful re-reading of President Nixon's March 16 announcement of Safeguard, I am convinced he carefully evaluated each uncertainty and weighed each alternative before making it. For myself, I find the reasoning underlying the President's decision altogether persuasive.

CHAPTER 11

Statements and Official Testimony

STATEMENT OF DR. WILLIAM G. McMILLAN*

The distinguished scientist Dr. William G. McMillan, professor of chemistry at the University of California at Los Angeles, is a noted specialist on such strategic nuclear matters as reentry vehicle vulnerability, penetration aids, nuclear weapons effects, and missile vulnerability. Before the Senate Armed Forces Committee Dr. McMillan expressed his views in support of the Safeguard system as "an essential part of maintaining the viability and credibility of our strategic deterrent."

Mr. Chairman, and members of the committee, your invitation has provided me a welcome opportunity to offer my views on the issue of ballistic missile defense.

Since this is my first appearance before your committee, I thought I should begin by sketching my technical background and experience.

* Before the Senate Armed Forces Committee, April 22, 1969.

I received my doctorate at Columbia University during World War II in that hybrid field known as chemical physics. Immediately thereafter I joined the Columbia University branch of the Manhattan Project as a member of the Chemistry Division, where we were deeply involved in the design of the gaseous diffusion plant for the production of U-235. After the war, I spent a year as a Guggenheim Postdoctoral Fellow in theoretical physics at the University of Chicago. In 1947 I joined the faculty of the Department of Chemistry at UCLA, where latterly I served six years as department chairman. I have also taught at Harvard and Columbia universities.

During the fifties I served as consultant to the Engineering Department of Brookhaven National Laboratory and to the Lawrence Radiation Laboratory in Livermore. Since 1954 I have been a part-time member of the Physics Department of the Rand Corporation, where my work has been concerned primarily with such strategic nuclear matters as reentry vehicle vulnerability, penetration aids, underground nuclear testing and test detection, nuclear weapons effects, and missile vulnerability.

In mid-1961 in anticipation of the Soviet abrogation of the nuclear test moratorium I was charged with forming the Scientific Advisory Group on Effects to advise the Director of Defense Research and Engineering and the Defense Atomic Support Agency. This group played a large role in designing the U.S. nuclear test programs aimed at exploring many of the strategic nuclear problems mentioned above.

In 1963 I was asked to chair a study group on missile vulnerability for DDR&E, the Air Force, and the Navy. This group, which is still in existence, greatly extended our understanding of missile vulnerability and sponsored far-reaching changes in the design of our strategic missiles.

With the support of DDR&E and the Advanced Research Projects Agency, I founded in 1964 the Defense Science Seminar aimed at getting new young scientific talent in the Defense advisory business. This seminar ran for three successive summers, with a total attendance of about 120 individuals. In 1965 I helped establish the Defense Intelligence Agency Scientific Advisory Committee, which I have since served as vice-chairman. Also in 1965 I chaired a study for the JCS on the technical-military implications of possible extensions of the Limited Nuclear Test Ban Treaty. In 1966 I participated in a related study for the Arms Control and Disarmament Agency. Most recently from October 1966 through December 1968, I served in Vietnam as Science Advisor to COMUSMACV.

As Mr. Nitze so ably described, the intransigence of the Soviet Union after World War II left us no alternative to the development of a strong nuclear deterrent. The hope that the Soviets would join with us under the Baruch plan for sharing the great potential of the nuclear age was shattered with the first Soviet atomic explosion in 1949. Similarly the national debate over the decision to develop thermonuclear devices was punctuated emphatically by the first Soviet thermonuclear explosion in 1953.

Our policy of nuclear deterrence, which came to maturity under President Eisenhower, has I believe served us well. There are, however, two current Soviet developments that threaten the survivability and credibility of our deterrent: their ballistic missile defense systems; and their counterforce efforts.

For some years I have followed closely the growth of the Soviet ABM systems. By my reckoning there have been three systems involved: the first, partially deployed around Leningrad and then apparently abandoned; the second, deployed around Moscow and now approaching operational status; and the third or Tallinn system, very extensively deployed throughout the

Soviet Union, and which appears to me likely to have a considerable ABM potential.

I find very unpersuasive the argument that the Soviets are building in the Tallinn development yet another SAM antiaircraft system to the neglect of a defensive system aimed at what they must surely regard as the more current threat of ICBMs and SLBMs.

By the counterforce effort I refer to the current Soviet development of multiple warheads for their SS-9 missile. To me the evidence as I understand it points very strongly, if not unequivocally, toward a MIRV—i.e., a multiple, independently targeted reentry vehicle-system designed against the U.S. land-based Minuteman system.

To impart some feeling for the strength of my conviction on these two Intelligence issues, I would strongly support spending a substantial fraction of our defense budget to assure that neither of these Soviet developments be allowed to degrade our strategic deterrent.

Put differently, I am most certainly not willing to gamble the survival of our Minuteman force that such an interpretation is wrong.

In addition to the question of capability, Intelligence must concern itself with the question of intent. Here the writing of such high-level Soviet military planners as Marshal Sokolovsky abound with references to the need for a preemptive strategic first-strike capability. They tell themselves they must develop it, and now we see that development in progress. How much more notification do we need?

In this focusing on the survivability of Minuteman one often encounters the rebuttal "Well, there is always Polaris." This seems to me a hazardous position. The whole point of the mix of strategic weapons systems—Minuteman, Polaris, Poseidon,

299

B-52 bombers—is to have such diversification that our deterrent could never be totally negated. I am sure that if we are willing to write off Minuteman as a component of our deterrent forces, we would not have any difficulty inducing the Soviets then to focus their full counterforce genius against our submarine and bomber forces. In fact, I fully expect there has already been long established a Soviet group charged with developing specific means of countering such element of our deterrent. To them, Polaris may not look like six hundred missiles, or six thousand warheads if given a ten-fold MIRV multiplication, but rather as only forty-one boats to be neutralized. Certainly we know the Soviets are engaged in large-scale ASW developments. And our six hundred B-52 bombers may be viewed as a much smaller number of airfields to be attacked—for which they may think their Fractional Orbital Bombardment System (FOBS) is well suited.

Turning to the Chinese People's Republic [CPR], it is no secret that their progress in the development of atomic and thermonuclear weapons has been spectacularly rapid. While their missile program has been less spectacular, there can be little doubt that they are striving to achieve an ICBM capability. Now who will those ICBMs be aimed at? It should be a sobering thought that no Chinese ICBMs would be necessary if only the Soviet Union were their target.

As to intent of the CPR, we have the wonderfully candid statement of Marshal Lin Piao, Minister of Defense, in September of 1965. This document developed the theme that the U.S. nuclear capability is a paper tiger, and "cannot save U.S. imperialism from its doom." It also laid out a blueprint for what Marshal Lin euphemistically termed "people's wars of national liberation," a blueprint that is being followed by the North Vietnamese in their invasion of South Vietnam.

Thus, while I had no part even as an adviser in the Sentinel deployment decision, which occurred while I was on overseas assignment, it did seem to me a prudent move to anticipate a CPR ICBM threat.

It has been argued that even if there were a sound military requirement for the Safeguard ABM system it wouldn't work anyway. The technical reasons adduced for this view include:

1. It is too complicated.
2. There is insufficient reaction time for human decision-making.
3. It was designed for another purpose ("thin" defense of cities against a CPR attack) and is thus unsuited for the defense of Minuteman.
4. The radars can be blacked out.
5. Cheap and simple decoys can saturate the defense.

Before commenting on these points I must emphasize that I have no special expertise in the engineering of either missiles or radar—although I have studied Professor Panofsky's excellent book on electromagnetic theory. But we have all seen some other fairly complicated systems built by our aerospace industrial complex that work, and work well; for example, the Explorer, Surveyor, and Mariner space shots, topped by the magnificent performance of the Christmas round-the-moon Apollo excursion. The use of solid-state electronic components, which were invented only a few short years ago, has made possible a vast improvement in reliability. It would, of course, be folly to expect no difficulties, no start-up bugs in any new system. But both the Spartan and Sprint missiles have been successfully flown many times. At Kwajalein there has been constructed a Missile Site Radar (MSR) that will soon be tested in operational launches, and somewhat later in actual ICBM reentry vehicle intercepts. Already in operation are numerous

301

phased-array radars employing the same basic principles as the Perimeter Acquisition Radar (PAR). The computer required is well within the state of the art. The nuclear warheads are either already developed or can be tested underground. In other words there is a justifiably high confidence that each and every component is completely feasible.

The short time in which an ABM system must react is indeed a severe problem. But it seems to me far better to place that burden upon a defensive system which would not trigger a nuclear exchange than upon our ICBMs which certainly would if they had to be launched on warning.

Since the new Safeguard deployment has brought into question the rationale behind the original Sentinel deployment, I believe it may be useful to quote an important part that seems to have been overlooked in Secretary McNamara's San Francisco address on September 18, 1967. He said,

"Further, the Chinese-oriented ABM deployment would enable us to add—as a concurrent benefit—a further defense of our Minuteman sites against Soviet attack, which means that at a modest cost we would in fact be adding even greater effectiveness to our offensive missile force and avoiding a much more costly expansion of that force."

This statement is, of course, borne out by the proposed Sentinel deployment, in which 4-face MSRs along with complements of both Spartan and Sprint missiles were to be collocated at both Grand Forks and Malmstrom, the same two Minuteman bases to be given priority protection under the Safeguard proposal. In other words, the difference between the two deployments is more one of emphasis than of kind.

Of course, many other approaches to hard-point defense have been examined, but precious—perhaps even critical—years would be lost in starting over at this point.

A blackout attack, like that of a direct attack upon the

radars—the eyes and ears of the ABM system—is of course a possible enemy option, but is neither simple, guaranteed to work, nor cheap in ICBMs and nuclear warheads. To be sure, any defensive system can be burned through with enough concentration by the offense, but this absorbs time that would upset a concerted attack, and absorbs warheads that could have caused great casualties elsewhere.

Any nation, like the CPR, who can produce ICBMs and nuclear warheads can of course also develop penetration aids —given time. In my view we can only hope to buy time, time to give our political colleagues and their foreign counterparts an opportunity to realize a workable arms control agreement based upon mutual concern, mutual restraint, and mutual dedication.

In his San Francisco speech, Secretary McNamara made clear that intensive consideration was being given to other means of protecting our land-based deterrent: mobility, super-hardening, etc. It is strange to find some of those individuals who most strongly oppose ABM deployment because of the risk of escalating the arms race now advocating proliferation of our Minuteman system to assure its survivability.

In previous hearings of this Congress some have even suggested launching the Minuteman force on warning as a tenable course, or undertaking a preemptive strike against the CPR if their ICBM threat becomes intolerable.

I want to go on record as unalterably opposed to any intentional action—or intentional lack of action—that would maneuver the United States into such a position that only a strike-first option remained.

One of the most often expressed arguments against ABM is that it will inaugurate a new cycle of escalation in the arms race.

303

Some of this fear may have been allayed by the reorientation of Safeguard to the defense of our deterrent forces. But it is noteworthy that the Soviets first formally announced their interest in arms limitation shortly after the U.S. decision was reached to deploy the Sentinel system. The Safeguard deployment in no way reduces the deterrence inherent in the Soviet retaliatory capability. That the Soviets understand the desirability and innocuousness of such a defense is illustrated by Premier Kosygin's declaration that their ABM system is a threat to no nation and does not contribute to an arms race.

Personally I should be sorry to see even the thin city defense permanently rejected. I believe such a defense might serve to dampen an unwelcome CPR adventurousness, and thus to maintain for us a wider class of options and more room for political maneuver.

Finally, I believe the maintenance of the credibility of our deterrent—to which Safeguard would contribute—is absolutely essential in our relations with NATO and our other allies around the world.

There are two additional reasons, which may even be the strongest of all for an early deployment of the Safeguard system. First, a review of the Soviet ABM programs indicates that they have for a number of years been gaining operational experience from actually deployed systems, whereas we have not. We can ill afford to allow an important gap to develop in the learning process concerning such an important capability. Second, it is only through the actual deployment of the major system elements that we can learn with certainty how to cope with the problems that will surely arise in command, control, communications, and the interaction and internetting of the radars with each other and with the rest of the system.

I believe that the great majority of the American people, with their down-to-earth common sense, are having as great a difficulty as I am in swallowing the sophisticated arguments that conclude it is somehow bad to defend ourselves. I simply do not understand why it is provocative for the United States to deploy an ABM system as we are here considering today, but not provocative of the Soviet Union to have already deployed two ABM systems; nor why it would be provocative of us to defend our Minuteman forces against a developing Soviet pre-emptive first-strike capability, whereas it is not provocative of the Soviets to develop that destabilizing capability. We are told, in effect, to stop our provocative action of punching the Soviets on their fist with our eye. I sincerely hope that such an inverted Alice-in-Wonderland view of the world will not be allowed to prevail.

In summary, I support the early deployment of the Safeguard system as an essential part of maintaining the viability and credibility of our strategic deterrent.

Thank you, Mr. Chairman.

STATEMENT OF THE HONORABLE DEAN ACHESON

(Adapted from Testimony on June 11, 1969, before the Subcommittee on Economy in Government, Joint Economic Committee, U.S. Congress)

Some years ago Joseph Alsop, who is an old friend, said that my views on affairs might be described by a line from Coleridge's "Kubla Khan": "Ancestral voices prophesying war!"

I have taken a rather grimmer view of the world around us than do many who have recently testified before Congress, and I shall continue to do so now.

I would like to make four basic points.

First, in the more than seventy years during which I have been conscious of the world around me, I have been strongly impressed that the Congress throughout this entire time has underspent rather than overspent on the defense of the United States.

Second, during this time, the Congress and the people of the United States have been greatly distracted from considering the real problems they have to face by witch hunts and clichés, all of which have taken their minds off the point.

Third, the old world that many Americans still consider normal has completely disappeared. In former times we could count on time and distance as safety factors. That situation has vanished, probably forever. The development has not been due to some correctible error of judgment and practice on our part. The determining factors are the disintegration of the Europe-centered world, the establishment of a great power base for revolutionary purposes with universal ambitions, and the dynamism of technology. From here on, as far ahead as one can imagine, the nation will continuously be in the front line, and coping with adversary forces will be an unrelenting requirement. The war in Europe and the war in Asia have utterly destroyed the great empires upon which the nineteenth century world order and all its precepts and ideas were founded. They have gone entirely, every one. Out of it have emerged two of the great powers confronting one another with diametrically opposed ideas, ambitions, influences, and purposes. The possibility of compromise is only that referred to by Churchill when he spoke of a balance of terror, which makes coexistence possible. This is the basis on which we live, and it is a vast mistake to believe that it is anything else.

Fourth, as we add to, maintain, and protect our power, we do not in any way diminish the possibility of an agreement with the Soviet Union. In fact, we strengthen it. By power I mean that combination of population, resources, technology, and will

306

that enables a people to have an impact beyond their own boundaries.

The idea that the Soviet Union will negotiate with us in the sense in which we use that term is quite untrue. I am a Connecticut Yankee, and my conception of negotiation is a David Harum type of negotiation and deal: You have a horse, and I want to buy it. We are both trying to accomplish a common result. You wish to get as much out of me as you can. I wish to pay as little as possible. Somewhere between those two desires we have a negotiation and make a deal, and perhaps I get the horse. This is not the Russian conception at all. The Russian conception of negotiation is the carrying on of war by other means. It is the converse of Clausewitz, who talked about war as carrying on diplomacy by other means.

Therefore, as we strengthen ourselves, we bring about the calculation of forces by the Russians that induces them to make a deal. They are not moved by argument, nor by exhortation, nor by considerations of morality. They are moved only when their calculations lead them to believe that it is more advantageous to make a deal than not to do so.

It is the duty of the Congress, of course, to appropriate the funds of the United States for the purposes enjoined upon it in the Constitution. It is the duty of the President to be the constitutional adviser of the Congress in the matter and to recommend what he believes is good for the nation. While his is a recommendation only, it is an important one, a recommendation members of Congress disregard at their peril and in doing so assume responsibility that requires careful thought. But it is the prerogative, the duty, the right of members of Congress, and therefore I address myself to the problem which confronts them now.

I see no basis for the notion that we tend to overdo the military aspects. To the contrary, the nation has repeatedly neglected

307

to provide a military basis to match its policy or to cope with aggressive forces. We tried unilateral arms reduction in the interwar period. We got Pearl Harbor. We reverted to habit after World War II. We got the Korean war. With respect to military power, I do not share the worries of those who discern and deplore dangers of too much. We had a temporary advantage in ratios of available military resources at the time of the Cuban missile crisis. Some would have called it a redundancy. That margin was not a surplus. It provided the basis on which President Kennedy was able to bring off an acceptable outcome.

General Marshall used to drill into me the vast importance of maintaining a mean of preparedness in armaments at all times and not to raise it to terrific heights during times of trouble and then scrap the whole thing and go down to almost zero between crises. We have always been unprepared for conflict. Our wars as a result have lasted too long. The casualties have been too high.

Many of you will remember our situation in 1914 to 1917. During that time the chances of our being drawn into the European war were tremendously high. As a bookmaker, one would have given odds that we would have become entangled in that war before it would be over, and yet we took almost no steps to prepare for it. After that we allowed what we had done to sink into disuse.

From 1933 to 1939 it was pretty clear that there was going to be trouble in Europe and that we were going to be drawn into it. Yet again the government of the United States did all too little to prepare for trouble. The President, as well as the Congress, was at fault for this neglect. What little was done amounted to virtually nothing when measured against the requirements imposed by the war that overtook us.

After 1945 we proceeded with a unilateral disarmament. Our

308

conventional forces practically disappeared. We made a unique offer to negotiate with the Russians, the British, the French, and all the leading states in the United Nations about the international control of this great new force, atomic energy. I myself worked on the plan we laid before the United Nations, and all the time it seemed to me that the chances were almost nil that the Russians would join in any such negotiation. Our intelligence was clear that they were already at work on a weapon of their own. Any knowledge of the Russian temperament would have led anyone to believe that they would not rest upon international agreements but would insist that they must have a power equal to the power of the strongest nation in the world.

However, we went ahead, both disarming and negotiating, until, when I became Secretary of State, the budget for defense for fiscal year 1951 was down to $14.5 billion. This, I may say, terrified me, then the President, and finally the Secretary of Defense. We had two working parties set to work in which the task of both chairmanships fell to me. One was a State-Defense organization that reviewed the entire foreign policy and military policy of the United States. Its work resulted in a national security paper called NSC 68, which is still classified and which has laid the foundation of both our foreign and our military policy ever since.

The second dealt with the question of what to do about a hydrogen bomb. Scientific opinion was divided. Some scientists believed that the hydrogen atom could be split and that a hydrogen weapon of much greater force than the atom bomb could be made. Others said it was impossible.

Almost everything that was said in the discussion that followed has been said about the ABM before committees of Congress in recent hearings. Hardly a new idea has been brought out. The same curious transformations happen now as happened then. The scientists to a large extent ceased to be sci-

309

entists and tried to discourse as moralists and political scientists. They talked then about the wickedness of going forward to find out whether one could make an even more terrible weapon than the atom bomb.

Then, as now, laymen could have no scientific opinion whether the weapon could be made or not. It was futile for me to try to understand that aspect of the problem. I listened to one scientist in favor of it; he seemed persuasive. Then I would listen to one against it, and he also seemed persuasive. I knew nothing about the basic physical considerations involved. We knew, however, that the Russians were going forward with work along these lines. It seemed absolute folly for us to deny ourselves knowledge of this sort when the Russians were developing such knowledge and to forgo capacity to produce in this field, dreadful as it might be, thus permitting the Russians to have a monopoly of that capacity.

It came about that eventually, in November, 1952, we had a test of a thermonuclear device. Less than a year later the Russians announced and then tested a fully developed hydrogen bomb. They were ahead of us in weapon development, not behind us. Any idea that our venture into this field was what had stimulated the Russians to enter it was substantially refuted. It was not until March, 1954, that we produced a hydrogen bomb.

As I pointed out, after 1946 we continued our own disarming. The result was the war in Korea, which was again the obvious result of a calculation that we could not and would not undertake to oppose a move in so remote an area even though it was an area over which we were at the very time exercising responsibility. Korea gave the recommendations of NSC 68 life and importance and led Congress to support a great rearmament of the United States. It also quickened our efforts on the thermonuclear weapon.

310

I have mentioned this long sequence of events to show that, every time we relax our efforts in defense, we regret it, and that, by increasing our efforts and maintaining a solid and prudent stance, we do not discourage or impair negotiation with anybody.

One of our failings as a people, I think, is a preoccupation with witches. For some among us it is hard to get accustomed to the new circumstances. The temptation is to take the old situation as normal, to regard the huge expense and unremitting danger as aberrant, and to blame malign or heedless forces within our own establishment. Identify them, expose their machinations, cut down their powers, and, lo, the difficulties will be abated. So goes the argument, in a succession of faddish versions.

A version in vogue in the 1930s cast the munitions industry as the malefactor—and the banker. A few overzealous weapon merchants and bankers were supposed to have cast an evil spell over the nation. Mr. Nye took care of the munition makers by passing legislation that made it almost impossible to help the Allies in the early part of World War II. The outstanding episode in getting control of the banker was when somebody put a midget on Mr. J. P. Morgan's lap and had him photographed at a congressional hearing. That was the mood of reformist activity of those days.

In the 1950s, a handful of faithless persons at the center of policy-making were supposed to have manipulated the world to disparage our interests and undercut our security. We had the contribution of Senator Joseph McCarthy in running down internal subversives. This was a time when I had perhaps my greatest prominence in the press as the well-known so-called Communist who was at the head of a group of so-called Communists in the State Department.

The current substitute for serious thought is a cliché about a military-industrial complex. Our involvements abroad, alleged

311

to impede great strides in domestic improvement, are portrayed as something put over on a gullible nation by an excess of professional zeal at the Pentagon coupled with overactive entrepreneurship in industry. This I find the strangest one of all. As most of the other witches were not known certainly to be Communists, I cannot imagine that the Congress could take seriously the thought that such great people as General Marshall or Joe Collins or Hoyt Vandenberg or General Bradley or Admiral Forrest Sherman or Admiral Alan Kirk would be engaged in a conspiracy to waste the funds and money of the United States uselessly. And today their counterparts are equally incapable of such action. I should hope that that foolish cliché will be dropped for good.

What I decry is the effort to portray marginal problems as centrally important. It was probably a good idea to regulate the munitions industry in the 1930s. It was folly to try to put American strategy into a straitjacket in the Neutrality Acts. Tighter security regulations were in order in the 1950s. What was reprehensible was the attempt to exploit the situation as a lever for overthrowing due process and subverting our pattern of constitutional authority. Intensified rigor in congressional review of defense appropriations may well be appropriate now. What I wish to warn against—and I do so with all the emphasis at my command—is any effort to use the attendant issues as an excuse for tampering with defense and foreign policies that rise from external necessities and are vital to national existence.

The power of the United States alone blocks Sino-Soviet ambitions in this world. They may fall out between themselves, they may have difficulties, they may fight with one another in a minor way, but on one matter they are completely and wholly agreed: The United States is the enemy.

Our power stands in the way of their ambitions, and they have no doubt about that at all. We are alone at this pinnacle of

312

power. There is an idea that has been given some currency by Mr. Walter Lippmann that it is our commitments that have outrun our capabilities. This is exactly backward. Our capabilities are attempts to get aid in carrying out our responsibilities. Commitments have not created the difficulty. The difficulty is created by the outside world.

For example, the NATO treaty seeks to hold together the countries in Europe which, if held together, would deny their resources to the Soviet Union and make some of our problems more manageable. If they are not held together, if they are not under an umbrella of the United States, they can easily be put under Soviet direction, and then our difficulties would be very great. The same thing is true with the major treaties in the Pacific.

As I said before, the dominating fact is that our power alone can protect the amplitude of the free world, which makes our free life possible. In isolation, in a Fortress America, we could not have the kind of a country we have. We simply could not. And it is to our advantage, it is essential to our survival, that there should be a spacious area of freedom in the world.

In this setting, the Congress approaches its great task of deciding whether it thinks it wise as a priority matter to allot the resources necessary to go forward with the President's recommendation about the ABM.

How would one sensibly go about performing this duty? As I mentioned, when I had it to perform in connection with the H-bomb, I did my best to understand the technical arguments that were going on, but I felt that that was not my province. These matters had been discussed, and recommendation had been made by people who were charged with knowing more about them than I know or understand. It seemed to me that, in making the choice, one had to choose between the responsibility one took by going forward and the responsibility one took by stand-

313

ing still. I felt in the case of the thermonuclear bomb, with what I knew about the world, that the proper responsibility for me to take was to say go forward. Let us know as much about thermonuclear phenomena as anybody in the world. Let us not take the chance of later finding ourselves in a dangerous predicament. So it seemed to me that the simpler part of my duty was to accept the recommendation and go forward with it.

If you analyze the problem further, you must have in mind the size of it. A great deal of talk before congressional committees by opponents of the Safeguard ABM proposal gives one the impression that this is a vast program of such tremendous dimensions that it really forces a choice between a constructive domestic program and this ABM. That just is not true at all. It is not remotely true. The dimensions of this problem have been exaggerated out of all sense of reality. It just is not that sort of a problem.

The *Washington Post* sometime ago published an interesting little chart that gave the spending by the United States on non-defense and defense from 1965, which is the real start of the Vietnam war. One sees from it that non-defense spending has not only increased but has continued to be substantially ahead of defense spending. For instance, in the budget for the current fiscal year, non-defense is $106 billion and defense is $80 billion. As I look at the world, those magnitudes do not seem a disproportionate allocation of our resources. The part of the defense budget involved in the ABM program is $8 billion over a period of five years. If you add in the research and development costs, you get $11 billion. That is not a vast bet.

Suppose the expenditure is not made, and suppose the choice turns out wrong. The consequences could be disastrous. Turn the proposition around. Say to yourself that, to be on the safe side, we had better go ahead. Then suppose that the proponents of the ABM turn out to be wrong and that this weapon will not do all that they say it will do. Has anything disastrous happened?

Have you wrecked the United States? Have you ruined the internal economy? Certainly not. What you may well have discovered is that the other side is not doing any better than we. Therefore, the danger is not so great as the military thought it would be.

The bets seem to me wholly different in kind and quality. The responsibilities seem to be wholly different. To reject ABM may mean terrible trouble. To go ahead with it cannot mean terrible trouble. It may indeed bring great assurance. If you lose the whole investment, it is not a serious loss.

Will going ahead with the ABM minimize the chances of having a negotiation with the Russians? I can assure you that this is not so. Not because I set myself up as the wisest man in the world but because a good deal of experience has led me to believe what I mentioned at the start: The Russian conception of negotiation is based on what they call the calculation of forces.

Let me illustrate this by two experiences. The first one concerns the blockade of Berlin. The Russians began the blockade of Berlin to frustrate the attempt of the Allies to reconstruct Europe. What we were all trying to do was, first of all, to restore physically through the Marshall Plan our Allies and a defeated Germany and, having done that, to create some kind of a government capable of governing Germany, which would cease to be a menace to its neighbors.

What the Russians decided was that they were going to keep Germany divided. They would rather have complete control of East Germany than partial control of all Germany. So they started a series of actions against our actions, which finally led to the blockade of Berlin.

At this point, there were several discussions as to what should be done. Some said, "We have the nuclear weapon and can use it to frighten the Russians." Only a few of us knew how few were the nuclear weapons we had. They were not a frightening number. Furthermore, the only way we could then use these weapons was to drop them from aircraft. The Russians were in Germany, and we were likely to do more damage to Germany than we would do to the Russians. So this did not seem to be a wise response.

What did we do? We undertook a counterblockade—that is, we isolated East Germany from Europe and the West. As time went on, that measure hurt the Russians a great deal more than their blockade was hurting our side—particularly when we got the airlift going, and it turned out to be such a signal success. The Russians did not wish to push the situation to a military confrontation because we had not only a few nuclear weapons, which would have been unhappy for them at home, but also some local forces, which would have been difficult for them to deal with on the ground.

Time went on through 1948. Early in 1949, shortly after I became Secretary, a newspaper man asked Stalin some questions, which he answered. It seemed odd to me and my colleagues that Stalin would answer these questions, because they were not of immediate importance and they did not say much that had not been said before. In discussing them, we decided that this looked like a signal that the Russians were ready to quit if they could make a deal.

We had a secret negotiation known only to Philip Jessup, Charles (Chip) Bohlen, myself, and the President. Nobody else. Nobody telephoned. Nobody telegraphed. Nobody wrote. Everybody got on an airplane or a train and went back and forth to New York. This was done at the United Nations. Finally, Malik said to Jessup, "I have word that we will call off the blockade if you call off the counterblockade, call off the creation of a West German state, and call a meeting of foreign ministers." And we said that the first two could be a deal. We said we would not call off forming a West German state because that could not be achieved until the autumn anyway. It was then only spring. We would go ahead and have a meeting of foreign ministers as soon as the blockade was lifted. If we could solve the whole German problem, we would not go ahead. If we could not, we would go ahead with West Germany. After a great deal of groaning and grunting the Russians agreed to the deal.

The other matter was the ending of the Korean war. We had finally stabilized the Korean front and had dismissed General MacArthur. General Ridgway had created the Kansas line, and this was holding strongly against all attempts by the Chinese to break it, but there were possibilities that the Russian air force might intervene or that they might land some troops. If this happened, we were in for it as this would be World War III. We wanted to be sure that everybody understood everybody else's attitude. I suggested to George Kennan that he write a note to Malik and say that he would like to come up and have a chat, not having seen him for a long time. Malik suggested that Kennan meet him at his place on Long Island.

So he did. Kennan pointed out the way things were going; we were on a collision course here, which we did not desire. They would be crazy to desire it because it would be a Chinese gain and not a Russian gain if it came off. But inevitably, if matters were pushed to the point of an attack, we would all end up in war. And we warned them that this had an end that they had better think over. The answer came back that we quite misunderstood them. They did not want to push hostilities and believed that there should be an armistice. Malik made a public speech and presented this view on a U.N. radio program.

We had an awful time with the Chinese and the North Koreans after that for two years, but the Russian part of it was very, very simple. It was just a matter of putting to them a proposition they could take or leave. They took it. They did what they could, and they stepped out.

The idea has been expressed that, if we move on the ABM as proposed by the President, it is going to make negotiation much more difficult. It is not going to make it any more difficult. Any

317

negotiation will be difficult to start with. All the problems are very difficult. They are not made any more difficult by adding to our defense.

I doubt emphatically that some great transformation of relations with the Soviet Union is about to move us from an era of confrontation to a phase of negotiation. We have been negotiating with the Soviet Union all along. We shall be involved in confrontation into an indeterminate future. The two go hand in hand in the Soviet view, and perforce we must see the matter in that perspective. The Soviet Union will come into agreement with us only in the measure that it discerns advantage in doing so and detriment in doing otherwise. I certainly do not oppose such negotiations. I am merely warning against the notion that the Soviet Union is on the verge of a conversion to tractability and accommodation.

This ABM proposal is a defensive action. The Russians realize that quite as well as the free world or anybody else does. They are working on it themselves. They are deeply into it. They know what it will do, and their whole purpose is to take out an incoming weapon. They may use it to take out a weapon before it is incoming, in which case it becomes an offensive weapon, but they know that what we are proposing is to meet what they might send against us.

If I were a Russian looking at this and I heard an argument saying what we should do is to have Safeguard here so it will disarm the incoming Russian weapon and if they build more weapons we will build more ABM's, I would feel different about that than I would toward a proposal that has been made several times before various congressional committees by opponents of the ABM that we do not try to safeguard the Minuteman but fire everything we have at the first radar sign of trouble. This, I think, comes about as close to madness as one can come. If I were a Russian, it would scare me to death, because this gives you no time to think. It really gives the President no time even to read a report that he gets from radar operators. It puts the control of policy in the hands of technicians. This, I think, would be really disastrous policy. Yet several members of Congress in one House or the other have actually advocated this policy!

The ABM proposal in the United States, viewed from the Russian side, is not one more aggressive round. It just is not. This defensive move does not raise any problems with them. They are not children. They are not frightened. They are not easily scared. And if ABM works out and if it is true, as I believe it has been testified before committees of the Congress, that this operation as proposed can help protect the Minutemen and that, if the Russian effort is increased, the defense can be increased at a lower cost than the offense, then the ABM does not add to the problem; it simplifies the problem.

If I had the responsibility, which is laid upon the Congress, I would accept the recommendation of my constitutional adviser and go forward with the ABM, confident that if it turns out to be good advice, we have greatly benefited the country. If it turns out to be unworkable, we at least shall know it is unworkable, and we shall know also that what the other fellow is doing is unworkable. We will have a parity of knowledge, and we will not have wasted the nation's resources in finding out.

STATEMENT OF DR. JEROME B. WIESNER*

Mr. Chairman, Members of the Committee:

I appreciate very much your willingness to allow me to testify before you on this very important subject. If you will permit I would like to qualify myself to speak on the matter of the ABM,

---

* Before the Senate Committee on Foreign Relations, May 14, 1969. Dr. Wiesner, provost of the Massachusetts Institute of Technology, is generally regarded as the leading scientific opponent of missile defense systems.

both in respect to its technical aspects and in regard to its strategic implications, and particularly its effects on the arms race and the possibilities of arms control agreements.

I have been concerned with the technical aspects of military systems since 1942 when I joined the staff of the M.I.T. Radiation Laboratory where I worked on a variety of radar systems that were used in World War II, including ones for air defense and blind bombing. At the end of World War II I spent a year at Los Alamos helping to develop more reliable electronic components for nuclear weapons, and then I returned to M.I.T. to become a member of the faculty. When the Cold War intensified in the late 1940s and the United States began to fear a massive surprise attack by Soviet bombers, a major air defense effort was begun by the United States Air Force, and I participated in many of the studies it sponsored. I˙ helped conceive the SAGE computer-aided, air defense system and the D.E.W. line. During this period I participated in many other studies for the Department of Defense relating to strategic missiles and missile defense. Also, in 1958 I was the staff director of the U.S. delegation to the Conference on Means of Reducing the Danger of Surprise Attack.

From 1957 to 1960 I was involved in various strategic weapons and arms control studies for the President's Science Advisory Committee, and in 1961 and 1962 as President Kennedy's Special Assistant for Science and Technology I was deeply involved in the studies and discussions which led to the decision not to deploy the Nike-Zeus ABM system and to begin research on a more advanced ABM system, then called the Nike-X, which was converted into the Sentinel system in 1967 and whose radars, computers, and missiles in a different configuration form the basis of the Sentinel system. Through these involvements and a continuing advisory role I have been able to stay reasonably familiar with ABM developments and the related intelligence.

320

In the course of my advisory roles in the White House and the Pentagon during the Eisenhower and Kennedy administrations, I became deeply conscious of the tremendous pace of the arms race and the desperate need to bring it under control. I have also become aware of the fact that there have always been ways to reverse this dangerous situation without jeopardizing our security, but for many reasons we have not been able to take advantage of these opportunities in the past. In my opinion, it is possible to greatly enhance our security by halting the arms race. And when I say this, I am referring to our military security, not our domestic security, though this too would greatly benefit if we were able to turn our minds and our resources to constructive tasks. I would be glad to talk more specifically about how we might do this if you would like me to during the question period.

I believe that the Safeguard ABM system is a prime example of a weapons system that will at best do very little good, most likely accelerate the arms race, and either way, waste large sums of money.

In my discussion today, I will concentrate my remarks on the current primary mission of the Safeguard system, the protection of the United States deterrent, but I will also say a few things about its potential for city defense. In this short paper it will not be possible to cover all of the issues that should be examined; however, these matters are examined in detail in the book *ABM: An Evaluation of the Decision to Deploy an Antiballistic Missile System*,[1] which Professor Abram Chayes and I

[1] New York: Harper & Row, 1969. *Editor's note:* The logic of the Chayes-Wiesner book is based on an evaluation of the threat to the U.S. strategic forces, a judgment of the reliability of the ABM system, a judgment regarding the effectiveness of countermeasures and opinions regarding strategic alternatives to ABM.

The subsequent discussion of four different missions (pp. 24 ff.) is based on numbers assumed from their estimates of reliability and their evaluation

edited and which I believe you have. I will only highlight what I believe to be the key issues and then go into as much detail as is desired during the question period.

My opposition to the Safeguard ABM is based on my judgment that:

1. It cannot be made to work reliably and in the fashion claimed.

2. Even if it could be made to perform according to plan, it could be overwhelmed and exhausted by relatively easy to

---

of counter-measure effectiveness. The broad national security issues then discussed (p. 49) take up the effect of ABM on the strategic balance and purport to do so apart from the technical effectiveness and capability to perform various missions. However, this discussion is again largely based on numbers derived from the previous reliability and penetrability assumptions. It is concluded in this section that Safeguard is destabilizing, that a Soviet reaction to increase its offensive power is certain, and that this will in turn lead to an intensive arms race.

The effect of Safeguard on arms control negotiations is the final topic discussed (p. 54). Two key but contradictory points are raised here. One, it is postulated that ABM complicates arms control agreement because the components of the proposed Safeguard are ambiguous (that is, the same components are used for hard-point and for population defense). Two, because Safeguard is primarily hard-point defense oriented and does not affect Soviet retaliatory capability, it is a worthless negotiation card.

From all of the foregoing, four main conclusions are then stated as follows:

1. Because the system is complex and realistic testing is not possible, the system is unlikely to perform according to specifications.
2. Because of a large variety of possible countermeasures, the system is highly susceptible to penetration.
3. The Sentinel/Safeguard is not well adapted to perform the missions assigned to it by either the previous administration or the present one.
4. Because of the ambiguity of the system, it is certain to evoke a Soviet response and complicate arms control.

Finally, while continued R & D [research and development] is favored, deferring deployment at this time is recommended.

achieve countermeasures, and so at best it could provide only modest protection for the deterrent forces.

3. It will not be possible to test the Safeguard system realistically, that is, against a large attack using nuclear weapons, so that we will never know its true capabilities or deficiencies before it has been used for real and then it will be too late to redesign it.

4. It is not needed to protect the deterrent forces. Even after a massive attack such as Secretary of Defense Laird suggests might be possible in the 1975 time period, if the Soviet Union continued the deployment of its large SS-9 missiles at the rate of the past several years and were successful with other developments, such as ASW [antisubmarine warfare], MIRVs, FOBs, [fractional orbital bombardment], etc., a very substantial United States retaliatory strike would be possible.

5. Its deployment would be a move in the wrong direction. Safeguard is more likely to reduce our security than enhance it and represents a complicating step in the arms race. Whether it evokes a Soviet response or not, it will certainly make more difficult the arms limitation problem.

From the point of view of the responsibility of the Congress, the fourth point is of particular importance, for if a large retaliatory force remains after the strongest attack by the Soviet Union that we can conceive of in the 1975 time period the desperate urgency to do something now disappears. There is plenty of time to decide what to do. Not the least of the choices is to continue to do nothing about new weapons systems while seeking the best way to insure the survival of the deterrent forces, whether through active defenses, or hardening, or increasing their numbers or through agreements limiting weapons deployments. It does appear feasible to design a hard-point defense that would be considerably cheaper and better than the Safeguard system, but it wouldn't look much like the Safeguard. It is not obvious that deploying even such a system, were it available, would represent a most attractive choice.

Why do I believe that the Safeguard system is not needed? If one accepts Secretary Laird's estimate of Soviet force—numbers and accuracies, and his projected form of attack for 1975—it is possible to show that a very creditable retaliatory force would survive it. According to calculations I made for our book, based on the assumption that not even elementary precautions were taken by the United States to protect its forces, such as redeploying aircraft or flying an air alert or protecting the Polaris submarines with our own ASW forces, and assuming that the Soviets achieve the projected capabilities, several hundred United States missiles and bombers capable of delivering more than 2,500 megatons of nuclear explosive would survive. This is a truly fearsome deterrent. In reality the situation would be better because in these calculations the attacker was given every benefit in regard to missile reliability, ability to accurately time and launch a global attack involving missiles and submarines, etc. A planner designing such an attack would obviously have to be much more conservative in his calculations, and to him the chance of success would seem even more improbable.

I want to make it clear that I don't believe that the Soviet Union is planning such an attack. I am examining the question of their ability to do so. That is, their capabilities. In fact, Secretary Laird has made it clear that he too is concerned about capabilities, not intentions. I do not claim that it would be impossible for the Soviet Union to achieve a first-strike capability, but for this they would have to build a vastly bigger force than that projected by Secretary Laird. It would require that a larger number of very substantial technical programs all be highly successful. They would need large numbers of high-accuracy multiple warheads, a much better air defense system, an effective ASW capability and a truly effective nationwide ABM system. Clearly, the Soviet Union is far from having these combined capabilities now, and there is essentially no reason to believe that they will move into such a position by 1975 or even later.

If we were actually worried about the safety of our forces, it could be improved quite readily. For example, moving the bombers from coastal bases to the center of the country would almost double the number that would survive a submarine-launched missile attack. An airborne alert would allow still more aircraft to survive. If we were still worried, a doctrine under which we fire after the first nuclear explosion if warning confirms an attack would assure that all workable Minuteman missiles would be used in retaliation. There are other steps which could be taken, some of them quickly, to strengthen the deterrent, but unless the possible threat gets more serious than Secretary Laird's current projection, I do not believe that any of them are necessary.

My second point was that the Safeguard system would not provide much protection from a large-scale attack for the deterrent force even if it did work as designed. It is generally agreed that the Spartan area defense system will not be effective against a large attack using countermeasures, so that it must be discounted in this case. Actually, the Sprint system is also vulnerable to countermeasures and saturation tactics, but even without such handicaps it will only provide modest help. The proposed first phase deployment would make hardly a measurable defense aaginst the SS-9 force predicted for 1975. The five hundred SS-9s carrying three warheads each would result in fifteen hundred objects to be intercepted by the defense (one thousand two hundred) if we assume that the SS-9 has a reliability of 0.8). If the 150 Sprints all worked, they could destroy only 150 of the incoming objects so that most of the attacking warheads would still reach their targets. Realistically two or three times as many Sprints as incoming objects would be needed for an effective defense. It would be possible to increase the number of Sprints to say 1,500, but it would also be quite simple for the offensive to counter this by replacing the three warheads with a mixture of even smaller warheads and heavy decoys which would still saturate the system. Replacing the three SS-9 MIRVs presently assumed by fifteen smaller ones and fifteen decoys, which is certainly feasible, would make the ratio of attacking objects to Sprints stay the same as before with as little consequent defense.

In these examples I assumed that the attack was directed at the hardened missiles. The Safeguard system radars are much more vulnerable to blast effects than the missiles it is supposed to protect, and there are only a few of them. Since they are vital to the operation of the system, a well-planned attack would concentrate its first fire on them in the hope of neutralizing the entire system.

The foregoing assumed that the Safeguard system actually worked. There is good reason to question the system's reliability. There are several interrelated aspects to this question. First, there is the reliability of what is called the hardware—that is, the physical components, radars, computers, missiles, communications facilities, etc.; second, there is the question of whether it can be kept functioning by the normal military crews; third, I doubt the reliability of the computer programs, and finally, we must be concerned about a different kind of reliability, whether it is possible to imagine and simulate the actual environment in which this complex system will have to operate.

The creation of the Safeguard system, like any large-scale system that depends upon computers to control the operation of its parts and their integration, really involves two engineering tasks: the design and development of the physical equipment and the design and development of the computer program for operating the system. Few people realize that the second task may be much more formidable than the first and cannot proceed independently of it. In a very loose way I can liken this to the physical and mental development of a child. The two must go along together at the start until the physical computer exists and is operating reliably, which may take some time, and then the program development can be undertaken seriously.

While I do not have the time to examine the equipment reliability in detail now, a section of our book is devoted to the matter. It can be said without danger of contradiction that the ABM system represents the most sophisticated and intricate system that man has attempted to build, greatly exceeding the SAGE system or any other previous military system in complexity. Each individual component must perform considerably better, that is, be more reliable, than those in present-day units if the system is to achieve the needed over-all reliability. In a recent article, Dr. Dan Fink, former deputy director of Defense Research and Engineering, indicated that operational missiles might be expected to have an availability of approximately 50 percent. Though he was talking about offensive missiles, they are hardly more complex than the Sprint or Spartan devices which furthermore are subjected to considerably greater accelerations in flight. The radars and the computers of the Safeguard system are much more complex than any previously used in a military application, and in my judgment, the pattern of delays and failures in electronic systems reported by Mr. Richard Stubbing, a staff member of the Bureau of the Budget, in his study of the performance experience of major weapons systems developed since World War II, will be duplicated here. It is very likely that a high failure rate will be encountered during the early life of the system and probable that components and subsystems will need to be reengineered and replaced.

More difficult than creating the "hardware" is building the computer program. This was never adequately done for the

327

SAGE system, and I am under the impression that the effort has been given up. Every new large-scale computer system has had serious operational trouble with its software or operational program. First, the task of designing and debugging a program always takes much longer than anticipated at the start. Second, even after extensive development and shakedown, the programs for complex systems contain many defects or conflicts that come to light only during the stress of operation, and so it is quite common for a computer system to fail completely ("crash," as it is called in the profession) as some new demand is put on the system. Program "bugs" are at least as serious a source of down time on many large systems as actual component failures. Large computer programs have proven to be extremely difficult to modify or "repair" without inadvertently introducing new "bugs."

The Safeguard programs are enormous. From published data it is easy to see that the computer is designed to execute programs consisting of many millions of instructions. It is therefore both reasonable and necessary in analyzing the presumed reliability of such a system to make comparisons with other systems involving programs of similar size. There are no working examples today of huge computer programs on the scale required by the ABM program, but the body of experience with complex problems of a smaller scale inspires no confidence in the ultimate reliability of the ABM system. There is, today, no theory to account for the method of "debugging" a program; it remains an art. Moreover, it is possible *to show mathematically that no such theory can be constructed.*

Large computer programs can only be tested properly in their operational environment. It is not likely that it will be possible to simulate a nuclear attack well enough to have high confidence that the Safeguard system will actually function as planned when it is truly challenged. In fact, I believe that the odds are against it.

In recent weeks the two planned Safeguard sites have been

termed R & D sites, and the impression conveyed that they will make possible more realistic testing of the system than can be done at Kwajalein. While some useful knowledge may be gained because of the greater complexity of the interconnected systems, it clearly will not be possible to have the important tests, those in which the system attempts to defend the Minuteman force against a large attack in a nuclear weapons environment. In fact, I suspect that more realistic tests could be made on the test range.

Many people propose that we deploy the Safeguard system, regardless of the fact that it may not provide any protection, saying for example, that it can't do any harm, or if there is any chance that it will work, it may make an incremental contribution to our security. In my view, the most likely consequence of the attitude that we must prepare against any conceivable eventuality no matter how unlikely and that we must buy every weapons system no matter how poor, is a continuing upward spiral in the arms race and a continuing decrease in our security rather than any improvement. If the United States deploys the Safeguard system, the Soviet planners will have to be conservative and overestimate its capabilities. Their response, which would most likely be out of proportion to its actual value, could take the form of extending their ABM system or increasing still further their missile force. In either event we would undoubtedly have to respond again and so on. Such a reaction is expected by General Twining and his colleagues in the American Security Council. They recently put out a pamphlet supporting the ABM, in which the following statement appears: "Safeguard will work in the sense it is intended to work—it will force the enemy to greatly multiply his arsenal with greatly sophisticated missiles before he could dare to attack." One could go on to say that this would undoubtedly be the Soviet reaction even if they only wanted to deter an American attack. The United States would react similarly to a substantial Soviet ABM. Clearly we agree on the escalating effect of an ABM deployment but disagree on the desirability of it.

Freezing the present system and putting it into production even on a small scale will tend to preclude the development and deployment of an effective hard-point defense if one is in fact possible and needed. The energy and resources that would go into the Safeguard system will clearly not be available to continue the search for something more useful.

It is now generally agreed that ABM systems of the Sentinel type cannot provide city protection against large attacks, but defending cities against a small Chinese attack remains one of the objectives of the Safeguard system. The argument seems to be that our massive aircraft and missile force will not deter the Chinese after they have achieved an ICBM capability and that we will need Safeguard to protect us from them. Furthermore, the argument goes, the Chinese weapons being "first generation" would be simple and make no use of penetration aids so that the "thin" Spartan defense would work against them. I believe that both of these arguments are wrong. First of all, it is perfectly clear that we could inflict almost complete destruction on Communist China should they launch an attack on the United States. It is also perfectly obvious from their behavior that they understand this, so I find it difficult to imagine a creditable circumstance under which they would attack the United States. Also, the United States obviously would have a first-strike capability against China, even after she achieved a modest missile force. It is conceivable that an ABM system would prolong the period during which this was true. However, it is not sound to assume that the Chinese will not produce simple penetration aids, amply described in the literature, very early in their program, and these could allow their warheads to breach the Spartan defense. Thus, the U.S. first-strike capability

330

could be short-lived and hardly prolonged by a "thin" ABM system. Finally, a "Chinese"-oriented system could well raise fears that the United States actually intended to launch a first strike and thus contribute to the very "irrationality" that some people fear.

I would like now to make a few general observations. I am troubled by the argument that the Safeguard system, by protecting the deterrent force, would strengthen the President's resolve in a crisis. Considering how unlikely it is that this ABM system will make a significant change in the strategic forces surviving an attack, it would be most unwise to build it just to back up a game of "chicken." The strategic superiority enjoyed by the United States is often cited as the reason for the Soviet withdrawal during the Cuban missile crisis and used to support this argument. I believe that geography and disparity of interests were much more important than relative nuclear strengths. It was easy for the United States to bring its conventional forces to bear on that situation and extremely difficult for the Soviet Union to do so. Strategically it was much more important to the United States than to the Soviet Union. Recall that the United States had absolute nuclear superiority at the time of the 1948 Berlin crisis, but this helped very little in resolving the crisis. The United States also had vast nuclear superiority at the time of the suppression of the Hungarians by the Soviet Union and yet it could not affect the outcome because the Soviet forces were much nearer and the question of who controlled the area was much more vital to the Soviet leaders. I would also point out that the Soviet leaders have always been extremely careful not to cause an irresolvable confrontation around Berlin where they appreciate the extent of the U.S. commitment and interest.

It is frequently said that there were, in the past, debates

similar to the present one over the ABM relating to the hydrogen bomb, the ballistic missile, and on the Polaris submarine with the strong implication that scientists and engineers were wrong on those issues and so are likely to be wrong again. This is a very wrong interpretation of history, and I would like to tell you why. I was not directly involved in the arguments about the H-bomb, and though I have the impression that the debate started around the question of whether a specific process would work at all, not whether they would be reliable in service, I will leave this question to Dr. Teller. I was involved in both the Polaris submarine and the ICBM issues, so I can talk about them with some authority.

In the case of the ICBM the outside scientists were actually advocates, fighting people who didn't believe that intercontinental missiles were possible. I was a member of the von Neumann committee and one of our major efforts was to convince the leaders of the Department of Defense—many of the Air Force generals and the civilian secretaries of both the Air Force and the Defense Department—that missiles were practical weapons. In the case of the Polaris submarine the issues were also different. Most of us who were involved in the development of the United States strategic missile systems during the 1950s believed that the nuclear submarine provided an ideal base for a ballistic missile because of its invulnerability and because, to the extent that it would be the target of a counter force attack, that attack would be drawn away from our shores. The argument was a technical one and had to do with the type of missile to put on the submarine. Secretary of Defense Charles Wilson was only willing to permit the Navy to proceed with the Polaris submarine program if it would use the liquid-fueled Thor IRBM developed by the Army at the Redstone Arsenal. Many of us thought that to do this was a serious error and argued for the development of a solid-fuel rocket. Our objections

332

were twofold: The Thor system was a very complicated system that required the use of liquid oxygen and dangerous liquid fuels. In our opinion it created a very major safety hazard on board the submarine. In addition, we believed that it was possible to achieve a much higher degree of readiness and reliability with a solid-fuel rocket. In the end we were able to win people over to our views and the present Polaris missile was developed. I believe that Admiral Rayburn, who was the director of the Polaris project, understood our objectives and to the best of my knowledge appreciated our efforts. It is hard to see what lessons can be learned from those situations that would apply to the present debate.

I would summarize my position as follows:

1. I have very serious doubts about many technical aspects of the Safeguard system.
2. I do not believe that the Soviet Union can achieve a first-strike capability against the United States in the 1975 time period by following their present course of action.
3. Even if Safeguard could be made to work as designed, it would be relatively simple—compared to the difficulty of building Safeguard—for the Soviet Union to deploy effective countermeasures against it.
4. Safeguard is unnecessary and building it would waste a great deal of money.
5. If the survival of our deterrent was in danger, I would still oppose Safeguard, and I would search for more promising ways to maintain it.
6. We must make a more determined effort to halt the arms race. Neither building the ABM nor stopping it will insure our security. We must find a way

to stop the development and deployment of new strategic weapons systems, MIRVs, FOBs, etc., and to reduce the existing attack forces on both sides. Similarly, we must support means of preventing or controlling limited conflicts. There are obvious steps that should be explored for these objectives.

I would give the highest priority to beginning the bilateral discussions with the Soviet Union on strategic weapons. I hope that your committee will give urgent attention to this broader range of issues.

7. The views I have expressed here are shared by the persons who worked with me on the ABM book.

Addition to testimony by Dr. J. B. Wiesner before Committee on Foreign Relations, May 14, 1969:

Since I prepared my testimony, Dr. Foster has suggested that my calculations regarding the surviving Minuteman force were in error. He estimated that only 50 missiles would survive a Soviet SS-9 attack instead of the 270 shown in our ABM book. My calculations were based on Department of Defense data released in March and April of this year. Dr. Foster has now changed those figures. He says that the SS-9 warhead will have a 0.95 probability of destroying a Minuteman rather than the 0.8 previously predicted. This involves a new estimate of the SS-9 MIRV accuracy and reliability, a reliability which is hard to accept. He also has changed the estimate of Soviet SS-9s from 500 to 600.

Dr. Foster also says that the Soviets might have the capacity for monitoring their MIRV warheads and only using a second one against a target when the first has obviously failed. This is a technical complication in addition to the MIRVs and I don't believe would be used. Even if it were, there is an easy counter to it. The attack will have to come in two waves spaced by a few

minutes so that the attacker can determine which reentry vehicles have failed and need backup. Our early-warning system
will certainly indicate that there are two components to the attack.
It seems unlikely that we would wait for the second attack to hit,
rather than fire the remaining missiles after the first weapons
explode. In this case about 290 land-based missiles (Minuteman
and Titan II) would be available for counterattack. As our book
indicates, there will also be a great many aircraft and Polaris
missiles available as well.

I find it hard to believe that the changing rationalizations,
data, and intelligence estimates in support of the Safeguard
system can be based on a truly careful study.

THE ROLE OF THE ABM IN THE 1970s*

*Albert Wohlstetter, professor at the University of Chicago
and a fellow of its Center of Policy Studies, was for many
years a member of the Rand Corporation, eventually becoming an Associate Director of Projects. He specialized in problems of deterrence and arms control.*

*Dr. Wohlstetter's brilliant article, "The Delicate Balance of
Terror" (Foreign Affairs, January 1959), is generally recognized as a primary intellectual source for subsequent strategic
debates. His studies have developed such concepts as the first-
strike/second-strike distinction, fail-safe procedures against
accidents, and programs for hardening strategic missiles.*

I appreciate the honor of testifying before this committee
on the role of an antiballistic missile system in the 1970s.

Since I believe the Safeguard program warrants the sums
involved, and I support it, perhaps I should begin by saying

* Statement of Albert Wohlstetter before the Senate Armed Services Committee, April 23, 1969.

that I am entirely sympathetic to a rigorous review of the defense budget. I favor getting our safety as cheaply as we can. Moreover, I believe the defense budget has a good deal of fat that can be cut without substantial harm. I would recommend, for example, a careful look at the equipment and support costs of our ground forces, and at our tactical air forces, both land- and sea-based. Some of these seem ineffective, or leveled at threats that are poorly defined or not grave enough to be worth the cost.

Sensible efforts to reduce the defense budget, however, would not center on the strategic offense and defense force. There are, of course, arguable choices about strategic offense and defense. But the $8 billion plus strategic budget makes up a small part of the total defense budget. It has a paramount importance for the safety of the country and indeed of international society. Deterring nuclear coercion and nuclear attack on ourselves or our allies, reducing the damage done in case deterrence fails are complex and uncertain functions; but because they are crucial, the part of the defense budget devoted to them has been the most studied and is better understood than any of the rest.

Nonetheless, sizable uncertainties are intrinsic. They affect the predictions of scientists as well as the military and limit the reductions we can make without excessive risk. The strategic forces will need continuing adjustment to predicted and to some unanticipated changes in the state of the art. But such adjustments need not entail drastic changes up or down in long-term levels of spending.

A start in deploying ABM, I believe, is a prudent response to changes in the state of the art available to ourselves and to our adversaries. As strategic systems go, it is a modest program. It is subject to review and can be halted or stretched out. The average annual cost of the completed program, on a five-year basis, is less than one fifth of what we were spending for active defense against manned bombers at the end of the 1950s. Nor

336

is it at all likely to start a quantitative arms spiral. Indeed, despite the stereotype, there has been no quantitative arms race in the strategic offense and defense budget, no "ever-accelerating increase," nor, in fact, any long-term increase at all. The budget for strategic offense and defense forces in fiscal 1962 was $11.3 billion.[1] The proposed fiscal 1970 budget, I understand, comes to about 8.3 billion dollars. Adjusted for price changes, the 1962 figure was well over 50 percent higher than that for 1970.

There is an important difference between making qualitative adjustments to technical change and expanding the number of vehicles or megatons or dollars spent. The difference has been ignored in a debate on ABM that seems at the same time impassioned and very abstract, quite removed from the actual political, economic, and military history of nuclear offense and defense. For example, one alternative to protecting Minuteman is to buy more Minutemen without protection. But adding new vehicles is costly and more destabilizing than an active defense of these hard points, since it increases the capacity to strike first. A one-sided self-denial of new technology can lead simply to multiplying our missiles and budgets; or to a decrease in safety; or to both.

Active defense against ballistic missiles in the 1970s will have an important role to play in maintaining a protected and responsible second-strike capacity. (The projected Safeguard defense of the national command authority and of the bomber and Minuteman bases are directed to this end.) And it has a useful function in providing an area defense against attacks involving modest numbers of apparent incoming missiles.

There have been so many charges that the Safeguard program was invented in bad faith in March of this year as a gimmick

[1] DOD Appropriations for 1969 Hearings, Part I, Financial Summary. Expenditures in the 1950s were not then broken down by mission but strategic budgets appear to have been even higher in the late 1950s than in 1962.

to answer critics of the Sentinel city defense that I would stress that in 1967, long before the present administration quite independently decided on the Safeguard, the evidence of advancing technology convinced me that ABM in the 1970s would have essentially the uses the administration suggests for Safeguard, and in the same order: to defend the offense and, given this, at a small extra cost to provide a light area defense of population.[2] In fact, there is a substantial continuity between the ABM decisions of the present and past administrations. The last administration called for an ABM area defense but said it would furnish an economic basis for defending Minuteman if the threat grew. It had been weighing and it continued to weigh this for some time—indeed itself requested some funds for hard-point defense in its own version of the 1970 fiscal budget.

Like the Republicans now, the Democrats in 1967 were charged with directing their ABM decision against the opposing party. I would recommend to opponents of ABM that they contemplate the possibility that the decisions were made in good faith in both cases and that we turn to the substance of the issues.

There are other political and military functions of an ABM

[2] "*First,* an offense force with such increased accuracies and reliabilities and with an extensive use of MIRVs is very much more efficient in attacking the fixed offense force or the important fixed elements of the mobile force of an adversary. . . . *Second,* one result of this sort of change in Russian offense forces is to make improved antiballistic missiles (rather than simply more hardening or more missiles) an economic way for the United States to protect the hard fixed elements of a strategic force. . . . *Third,* at a minor increment in the modest cost of a hard-point ABM defense, it is possible to make available a light ABM for defense of civil societies against a small submarine or land-based missile force or part of a large one launched by mistake or without authorization. . . ." Address to the Sepetmber 1967 Institute of Strategic Studies Conference on the Implications of Military Technology in the 1970s at Elsinore, Denmark. Adelphi Paper No. 46, p. 4.

system than protecting the offense and offering an area defense of civilians against light attack. I would like to say something about each of these two latter roles and also something about the doctrine of minimum deterrence on which much opposition to the ABM is based, but time permits comment mostly on the protected offense function.

For one superpower as against another, getting and keeping a responsible strike force is feasible but hard. It requires thought, effort, and continuing realistic adjustments to technological change. Minimum deterrence theorists, who call for no defense of our civilians and nearly total reliance on a threat to bombard enemy civilians, have always claimed that the attacker inevitably must expend many strategic vehicles to destroy only one of the vehicles attacked. No such generalization holds. It has depended and always must depend on the changing capabilities of the offense and on the kind and degree of protection of the force attacked. At one time, for example, both we and the Russians had very many unprotected aircraft concentrated on a base within the lethal radius of a single bomb. On a two-wing base, for example, we had as many as 130 aircraft; on a one-wing base 65 medium bombers and tankers. And the planned response time was too slow for the reliable warning likely to be available. Small numbers of vehicles could have destroyed much larger numbers of the vehicles they attacked. Under some realistically determined conditions, the ratio would have favored the attacker by 1 to 8 or more. These vulnerabilities had nothing to do with the supposed missile gap. In fact they preceded such predictions.

There is always a temptation in such circumstances to resort to responses that are automatic or that bypass national command. Advocates of sole reliance on city bombardment forces have from the time this doctrine first gained currency been tempted to prove that response was certain by making it automatic, by shortcutting responsible political decision.[3] But the decision to launch ICBMs against Russian cities would be perhaps the most momentous choice ever made in all of history. It would be the decision for World War III. If this awful decision is ever made, it should be based on as much information as we can get and it should be made by as high a political authority as possible. It is the last decision we should contemplate delegating to a computer.

The revival today, by several distinguished senators and some able physicists opposing ABM, of the suggestion that, rather than defend ICBMs, we should launch them at Russian cities simply on the basis of radar represents a long step backward. If we were willing to do this, we would dispense with silos or Poseidon submarines or any other mode of protecting our missiles. And we would increase the nightmare possibility of nuclear war by mistake.

Understanding of the complex problems of designing a protected and responsible nuclear strategic force has grown slowly among scientists as well as laymen, civilians as well as soldiers, Democrats as well as Republicans. But it has grown, and decisively. The United States has designed and deployed a second-strike force capable of riding out an attack; and there have been large improvements in protecting responsible command. This was accomplished not by merely expanding nuclear bombardment forces, but in essence by shifting to forces with protection against the changing threat. The stereotype repeated throughout the 1960s that our security has declined while our strategic force grew at an accelerating rate is grossly wrong on both counts. In the past some key programs increased the protected second-strike capacity of the force, while cutting at the same time billions of dollars from the spending projected.

[3] See, for example, one of the first classic sources of minimum deterrence doctrine, *NPA 1970 Without Arms Control,* Special Committee Report, 1958, pp. 32–33, 44.

In the 1970s unless we continue to make appropriate decisions to meet technological change, once again the viability of a large part of our second-strike force will be put in question. Several related innovations, but in particular the development of a rocket booster carrying many reentry vehicles each aimed precisely at a different target, raises once again the possibility of attack ratios favoring the attacker. One reentry vehicle may kill a booster carrying several. One booster can carry the means of destroying many boosters.

Raising a question about the future second-strike capacity of any part of our strategic force implies nothing about the present intentions of an adversary to strike first or even to be able in the future effectively to strike first. The recent debate on whether the SS-9 is a "first-strike weapon" or whether the Russians intend it to be is beside the point. If by maintaining our second-strike capability we can make the risks of striking very great, this can affect an adversary's intentions favorably to ourselves. It can deter him even in a crisis, like the one over missiles in Cuba, when the alternative to striking may look bad, but not, if we are careful, as bad as striking. Moreover, we ought not to talk of "first-strike weapons" and "second-strike weapons" as if this could be settled simply by looking at the weapons on one side. Whether or not a weapons system can preclude substantial retaliation will depend on many uncertain future performance characteristics of the forces on *both* sides. The test of whether one has a responsible second-strike capacity is whether one can, under nuclear attack, preserve vehicles, decision centers, and the flow of communications among them, whether one can transmit the order to retaliate and penetrate adversary defenses to reach targets. If we were unwilling even to entertain the hypothesis of a first strike, we would do nothing to protect any part of our strategic forces or its control centers by making it mobile or hard or by ABM. Some leading scientists who oppose currently deploying ABM say they will favor it for the defense of Minuteman when precise MIRVs and the related offense technologies are likely to be available to the Russians. That calendar date, and not present Soviet intent, is then a major substantive issue for these opponents. And their position recognizes that we want to maintain the second-strike capacity—not of just one, but of all major vehicle types in our strategic force: Minuteman, bombers, and Poseidon.

In designing a second-strike force, there are excellent reasons for making it a substantial mixture of vehicles of several quite different types: land- as well as sea-based, manned as well as unmanned, each with its own mode of protection. Such systems have differing limitations, are subject to varied and independent uncertainties, require distinct modes of attack and, if each type is protected, greatly complicate the attack. It is a serious matter, then, if a large part of this mixture is badly affected by changing adversary forces and technologies. The forces deployed and the state of the art available to the Russians will influence other parts of our strategic force than Minuteman silos. And ABM has a role to play, for example, in protecting the important fixed elements of a mobile force, including the politically responsible command centers. Preserving command, control, and communications is always hard, and particularly so for mobile sea-based systems.

My remarks, however, center, so far as the second-strike function of ABM is concerned, on the problem of protecting Minuteman. We have good cause to preserve the second-strike capability of so large a proportion of our strategic force. Even if it were true that the United States needed only a few strategic vehicles surviving, buying and paying for the operation of a great many that had become vulnerable to attack would be a very poor way to obtain those few surviving. There are safer and cheaper ways of getting a force of a given size than to buy a much larger one, most of which is susceptible to annihilation.

How does the planned timing of our ABM deployment compare to the date when it is reasonably likely that Russian offense technology could badly worsen the effectiveness of our projected Minuteman III? The first point to note is that the proposed Safeguard deployment has extended lead-times. It can stretch out further if continuing review of intelligence suggests it should, but the shortest schedule calls for completing this program early in 1976. If, as ABM opponents stress in other connections, there is likely to be a substantial shakedown period, we are talking of 1977 or later. If, as has been suggested, we delay decision for another year or more and then proceed to design and develop an entirely new ABM, we are talking of the 1980s.

Second, predicting exact calendar dates at which technologies will be available to adversaries and what their strategic significance will be is very hard, and we are not very good at it. Moreover, we have erred not only on the side of overestimating Russian capabilities, but often by underestimating them. At earlier dates we were surprised by the rapid Soviet achievement of the A-bomb, the H-bomb, advanced jet engines, long-range turboprop bombers, airborne intercept radars, and large-scale fissile-material production. And scientists have been surprised; not only military men.[4]

[4] We have not been very good at predicting our own or our adversary's technologies. These matters are intrinsically uncertain. Eminent scientists at the end of the 1940s predicted that fusion weapons would be infeasible, and if feasible undeliverable, and if delivered of no strategic significance, since they thought (erroneously) it could be used only against cities. (Some of those who then thought the threat of fusion bombs against cities neither moral nor important strategically now take it to be both.) In February 1953 an important scientific study group expected the Soviets would have no ICBMs before the late 1960s—a prediction plainly in error by the end of the year. Writing in October 1964 some scientists opposing ABM were quite sure that no technological surprises could substantially change the operational effectiveness of intercontinental delivery systems, and thus entirely missed the major strategic potential of precisely aimed MIRVs, a concept that was at that very time emerging in the classified literature. These were able and informed men. But exact prediction on these matters defies confident assertion.

Third, the public discussion has not stressed how sensitively the accuracy of attack affects the viability of the hardened force attacked. Accuracy affects the number of weapons required to destroy a hard target very much more than the bomb yield or the overpressure resistance of the target. Roughly speaking, for such targets, improving accuracy by a factor of slightly more than 2 is the same as increasing bomb yield ten-fold and serves essentially to offset a ten-fold increase in overpressure resistance.

I have tried to reconstruct various numerical proofs recently presented or distributed to the Congress that purport to show our Minuteman will be quite safe without any extra protection; these proofs depend heavily on optimistic estimates of limitations in Russian delivery accuracies, reliabilities, and associated offense capabilities and sometimes on very poor offense tactics. Suppose, however, that by 1976 when Safeguard is deployed, or by 1977 when it may be shaken down, the Russians have:

1. Accuracies like those of the systems we are deploying *now*.
2. Overall reliabilities currently attributable to them.
3. Methods familiar to us for using extensive and timely information as to which missiles have failed so that others can replace them.
4. Continued production of SS-9 boosters at past rates.
5. Modest numbers of MIRVs per booster (*e.g.*, the three five-megaton reentry vehicles stated by Secretary Laird for the SS-9).

Then the percentage of the Minuteman force that would be destroyed, if undefended, comes to about 95 percent.

These results are based on quite moderate assumptions about Russian capabilities. Better accuracies, for example, may be expected in the late 1970s, and higher degrees of MIRVing. Reliabilities of any given offense missile system improve with use. Do those who favor a hard-point defense but would postpone a start really consider these Russian capabilities I have outlined "extremely implausible"? Or at *all* implausible?

There is a striking inconsistency in the way ABM opponents treat the Chinese and the Russians. In contemplating the possibility of a Russian offense against our Minuteman, they assume Russians who cannot by 1976 or 1977—twenty years after Sputnik—do what we know how to do now. When considering the ability of the Chinese to penetrate an ABM defense, they attribute to them penetration systems that cost us many billions of dollars, a dozen years of trials and many failures to develop —and they assume this for first-generation Chinese missiles. These are rather backward Russians and very advanced Chinese. Moreover, since in the Russian case we are considering a potential threat to our second-strike capability and we want this to be highly reliable, we want particularly to avoid underestimating the threat. But we should undertake a modest defense of population if it works in the expected case, even if on extremely pessimistic assumptions it might not. Here again it seems to me the ABM critics get things exactly backward.

Finally, the fact that such impending developments in Russian offense may make it necessary to do something more to protect the fixed elements of our force should come as no surprise. It was the sensitive effects of missile inaccuracy that in the early 1950s suggested to the original proponents of programs for hardening strategic vehicles against ICBM attack (a) that hardening would be an important and effective method of protection against ICBM attack in the 1960s, and (b) that by itself hardening would not be adequate for much past the 1960s. The ICBMs then expected in the 1960s were, of course, enormously faster than manned bombers, and therefore would outmode some programs that served very well in the 1950s; but the early ICBMs were likely to be very much less accurate than the manned bombers. They were expected to have inaccuracies

345

measured in miles, perhaps, it seemed then, as large as five miles, compared to the quarter of a nautical mile or 1,500-feet median miss distance associated with manned bombers. Since just doubling inaccuracy could affect weapons requirements by a factor of 4, hardening clearly seemed a good idea. The paper proposing hardening for the 1960s was entitled "Protecting a Strategic Force after 1960" and was put out on February 1, 1954. That paper included a very short section called "After After 1960" that is quite relevant for understanding why we should expect that we will have to adapt the current Minuteman to impending changes in opposing offense technology. The section read in full:

> The foregoing also suggests that even against the ballistic missile this defense would have a finite life. The missile might improve drastically in accuracy and payload. However, the date at which the Russians will have a missile capable of carrying a 25-MT bomb with a 1,500-ft. CEP appears sufficiently far removed to make the defense good, let's say, until the end of the sixties [p. 19].

That the numbers cited in this paper of February 1954 so closely match some of those being talked of for the SS-9 is, of course, purely a coincidence. They were performance characteristics of bombers then current. However, the quotation illustrates that, from the outset, it was to be expected that sooner or later and probably in the 1970s, hardening would not be enough by itself. The discussion also suggests that to depend merely on further hardening would make the system vulnerable to further improvements in accuracy.

Hardening can be outpaced by further development in precision. This does not mean that for some possible threats a combination of ABM and extreme hardening might not be useful. It might. But as a complete substitute for ABM, extreme

346

hardening has drawbacks. It is subject in my opinion to much larger uncertainties as to both performance and costs than the ABM.

The major components of the Safeguard system have received elaborate study and testing. Ideas for brand-new ABM systems to defend hard points that I am familiar with are not serious competitors in this time period. We should start deploying the system now on the schedule suggested, and we should expect, as in the case of every other offense and defense system, that we shall learn a great deal from operational experience, make some changes and retrofits. This seems to me a sound way to supplement the protection of the Minuteman in a period when we can expect it to be endangered.

I have used the time available to comment mainly on the role of ABM in defending Minuteman. I also support its utility for a thin area defense of population and shall be glad to try to answer questions about that subject as well.

ADDENDUM

In The New York Times, *June 15, 1969, there appeared an exchange of letters between Professors Rathjens and Wohlstetter on the general subject of the vulnerability of the U.S. land-based Minuteman system to various Soviet SS-9 attacks. In view of the fact that Professor Rathjens was an associate of Dr. Wiesner in the Chayes-Wiesner book, this exchange is pertinent not only to Dr. Wohlstetter's Senate testimony but also to that of Dr. Wiesner.*

The exchange of letters follows:

To the Editor:

You recently carried a story about Albert Wohlstetter's criticisms of an estimate I made that 25 percent of our Minuteman force could be expected to survive a preemptive attack by a

Soviet SS-9 missile force in the mid-1970s. Mr. Wohlstetter is reported to claim that the "correct" number is 5 percent.

I have dealt with Mr. Wohlstetter's criticisms in a classified letter, but also feel I should comment on them publicly.

First, there is the question of whether I used the right "hardness" for Minuteman silos in my calculation. I used a chart released by Deputy Secretary of Defense Packard and data made available by former Deputy Secretary of Defense Nitze on Nov. 8, 1967.

One cannot determine unambiguously either the hardness of a Minuteman silo or the accuracy we expect with MIRVs from this data. However, by using both releases one can derive a probability for a Minuteman silo being destroyed without knowing the exact hardness. This I did. Any error in estimation of hardness is irrelevant because it is offset by a compensating difference in estimation of accuracy.

Second, it is alleged that I made an error in assuming four one-megaton [MT] warheads per SS-9 missile rather than three five-MT warheads as Mr. Wohlstetter assumed. My statement for Senator Albert Gore's subcommittee was prepared before anyone had suggested that the Soviet Union could employ the latter option with the SS-9. I saw no reason to change it, since I continue to regard a payload of less than three five-MT warheads as a plausible threat and because the difference is small compared with the following more important points.

The major difference between Mr. Wohlstetter's analysis and mine is with respect to the extent to which the Russians could retarget some of their missiles to take account of failures of others.

Mr. Wohlstetter has assumed perfect information would be available to them about missile launch failures, failures during powered flight, and failures in separation and guidance of the individual warheads, and that they woud be able to use that

348

information with the high confidence required to make a pre-emptive attack a rational choice. I have assumed they would not be able to obtain and use information about such failures in a timely fashion. This accounts for most of the difference in our estimates of Minuteman survival.

There are five far more important points to be made.

There is no hard evidence that the Russians are determined to build a capability to effectively attack our ICBMs.

If they wish to do so, they can build such a capability by the mid-1970s.

If they do so, implementation of the Safeguard plan could be offset by a very small additional Russian effort. Even an expanded Safeguard system would be less satisfactory than other alternatives for strengthening our retaliatory capabilities.

Even if the Russians built the capability to destroy our Minuteman force, preemptive attack by them would be madness unless they could discount completely the possibility that we might launch some Minutemen before the arrival of their ICBMs, and unless they could be highly confident of also destroying the other components of our retaliatory strength essentially simultaneously, a possibility that is all but incredible.

The most effective means of insuring the continued viability of the Minuteman force is early agreement to stop MIRV testing and to preclude a large build-up in Soviet ICBM strength. Negotiations to achieve these ends clearly merit higher priority than the deployment of Safeguard.

George W. Rathjens
Cambridge, Mass., June 5, 1969

To the Editor:

Responsible scientists like Drs. Bethe and Ruina, who feel we can delay starting ABM to protect Minuteman, testify that "any one . . . system, bombers, Polaris, Minuteman, has its own

349

vulnerability"; that we need all three; that a threat to Minuteman concerns us gravely. One key issue then is whether that threat will develop by 1976 or 1977 when at the earliest Safeguard will be shaken down—or whether it is safe to wait years for a better ABM.

A disparate variety of calculations by Drs. Rathjens, Weinberg, Wiesner, and Lapp purport to show that it is safe to wait, that an attack by five hundred Russian SS-9 missiles would leave untouched anywhere from one fourth to three quarters of our Minutemen.

They claim to square with official intelligence. Such confident inferences by scientists carry great authority and ought to be made with the utmost professional care. But despite their widely publicized claims, it is they (not those who would start ABM) who are careless of pre- as well as post-Nixon intelligence, and quite casual in their calculation.

They attribute to an SS-9 in the late 1970s poorer combinations of bomb yield, number of MIRVs, and accuracy than intelligence expects in the early 1970s; and compound these errors by presuming poor Russian tactics or higher blast resistance than designed.

In a note to me on his calculations, Dr. Rathjens assumed our silo could resist overpressures two-thirds higher than its design performance; and derived a probability some three-fourths too high that it could survive a one-MT burst. He bases his probability calculations on doubtfully relevant 1967 testimony about U.S. attacks on adversary silos of unspecified hardness with a range of destruction probabilities. Dr. Rathjens applies the low end of this range to late 1970 SS-9s attacking our silos —which hardly fits a proof that "the most worrisome projections" leave us nothing to worry about. The other end of the range yields roughly the appropriate lower survival probability.

350

Dr. Rathjens assumes only four one-MT MIRVs in the late 1970s SS-9. But (a) more than four one-MT MIRVs were attributed by pre-Nixon intelligence to the SS-9 in the early 1970s; and (b) an alternative of three five-MT MIRVs is now public. Five hundred SS-9s equipped with either of these MIRV options could destroy about 95 percent of Minuteman if the Russians use well-established techniques for reprogramming missiles to replace known failures. Using no reprogramming at all, the one-MT MIRV force would destroy 92 or 93 percent of Minuteman. The ability of the five-MT force to destroy 95 percent of Minutemen presumes only half the failures after launch are replaced—a figure well within the state of the art.

Even limiting the use of information to missile malfunctions before or during launch, the five-MT MIRV force would leave only 8 or 9 percent surviving. These numbers are intrinsically uncertain—sensitive especially to changing accuracy.

Four hundred SS-9s with one-MT MIRVs and accuracies better by only 250 feet would destroy more Minutemen than five hundred with the accuracy expected in the early 1970s.

Dr. Rathjens' belief that variants of Safeguard help retaliation less than available alternatives is based on estimates of costs of these alternatives which I find as casual as his calculations on the threat to Minuteman.

Finally, unlike him, I don't believe a stable, monitorable agreement to limit strategic offense and defense would freeze ABM at zero. ABM can counter improvements in offense accuracy unlikely to be monitored; and can protect population against smaller powers that violate or do not sign the agreement. I doubt the Russians would accept a total ban on ABM.

Albert Wohlstetter
University of Chicago
Los Angeles, June 11, 1969

STATEMENT OF EUGENE P. WIGNER*

Dr. Eugene P. Wigner, now at Princeton University, has doctorates in physics and engineering. A former member of the general advisory committee of the Atomic Energy Commission, and a director of the Civil Defense Research Project at Oak Ridge, Dr. Wigner has received many honors and accolades for both his scientific and administrative work. Among these are a Nobel Prize in physics (1963), the Max Planck Medal of the German Physical Society (1961), the Enrico Fermi Award of the Atomic Energy Commission (1958), the Atoms for Peace Award (1960).

When thinking about the problems facing this committee, I came to conclude that the two principal questions are: do our defenses need strengthening and, if so, what are the best ways to do this. I realize my own inadequacy for answering questions as difficult and important as these, but I sincerely and earnestly tried to come to valid conclusions.

The case for strengthening the defense of our country is easy to make. The Soviet Union has surpassed us in the most effective weapons system: its capability to deliver ballistic missiles exceeds ours by a considerable margin. It is instituting civil-defense measures which are calculated to impair our deterrent capability. I wish to enlarge a bit on these two points.

The total explosive power of the missiles which the Soviet Union can deliver exceeds ours by a factor between 3 and 4. This will surprise many, but it is well known in our Defense Department. As far as area coverage is concerned, we are somewhat better off: the area which we can cover with a certain overpressure is 70 to 80 percent of the area which the Soviet

* Before the Subcommittee on International Organization and Disarmament Affairs of the Senate Committee on Foreign Relations, May 21, 1969.

Union can cover with the same overpressure. Considering that our population is concentrated in cities to a greater extent than that of the Soviet Union, the disparity is great also in this regard. It is true that the number of nuclear warheads which the United States can deliver exceeds that which the Soviet Union can deliver, but the number of warheads is not a measure of the fallout or of the destruction of life that can be caused. In my opinion, the best measure is what I earlier called "area coverage."

The situation is aggravated by two other factors. The first is that this country will surely not be the one to initiate hostilities; the time of any armed conflict would be chosen by our opponents. I could quote many statements by leading personalities in the Soviet Union extolling what they call a preemptive strike against the imperialistic aggressors. The second circumstance aggravating the situation and, in my opinion, aggravating it gravely, is our neglect of civil defense. The Soviet Union has elaborate plans for evacuating its cities, and these plans can become effective much before we can establish an effective civil defense, even if we were to start this afternoon.

I may mention in this connection that the particular form of civil defense which plays a prime role in Soviet planning, the evacuation of the cities, was found objectionable to those participants in which, including myself, expressed opposition to evacuation plans because they felt such plans are "provocative." The time needed for the actual evacuation is long, of the order of a day at least. Hence, evacuation can be carried out in time only if the time of the confrontation is known well ahead of time. Since this is the case only for the party which initiates the confrontation, evacuation is most useful as a measure supporting aggression. The preceding is much condensed discussion of the rationale of evacuation planning but, unless asked to do so later, I will not elaborate on it further.

I will say, though, that the evacuation of the cities could

353

decrease the fatalities which an opponent can inflict by a very considerable factor. I calculated that, assuming evacuation of the cities of the Soviet Union into circles with fifty-mile radii, our present missile power, including that on submarines, could cause a fatality level of about 9.5 million if (a) all our missiles were used against the population, none against the military targets, (b) the ballistic missile defense of the Soviet Union were completely ineffective, (c) we suffer no losses whatever from a first strike, and (d) all our submarines are on station. Naturally, though only a fraction of the numbers often quoted, 9.5 million is an extremely high level of fatalities. It is based, however, on extreme assumptions and, of course, we do not know the lives of how many people a possible bellicose leadership of an opponent may be willing to sacrifice in order to assure permanent freedom from "imperialist war plotters."

Even though I wish to proceed to my next subject, I cannot help interjecting here that the tactic I am most afraid of is not an actual attack. It is, rather, the threat of an attack, preceded by the evacuation of cities. If the Soviet and U.S. armaments developed in the way the present trends indicate, I greatly fear that we would have to accede to whatever demands accompany the threat just described.

The preceding comparison of the relative powers of the United States and of the Soviet Union is, I am sure, known to the members of this committee, except possibly the effectiveness of the evacuation planned by the Soviets. To support this last point, in case it needs supporting, I'll quote from an article by Marshal V. Chuykov, head of the Soviet civil-defense establishment, which appeared in the January issue of a rather popular periodical, *Science and Life*. It came to my attention just a few days ago.

In our country, everything possible is being done to build reliable means enabling us to protect lives in a possible

354

war. It is well known that the task of defense of the population can be accomplished by two methods—by evacuation and dispersal of the population out of the regions which would probably be struck by the enemy, or by sheltering them in special defense installations. There are no other possibilities, but even these two give us a huge advantage over other countries, especially those of Western Europe. Our country has lots of space and a developed transportation network, our cities are surrounded by ample green belts. All this enables us, on short notice, to take people out of the cities and regions which are probable targets for the enemy into rural locations and thus sharply reduce possible losses.

Take for example city A. If today the average density of population in this city is seven thousand people per square kilometer, after the execution of dispersal and evacuation it would be lowered, on the average, to seven hundred to eight hundred people per square kilometer. In other words, the average would be lowered by eight to ten times. This means that after dispersal and evacuation, a nuclear explosion of the same magnitude would cause losses eight to ten times lower than before the implementation of these measures.

I should admit, though, that the density of the evacuated population, mentioned in this article, seven hundred to eight hundred per square kilometer, is much higher than the density which underlies my own calculations. If we adopt this figure for the density of the evacuated people, but still use the four rather unrealistic assumptions mentioned before, the number of casualties which we could inflict rises to about 13 million. I gave some details of these calculations a few weeks ago in an address to the American Physical Society, and Senator Miller of Iowa honored me by inserting the text of this address into the

Congressional Record. My original calculation has been repeated, independently, by Carsten Haaland of the Oak Ridge National Laboratory.

I can imagine only two conditions under which we could escape the conclusion that our defenses need to be strengthened. These are: (a) if our deterrent power, though inferior to that of the Soviet Union, would remain, nevertheless, "sufficient" and (b) if we could be convinced that our opponents are not interested, now or later, in imposing their will on us by threats or otherwise.

As to the first condition, I very much fear that it is absent. If the civil-defense plans of the Soviet Union, in particular its evacuation program, are carried out—and I cannot see what might prevent this—our deterrent power will be gravely degraded and may become insufficient. It has been argued that the deterrent will remain effective even if the number of casualties which we can inflict were reduced because we could still destroy much, if not most, of the industrial capacity of the Soviet Union. I doubt that we would be willing, as a result of a confrontation, to sacrifice the lives of many millions of Americans for the destruction of material goods in the Soviet Union. The Soviet Union could well threaten that it will demand the rebuilding of their industry as part of the price of any peace, should we carry out our threat of destruction. We know from past experience that it would be able to carry out that threat. As to the period in which the industrial production can be restored, I may recall that it took barely two years after the Second World War to restore Germany's gross national product to the prewar level, once a stable currency system was reestablished. The threat of the destruction of material goods is not a potent deterrent.

As to the second condition for the absence of a need to strengthen our defenses, that our opponents are simply not interested, now or later, in imposing their will on us, this committee can judge that much better than I can. As for myself, I am willing to believe the statements of their leaders which accuse us of being plotters of war and promise victory over us. The increasing emphasis on the mounting strength of the Soviet Union, as compared with that of the United States, is unmistakable in their statements.

If we accept the thesis that our defenses need strengthening, the next question is how this strengthening should be carried out. There are clearly two ways to increase our offensive strength, or to improve our defenses both of people and of installations, including military installations. The two could also be combined.

When I express a strong preference for the second, the defensive alternative, I admit to having principally the longer-range objectives and effects in mind. A world in which potential antagonists are relatively safe from each other is infinitely preferable to a world in which they can inflict, within minutes, tremendous damage on each other. The latter condition is inclined to promote antagonism, the former may lead to accommodation. Surely, disarmament is much easier if a few concealed weapons do not have decisive importance. If I accepted Dr. Rathjens' figures, I would have to say that less than one percent of the present ballistic missile armaments of the Soviet Union can inflict unacceptable damage on our country. Surely, no one believes that arms control can be detailed enough to uncover the concealment of one percent of the present arsenal of weapons. Hence, disarmament is impossible unless we can improve our defenses, and this remains true even if we do not accept the grossly exaggerated damage estimates of Dr. Rathjens—as I do not.

I will not dwell further on this subject—the preferable nature of defensive rather than offensive armaments. You have heard a powerful articulation of this point from Dr. Brennan. Let me instead address the question of the effectiveness of defense measures.

I cannot assert, with full confidence, that the BMD system

357

proposed by our Defense Department will be less expensive than an equivalent increase in our offensive power. I am not able to estimate the costs accurately and I know that members of this committee feel that no one can forecast the cost of as intricate a weapons system as the ABM with sufficient accuracy. I do know that civil defense, even the more expensive variety which the Little Harbor Study advocated instead of evacuation, would cost only a fraction of what the offensive weapons, able to annul its protective effects, would cost. As to the ABM, I cannot assert anything like this with confidence, though I am inclined to agree with Dr. Teller's guess, that "our expenditures on penetration aids were not much less and possibly were considerably higher than the Russian expenditures on defense." What he did not add, but what I wish to supplement, is that the installation of the penetration aids, the subdivisions, etc., led also to a certain degradation of our striking power. We paid in two ways when trying to counteract the ABM of the Soviet Union.

What are, then, the reasons for my confidence in the effectiveness of ballistic missile defense? The crudest one of these reasons is that our striking power had to be decreased when it was adjusted to the presence of the Soviet ABM. Similarly, I expect that the striking power of the Soviet missile force will be decreased when it will have to counteract our missile defenses. The modifications necessary for this will result in a significant decrease of the total damage the Soviet missile force can inflict even if our ABM became totally ineffective as a result of these modifications. As Secretary Nitze mentioned in the course of his testimony, our answer to the Soviet ABM will imply replacing ten-MT warheads by ten warheads, fifty-kt each. Such a replacement results in a reduction of the total explosive power to 5, the area coverage to 29 percent of their pre-replacement values. The total effect on our missile strength is not too great because we have few very large warheads—none of the twenty- to twenty-five-MT variety of the SS-9. However, the reduction of the striking power of the Soviet missiles could be very significant—they have mainly large warheads.

On a more purely technical level, I can see no fundamental problem that could not be solved by a competent group of engineers and physicists. If I may delve into my past experience, the situation may be similar to that which prevailed when the chain reaction was established by Fermi and the basic design for the Hanford reactors laid in Chicago. This may be a good opportunity to compliment those who laid the foundations for the present missile defense plans. The invention and development of the phased-array radar required, in addition to understanding and competence, a great deal of imagination and inventiveness. Naturally, such qualities will be of major help also in the implementation of the present plans but there are, as far as I can see, no outstanding problems which could not be solved in a more routine fashion than the information gathering could be solved. The phased-array radar was a breakthrough in this regard.

I do not mean to say that the present plans constitute a final solution of the missile defense problem. The situation is rather similar to that of a chess game. There is a countermove to every move, even the best one. This, however, is no argument against making a good move. The difference between our situation and that of the chess player is, of course, that we have no desire to win. It would be simply embarrassing. However, we have a fervent desire not to lose, and the hope that we do not lose is, I may interject, also the fervent hope of the people in Western Europe who cherish their freedoms.

I would not be entirely honest if I did not admit that another reason for my confidence is the ability, competence, judgment, and integrity of members of the Defense Department who discussed these matters with me. I am referring, among others, to Dr. John Foster.

359

My over-all confidence in the promise of missile defense does not mean that I am in agreement with all the details of the technical decisions. In fact, I concur in some of the technical criticisms of Dr. Panofsky, though of course not with his main thesis. On the other hand, I am convinced, as was also Dr. Seitz, president of the National Academy of Sciences, when he testified before the Armed Services Committee, that there is some flexibility in the plans. In one respect, and this is not a detail, I would go much further in modifying plans than previous witnesses have recommended: I would like to see the ABM deployment coupled with an expanded civil-defense program. However, this is not a subject on which I should speak today.

On the other hand, when I think of the possible consequences of a refusal to authorize the present relatively modest proposal for the Safeguard system, I become very deeply concerned. Such a refusal might be considered by potential opponents of this country as a sign of unwillingness of this country to defend itself. Nothing could be more provocative than this for people who constantly speak of the doom of the capitalist system, its downfall, the unavoidable victory of the progressive system in the future war, and so on.

On the contrary, that defensive measures are not provocative has not only been declared by Kosygin in the course of the famous interview on February 9, 1967; it has also been demonstrated by the vigorous civil-defense measures the Soviet Union has undertaken and which went virtually unnoticed by our country. Certainly, I never heard any of the passionate opponents of our own missile defense characterize the defense measures of the Soviet Union, civil or antiballistic, as provocative. The fact that some in the Soviet Union dislike seeing us adopt defense measures does not alter these facts.

Let me make three points in conclusion. First that I tried to avoid repeating arguments which you have already heard. It may be good to state, though, that I concur with the criticism which Dr. Wohlstetter offered in his supplementary statement concerning the calculations on Soviet first-strike capability offered by Drs. Rathjens and Lapp, and which were apparently accepted by other critics of the Safeguard program, such as Dr. Panofsky. I find also other inconsistencies in these statements but will not go into details now. Let me mention next that the statements of Drs. Bethe and Killian seem to be endorsing, nay, proposing, the Safeguard system and are opposed only to the Sentinel. This is particularly true of Dr. Bethe's statement, as originally presented to this committee: "A completely different concept of ABM is to deploy it around Minuteman silos, and at command and control centers. This application has gone in and out of the Defense Department planning. I am in favor of such a scheme." This part of Dr. Bethe's statement was, though, somewhat modified in the printed version.

Third, let me say that I fully concur with all of Dr. MacDonald's statement, in particular with his emphasis on the fact that a defense of the deterrent, such as the Safeguard, cannot be considered as an escalating move because it does not increase the first-strike capability. It would induce the opponent to increase his armaments only if he planned a first strike. The difference between Dr. MacDonald's and my own views is based on my grave apprehension stemming from the evacuation plans of the Soviet Union.

It is my belief that not responding to the threatening increase of the armaments of the Soviet Union would be the most provocative behavior in which we could engage. It would encourage the most aggressive part of the Soviet leadership by dangling a dangerous temptation before their eyes.

361

Soviet Views of the ABM
and Soviet Strategy

The following articles and excerpts from articles or books written by Soviet military experts are presented without any editorial comment, except for addition of emphasis where noted.

- N. Talensky, "Antimissile Systems and Disarmament," *Bulletin of the Atomic Scientists,* February 1965.

Antimissile systems and their effect on disarmament, prevention of nuclear war, and world security is a topic that has lately been prominent in Western writings. Various aspects of this question have also been dealt with by diverse public bodies; they were also discussed by the Eighteen Nation Disarmament Conference at Geneva, and the views of its members, the Soviet Union, United States, and Britain in particular, have been made quite clear.

I attended a number of unofficial scientific discussions of antimissile systems and disarmament and heard different views on the problem, and shall here try to outline them in general form.

363

The long development of the means of warfare has revealed one characteristic law: there is a kind of struggle between the means of attack and the means of defense. Sooner or later, every new means of attack leads to the emergence of a means of defense. The latter did not always have a specific form in its initial stage, and was frequently the same means of attack but improved and used in greater numbers. But in the subsequent stages of the "competition" between the means of attack and of defense, specific means of defense gradually became the rule. The classic examples are the sword and the shield, the shell and plate armor.

The new weapon initially gave its owner a clear advantage over his adversary; eventually their positions were balanced, mostly through the invention of adequate means of defense in the form of new weapons or new methods of warfare. The law can be clearly traced in the history of this contest between improved means of attack and of defense since the turn of the century.

The rapid development of the means of attack, especially of fire power (quick-firing weapons, long-range and heavy artillery) led to the emergence not only of new battle formations and fortifications on the field of battle, but also of armor (tanks). The use of aviation, chiefly bombers, produced specific means of antiaircraft defense: antiaircraft artillery and fighter planes, despite the fact that enemy bombers could be fought with bomber strikes at enemy airfields.

This is of course a somewhat simplified scheme of development of the means of warfare; the actual pattern was much more complex, but the exceptions merely went to prove the rule; every decisive new means of attack inevitably leads to the development of a new means of defense. The sword produced the shield; the improvement of naval artillery caused battleships to be clad in plate armor; torpedo-carrying submarines produced a specific system of antisubmarine defense; the growth of artillery fire and intensity of machine-gun fire created the armored troops, whose improvement and emergence as one of the main means of assault led to the appearance of specific antitank means of warfare; finally, as I have said, the development of effective means of air attack was accompanied by the creation of the means of antiaircraft defense.

It frequently turned out that a new type of weapon was more effective at its initial stages than later. This happened because, as the new means of attack was developed and accepted, new means of combating it were also developed. Every rationally designed arms system tends to be a harmonious combination of the means of attack and the means of defense against it, of offensive and defensive armaments.

This law appears to be operating in the age of nuclear rockets as well. It goes without saying that these weapons have worked a radical change in the nature of any possible armed struggle, but the law governing the search for reliable defense against nuclear-rocket attack continues to be in full effect, and antimissile systems will have an important part to play in this respect.

Nuclear-rocket weapons are an effective means of attack with tremendous destructive power. Rockets carrying multimegaton thermonuclear warheads can wipe out cities with millions of people and large industrial centers. They are weapons which have made war absolutely unacceptable as an instrument of politics. In our day, war is inevitably bound up with disastrous consequences for the whole of mankind.

The corollary is that war must be excluded from the sphere of international relations, and all armaments, especially nuclear weapons, the most destructive of them, must be eliminated.

Unfortunately, this logical conclusion has not gone beyond verbal acceptance, and numerous statements. The highly con-

365

crete and scientifically grounded proposals put forward by the Soviet government have been discussed in Geneva for far too long.

Meanwhile, the arms race continues, despite the fact that the international situation has eased. Unless the necessary decisions are taken soon, nuclear weapons will swiftly spread across the earth. Delivery vehicles are still being improved and in spite of the Moscow partial nuclear test-ban treaty, there remains a sizable loophole for the development of nuclear weapons in the right to conduct underground tests.

The danger of nuclear attack continues to threaten humanity, and this makes governments look for sufficiently effective ways and means of decisively reducing the danger of a nuclear rocket attack and if possible to neutralize it altogether.

There are no limits to creative human thinking, and the possibilities offered by modern science and technology are tremendous. And I think that it is theoretically and technically quite possible to counterbalance the absolute weapons of attack with equally absolute weapons of defense, thereby objectively eliminating war regardless of the desires of resisting governments. In our day, the human genius can do anything. Nuclear rockets could, of course, be fought with similar weapons, and in the West there has even appeared a special term for this, the "counterforce strategy," the gist of which is that nuclear rockets should not be used against cities and other vital centers but above all against the enemy's nuclear-rocket installations.

I shall not go into an analysis of this doctrine. Let me say, however, that it does not save the cities and vital centers from nuclear strikes or civilians from death. The modern level of nuclear rockets makes it possible to hit any target on the other side, including rocket installations, with a sufficient degree of effectiveness. But this method of defense has a basic flaw in it, for it is only the aggressor that can resort to it before the first

366

rocket salvoes are fired, before war actually breaks out. In order to destroy the enemy's nuclear-rocket installations they must be hit before they launch their rockets, which means that the peaceable side, the aggressor's objective, will in fending off nuclear attack be forced to deal the first strike, that is, actually to take the odious step of attacking first.

What is more, the effectiveness of any strike at the means of attack deployed on launching pads may be reduced by skillful camouflage against the other side's reconnaissance or by reliable hardening against any initial strike; finally the rockets may be fired by the aggressor before the nuclear warheads of the side on the defensive explode over his pad.

But specific means of defense against nuclear-rocket weapons in the form of antimissile rockets are quite a different matter.

There is no need to go into any technical description of these weapons. What is important is that antimissile rockets are designed exclusively for the destruction of enemy rockets and not for hitting any other objectives on the enemy's territory. They are designed to destroy enemy rockets in flight in such a way as to prevent the destruction of a nuclear warhead-carrying rocket from inflicting damage on the population of one's own country or of allied and neutral states.

Thus, antimissile systems are defensive weapons in the full sense of the word: by their technical nature they go into action only when the rockets of the attacking side take to their flight paths, that is, when the act of aggression has been started. The advantage of antimissile systems in the political and international law context is that their use is caused by an act of aggression, and they will simply not work unless an aggressor's rocket makes its appearance in flight over a given area. There will be no difficulty at all in deciding who is the aggressor and who the attacked.

While nuclear rockets offer only one solution to the problem of attack and defense, namely a nuclear strike, antimissile systems are a new form of nuclear rockets, namely their specifically defensive form. Their task is to destroy the nuclear-rocket means of attack as soon as these are set in motion, that is, without striking at the enemy's territory. This is a new factor which must be taken into account.

As soon as there was convincing evidence that the problem of antimissile defense was being successfully solved in the Soviet Union, many official and unofficial statements were made in the West concerning the possible consequence of the creation of an effective antimissile defense system.

A number of proposals were put forward with a view to eliminating these consequences which were almost all qualified as "dangerous."

Let us look into the chief arguments of Western spokesmen.

The main objection to antimissile systems, as seen by Western politicians and public figures, is that they tend to upset the nuclear balance, thereby undermining the system of mutual deterrence through nuclear rockets, that is, the system of "deterrence through fear." To prove their point they ignore the obvious facts and resort to verbal tricks instead of convincing arguments.

Take the official statements by Western spokesmen in the Eighteen Nation Disarmament Conference at Geneva. U.S. delegate Fisher, for instance, flatly declared that "antiballistic systems are no longer purely defensive; they become part of the balance on which our stability and peace now depend." This argument was taken up by the British delegate Mason. He said, "If one or the other side were to possess a really effective antiballistic missile defense system, that—ironic though it may seem—would be extremely dangerous, because it would upset the stability of the nuclear balance. It would be extremely dangerous because it would make one side or the other think that it was immune from potential nuclear retaliation. Any side which thought this would obviously not be deterred in its actions."

In other words, antimissile systems are defensive but, as the West insists, they upset the mutual deterrence based on the threat of a nuclear strike. This gives rise to the question: Who stands to gain and who is faced with "serious difficulties"? Let us take two countries, one peaceable and concerned with maintaining peace and security, and the other inclined to an aggressive policy and not at all loath to resort to nuclear rockets for its aggressive ends, but with a minimum of losses.

It is obvious that the creation of an effective antimissile defense merely serves to build up the security of the peaceable, nonaggressive state; the fact that it is in possession of a combination of antimissile means and effective nuclear rocket forces serves to promote the task of deterring a potential aggressor, insuring its own security, and maintaining the stability of world peace. A country not willing to abandon its aggressive policy will naturally not be too happy about such a state of affairs.

On the other hand, if the effective antimissile system is built by the side which adheres to an aggressive policy, a policy from positions of strength, this may well intensify the danger of an outbreak of war, but such a danger may also arise quite apart from the cretaion of any antimissile defense, for it may be brought about by other factors of technical progress or may spring from political causes, which, I think, would be the more correct assumption. But the creation of an effective antimissile defense system by a country which is a potential target for aggression merely serves to increase the deterrent effect and so helps to avert aggression.

It is said that the international strategic situation cannot be stable where both sides simultaneously strive toward deterrence through nuclear-rocket power and the creation of defensive antimissile systems.

I cannot agree with this view either. From the standpoint of strategy, powerful deterrent forces and an effective antimissile defense system, when taken together, substantially increase the stability of mutual deterrence, for any partial shifts in the qualitative and quantitative balance of these two component elements of mutual deterrence tend to be correspondingly compensated and equalized.

In that case, the danger lurks in politics. An aggressive policy and a course set for nuclear attack with "acceptable" losses for oneself as a result of a counterstrike create the danger of an outbreak of thermonuclear war, whether or not antimissile defense systems are at hand. But those systems considerably enhance the security of peaceloving states.

There are other big advantages as well in the creation of an effective antimissile defense system. After all, when the security of a state is based only on mutual deterrence with the aid of powerful nuclear rockets, it is directly dependent on the goodwill and designs of the other side, which is a highly subjective and indefinite factor.

"The main thing in the policy of maintaining the status quo by means of a threat," says French General Gallois, "is of course awareness on the part of both adversaries of the risk they take in resorting to the use of force. The more powerful the adversary's counterstrike forces appear to each side, the more stable the peace. It would be an excellent thing if the aggressive bloc in general overrated the enemy's forces."

But what if the aggressive bloc happens to underrate the deterrent and overrate its own forces of attack? There is a great deal of history to show that political and military leaders on the aggressive side are more apt to underrate the enemy's strength. The government and the Grand General Staff of Kaiser Germany miscalulated in assessing the enemy and clearly underestimated his strength. History has clearly demonstrated that great revolu-

370

tions cannot be crushed with armed force, but that did not prevent the governments of the capitalist states from launching their armed intervention against Soviet Russia between 1918 and 1920.

Hitler's aggression and the Second World War, started by the Nazis, were from the purely military standpoint a clear case of miscalculation, an underestimation of the enemy and an over-estimation of their own possibilities. Now if for past errors of judgment humanity has had to pay the price of tens of millions of human lives, the cost in the future will run to hundreds of millions of lives and the destruction of whole states.

If that is so, can we afford to rely on deterrence through the threat of a nuclear-rocket force? An American writer, Arthur Waskow, supplies the answer. He writes: "In the real world, frightened by unprecedented catastrophe in the offing . . . men and nations may not react in any rationally predictable way. . . . At such a moment, when deterrence is most needed, there is some evidence that deterrence disappears. As is generally recognized, deterrence exists in the minds of the major policy-makers of the nations deterred. There is evidence that under conditions of extreme and growing tensions, the major decision-makers in every great power become unable to pay attention to the warnings, the threats, the deterrents of their potential enemies."

He analyzes the American doctrines of deterrence and arrives at the conclusion that "they ignore the complexity of decision-making inside each power and the possible irrationalities of governments competing for high stakes in periods of great crises." All these theories "trust all the governments to react rationally"—that is, as we want and expect them to act—to control their own reactions, and to abide the arms race or the arms stalemate without growing impatient, unstable, or irrational."

In such conditions, the creation of an effective antimissile system enables the state to make its defenses dependent chiefly

371

on its own possibilities, and not only on mutual deterrence, that is, on the goodwill of the other side. And since the peace-loving states are concerned with maximum deterrence, in its full and direct sense, it would be illogical to be suspicious of such a state when it creates an antimissile defense system on the grounds that it wants to make it easier for itself to resort to aggression with impunity.

Some say the construction of antimissile defense systems may accelerate the arms race, and that the side lagging in such systems may build up its nuclear-rocket attack weapons. That is one of the arguments against defensive systems.

Such a development is not all ruled out, in much the same way as the possibility that the nuclear-rocket race may be stepped up quantitatively and qualitatively even without any antimissile systems. In any case, there is this question: Which is preferable for security as a result of the arms race, a harmonious combination of active means of deterrence and defense systems, or the means of attack alone? An exhaustive analysis of this can be made only on the basis of highly concrete military and technical data, but at any rate the side which makes a spurt in the means of attack will instantly expose its aggressive intentions, and stand condemned as the aggressor with all the negative political consequences that this entails.

Another argument is that it is not in the Soviet Union's interest to spend large sums of money and resources to build antimissile defenses for cities and economic areas because the West has adopted the "counterforce" strategy and will not use nuclear weapons against nonmilitary objectives. This argument will hardly convince anyone. History has taught the Soviet Union to depend mainly on itself in insuring its security and that of its friends. The Soviet people will hardly believe that a potential aggressor will use humane methods of warfare, and will strike only at military objectives, etc. The experience of the last war, especially its aerial bombardments and in particular the combat use of the first atomic bombs, is all proof to the contrary. That is why the Soviet Union attaches importance to making as invulnerable as possible not only its nuclear-rocket deterrent but also its cities and vital centers, that is, creating a reliable defense system for the greatest number of people.

The Soviet State, its government, and people have a vital stake in creating a reliable defense system and will strengthen it in every way to insure their country's security and that of their allies.

As I have said, antimissile systems are purely defensive and not designed for attack. It is quite illogical to demand abstention from creating such weapons in the face of vast stockpiles of highly powerful means of attack on the other side. Only the side which intends to use its means of attack for aggression purposes can wish to slow down the creation and improvement of antimissile defense systems. For the peaceloving states, anti missile systems are only a means of building up their security.

There is one reasonable alternative to a race in antimissile systems, and it is the early implementation of general and complete disarmament. The elimination of nuclear-rocket means of attack will automatically result in the elimination of the means of defense against them.

General and complete disarmament at an early date is fully in line with the interests of all states desiring to avoid a step-up of the arms race and expenditure of vast resources. It holds out a radical and effective solution for all security problems of big and small states and all peoples.

The "restraint" in building up antimissile systems which some Western spokesmen propose can and must apply only in the context of general and complete disarmament, with measures to ease international tensions and abandonment of the "positions of strength" policy. There will naturally be no sense in expending resources and effort to set up systems which may soon go by the board together with disarmament.

But if disarmament and its attendant measures are put off indefinitely, while the means of nuclear-rocket attack are being built up, it would hardly be in the interests of any peaceloving state to forgo the creation of its own effective systems of defense against nuclear-rocket aggression and make its security dependent only on deterrence, that is, on whether the other side will refrain from attacking.

- Col. I. Grudinin, "Qualitative and Quantitative Force Determinants," *Communist of the Armed Forces,* No. 11 (1968), pp. 15–22. (*JPRS,* No. 457, August 1, 1968, pp. 1–10.)

The Communist party and the government of the Soviet Union in recent years have given great attention to increasing stockpiles of various types of nuclear warheads, as well as to the sharp increase in equipping all services of the armed forces with means of using the nuclear weapon. Over this time a number of fundamentally new types of rocket weapons have been put into use, and a large quantity of new mobile launching units has been built for the Strategic Rocket Troops. . . . (*JPRS,* p. 8.)

It seems to us that Lenin's formula (the necessity of concentrating the basic efforts of the troops on the decisive direction) points to the necessity of having a predominant superiority of forces in the decisive directions . . . a concentration of superior forces at the decisive moment in selected directions at the present presupports primarily the creation of a superiority in the rocket and nuclear weapons. . . . The correct and prompt use of weapons—not only in the strategic but also on the operational and tactical scale—is the main problem in modern costs. (*JPRS,* p. 10.)

• Defense Minister Marshal R. Malinovsky, *Red Star*, August 10, 1965.

The appearance of nuclear weapons that are unprecedented in destructive power has made it imperative that air defense be not only antiaircraft, *but first of all, antimissile.*

• Defense Minister Marshal Andrei Grechko, *Sovietskaya Litva*, Interview, May 9, 1966.

. . . in the event that aggressors unleash a war, *the PVO Troops' primary task will consist of not permitting enemy planes and rockets into protected zones.* [Emphasis added.]

• Premier Alexei Kosygin, Excerpts from speech to Minsk Province Party Session, *The Current Digest of the Soviet Press*, Vol. XX, No. 7 (February 16, 1968).

In our days the path from the invention of something to industrial use of it is being sharply reduced.

At your conference here several comrades who delivered speeches put the accent quite rightly on attention to the need for accelerating the introduction of new technology in production. The huge outlays for science, which ensures technical progress, are explained precisely by the fact that the path from invention to use is being reduced by tens and hundreds of times and will continue to be reduced further.

We shall systematically increase allocations for the development of science and scientific research. The development of science represents the future of our country, growth of our economy and sharp increase in the people's standard of living.

Of course, such resources must be expended wisely so as to

obtain the fastest possible return from science. This is why the responsibility of men of science to the people and the country is growing.

In this connection it is necessary to criticize the work of many of our research and design institutes, design bureaus and enterprises' engineering services. Often scientific and engineering personnel engage in reproducing things invented long ago abroad, and often not the best of these.

Why does this happen? Primarily because of intolerable delays in designing and mastering the production of new types of machines. Slowness and poor organization in the creation and introduction of new machinery are major flaws in our practical work.

We cannot tolerate the fact that it takes us many years to move from the start of scientific and technical projects to their use in production. This is the way we can be left behind. In the capitalist countries the monopolies are obliged to wage a sharp struggle for profits and must react quickly to the consumer's demands, produce up-to-date types of goods and seek the most rational forms of organizing and managing production. We cannot tolerate a situation in which attempts are made to justify the manufacture of bad goods by citing the fact that the enterprise is new, that it is only beginning to master the production of this item. We must try to achieve the opposite, we must see to it that each new enterprise turns out better products.

It would be shortsighted of us not to make use of the latest foreign scientific and technical achievements. To know everything new and to introduce it in practice is an obligatory requirement not only for scientific and design personnel, but also for the executives of any production unit. We should make use of all the best new technology, employ every opportunity to purchase licenses and improve the work of utilizing the purchased licenses in order to speed technical progress in our economy.

- Foreign Minister Andrei Gromyko, Excerpts from "Gromyko Reports to Supreme Soviet on World Situation," *The Current Digest of the Soviet Press,* Vol. XX, No. 28 (June 28, 1968), pp. 11–13.

Statistics have shown that during the first half of the twentieth century the arms race and wars have swallowed up 4,000 billion dollars. It is difficult even to imagine the benefits this money would bring people were it at the disposal of a society free from exploitation of man by man and from the domination of monopolies! . . .

The Soviet Union has advanced a detailed program of universal and complete disarmament under strict international control. What do we hear in reply? They are ready to discuss it. For years upon years. But they are unwilling to get down to business.

The Soviet Union has tried other paths as well. The Soviet government has urged the Western powers literally dozens of times to make a start by reaching agreement on more modest measures, for instance on reducing military budgets, liquidating foreign military bases, creating nuclear-free zones, and banning the use of nuclear weapons.

How did the West respond? The responses varied, but there were always reservations: One proposal goes too far, the other not far enough, a fifth is premature, and as for the tenth—it might create problems for NATO.

Experience suggests that without resolute and constant exposure of the policy that propagates militarism, it is impossible to expect the governments of the capitalist powers to agree on a solution of pressing international problems, especially on disarmament.

Experience also suggests that a persistent and skillful struggle to solve urgent problems can yield positive results. The Soviet

Union's consistency in promoting a line aimed at disarmament and the major initiatives it has taken, which have rallied the forces of peace, make it impossible to achieve definite results even if this does not immediately lead to concrete agreements.

Everyone now agrees that the problem of nuclear weapons is one of the most complex problems confronting mankind. What is to be done with nuclear weapons? Will there be continuous stockpiling, or will people find ways to liquidate these weapons of mass annihilation and ensure the use of nuclear energy solely for peaceful purposes, solely for the good of mankind?

The Soviet Union replied to this question as soon as the problem arose. Its reply was clear-cut and categorical: Nuclear weapons must be banned. Their use runs counter to the conscience of mankind. The world has long been at the point where nuclear weapons must be outlawed.

As early as twenty-two years ago the Soviet Union proposed that an international convention be concluded to ban the use of nuclear weapons. It also proposed complete elimination of nuclear weapons and systems for delivering them, as well as the switching of all nuclear energy to exclusively peaceful purposes.

The Soviet Union urges all states, and above all the nuclear powers, to discontinue underground tests of nuclear weapons at once. No justifiction can be found for attempting to evade this task. It is necessary to rebuff those leaders who, pleading the necessity of perfecting nuclear weapons, hamper the solution of this important task. The references, usually made in discussing this problem, to the necessity of some sort of control are unfounded and contrived. No one can secretly explode nuclear weapons underground without being detected.

A veritable wall of condemnation must be built around governments and statesmen that erect obstacles on the path to disarmament. This calls for activating on behalf of disarmament all political movements and public groups in all countries of the world. Such activity, converted into a popular movement, would be capable of compelling the opponents of disarmament, those who have linked their destinies and political careers with militarism and the arms race, to retreat before the voice of the people.

One of the unexplored areas of disaramament lies in the quest for understanding on mutual restrictions on and subsequent curtailment of strategic systems for the delivery of nuclear weapons—both offensive and defensive—including antimissile weapons. The Soviet government is prepared to exchange opinions on this question, too. [Emphasis added.]

Our foreign policy and our ideology present a sharp contrast to the dismal future visualized by many leaders of the capitalist world. They have nightmares when they think about the fate of the system whose policy and ideology they represent.

All we can say is: Let them draw grim pictures, those who have lost confidence in themselves and in their social system, who cannot discern the perspectives of history from behind the fence of their pitiful little world of money-grubbing and oppression. But the peoples building communism and socialism are full of optimism.

• Maj. Gen. Engineering Technical Services G. Pokrovsky, *Sovetskii Patriot,* Moscow, Sept. 11, 1967. (P. 10, SRI-W-68-4208.)

States possibility of ABM "to combat long range and intercontinental rockets." "In principle antirocket combat and defense are possible as is the defense against any other means of destruction."

• Col. Gen. of Aviation Zimin, National PVO Troops, Moscow, *Red Star,* March 3, 1965.

For the *instruction* of the Communist party and the Soviet government we are constantly perfecting our air defense and . . .

antirocket defense—by making certain that their development is superior to that of the weapons of attack. . . .

. . . that our country had successfully solved the problem of destroying rockets in flight . . . our scientists had designed and our engineers and workers had build complexes of numerous weapons to protect our country against nuclear rocket attacks. (22d CPSU Congress Minister of Defense, Malinovsky's speech.)

- Marshal R. Malinovsky (then Minister of Defense), *Pravda,* February 23, 1965.

The complex and extremely important problem of destroying any enemy rockets in flight has been solved.

- General of the Army P. F. Batitsky, Deputy Minister of Defense, Commander in Chief of National PVO Troops, "The Rule of Life—Readiness," *Red Star,* December 28, 1967.

Experience of the past testifies that the aggressor . . . often tried to use the advantage of surprise attack. Today the imperialists, as a basic gamble, strive for a surprise massive aerospace attack. Therefore, as never before, the importance of the assured defense of the nation from nuclear blows from the air and from space is growing. National PVO Troops must frustrate the enemy's surprise nuclear attack by the absolute destruction of his rockets and aviation in flight and thus insure the protection of the population and economy, the vital activity of the state and the fighting ability of the Armed Forces.

In recent years, ballistic missiles have been adopted into armaments. They have become the main means for aerospace attack. *This means that the weapons of PVO must combat air-*

craft and also rockets. In other words, the modern PVO must be antiaircraft and antimissile. [Emphasis added.]

In battle with the enemy, guided surface-to-air missiles are highly effective. They do not depend upon weather or time of day. Day or night, in rain and in snow, surface-to-air missiles can destroy air targets.

I wish to stress that weapons and combat equipment of National PVO Troops are being continuously perfected.[1]

- Marshal V. D. Sokolovsky, from *Military Strategy*, 3d ed., 1968, Harriet Fast Scott translation.

Protection of the rear areas of the country and groups of Armed Forces from enemy nuclear attacks has the aim of preserving the vital functions of the government, of assuring the uninterrupted functioning of the national economy and transportation, and preserving the combat readiness of the Armed Forces. These aims are achieved mainly by annihilation of the enemy's means of nuclear attack in the regions in which they are based. However, there is no guarantee that considerable aircraft and rocket forces can be annihilated at their bases, particularly at the start of the war with a surprise enemy attack. Therefore it is necessary to have the necessary forces and means for destroying great masses of enemy aircraft and rockets in the air in order that there by no nuclear attacks against important objectives within the whole territory of the country. This can be done by military operations for protecting the country from attack by enemy aircraft and missiles.

[1] This December 1967 statement by the Commander in Chief of the Soviet Air Defense Troops is a reiteration of statements made in February 1967, to the effect that the Soviet Union had developed an antiballistic missile system that can "reliably protect the country from an enemy attack by air."

The basic means for protecting the interior of the country and groups of Armed Forces from enemy nuclear attacks are the National PVO and PRO Troops, and also civil-defense forces. They have the task of creating an invincible system for the defense of the entire country, and also preparing measures for rapid removal of the results of enemy nuclear attacks. Such a system should be prepared beforehand, in peacetime, and should be in a constant state of high combat readiness. The air and antimissile defense of the frontal zone will be in the hands of forces and weapons of PVO and the fronts in conjunction with the National PVO Troops. Modern air defense is built to be antiaircraft, antimissile, and antispace, united in a single system.

The destruction of ballistic rockets in flight is a more complex problem. During World War II England was unsuccessful in solving the problem of destroying the German V-2 ballistic missile. Attempts to create an antimissile missile ("Project Tamper") were unsuccessful since the level of technology did not make it possible to solve this complex problem at that time. In our country the problem of eliminating rockets in flight has been successfully solved by Soviet science and technology. Thus the task of warding off strikes of enemy missiles has become quite possible.

It is interesting to note that the problem of antimissile defense is far from being solved in the West. The United States has developed the Nike-Zeus and Wizard systems with nuclear warheads for the direct encounter between a missile and an antimissile missile. The foreign press has mentioned the possibility of throwing up a screen of fine metal fragments created by the fragmentation of conventional charges, into the flight path of a ballistic missile. Work is being conducted on the use of space means (antirocket "screening" system). It is intended to launch a large number of satellites (missile-carriers), aboard which are placed interceptor rockets with a guidance system which operates in the infrared or ultraviolet portion of the frequency band.

However, we should consider that no matter how effective the system of air and antimissile defense, we must have ready civil-defense forces and weapons for rapid removal of the results of nuclear attacks, evacuation of the population from regions subjected to nuclear attacks, the organization of emergency medical aid, the extinguishing of fires, the establishment of order, and other similar measures. Special civil-defense formations should be prepared to fulfill these tasks. In addition, there must be corresponding preparation of the population for operating under conditions of an enemy nuclear attack.

The methods of waging war as a whole are expressed by the totality of the types of military actions: nuclear rocket strikes for the purpose of simultaneously smashing the military and economic potential of the enemy, annihilation of strategic means of nuclear attack and groups of armed forces, and disorganization of military and government control; military actions for protection of a country and of its armed forces against nuclear rocket strikes; military actions in land theaters; and military actions in naval theaters.

Taking into account that military affairs do not mark time, but continuously develop under the action of various conditions, the authors have attempted as much as possible to anticipate and depict certain prospects in the development of various branches of military strategy.

At the same time, it is necessary to take into account that the theories expressed in this work were cited in each individual case by relying on an evaluation of the political and economic conditions of today. Therefore, it is impossible to consider them as final and unchanging data. Only a creative approach from the position of Marxist-Leninist dialectics will enable Soviet commanding cadres to understand properly and use the various conclusions and recommendations of this work.

Under conditions of nuclear rocket war, the strategic principle of the economy of forces appears in a new light. It is apparent that when the very outcome of the war depends largely on the number and the effectiveness of the strikes at the very beginning of the war, it is hardly reasonable to count on the potential capabilities of a country and to reserve a large part of the manpower for military operations during later periods of the war. An overwhelming majority of military theoreticians in the highly developed countries of the world are coming to these conclusions.

Public ownership of the means of production excludes all unhealthy competition in the economy and permits all efforts to be concentrated on the achievement of the general aims of the state.

In connection with this, it is noted that the United States must increase the capability of its armed forces to "respond quickly and effectively" to any action of the enemy. Under conditions of a world war, this means that the part of the armed forces "which survives the initial strike" must retain this capability. It is most important to guarantee the possibility of surviving the enemy's first attack and of delivering a retaliatory strike of destructive force, "which shall cause him far greater losses." In addition, it is stressed that the ability to force the enemy to refrain from attacking depends not only on the number of missiles and bombers, but on the degree of their preparedness, the ability to survive in case of attack, and the flexibility and reliability of their guidance for the achievement of strategic goals.

It is not accidental, therefore, that American theoreticians are carefully studying the pros and cons of preventive war and of first and preemptive strikes.

The theory of preventive war was first advanced by the most reactionary representatives of the U.S. political and military leadership at the end of the 1940s. However, subsequently the propaganda for this theory abated somewhat. Under present-day conditions, the official agencies of the military leadership and the military scientists of the United States have again returned to the question of preventive war, considering it one of the possible and permissible alternatives. What is preventive war? Bernard Brodie, in his book *Strategy in the Missile Age*, gives the following definition: "I am using the term to describe a premeditated attack by one country against another, which is unprovoked in the sense that it does not wait upon a specific aggression or other overt action by the target state, and in which the chief and most immediate objective is the destruction of the latter's over-all military power and especially its strategic armed forces.[2] Naturally, success in such an action would enable the former power to wreak whatever further injury it desired or to exact almost any peace terms it wished."

The case for preventive war, in Brodie's opinion, has rested primarily on two premises: first, that in a strategic aerospace war using nuclear weapons, the country that strikes first undoubtedly has crucial advantage, which with reasonably good planning will almost certainly be a decisive one; and second, that total war is inevitable.

"The least that can be said," states Brodie, "is that our plan for offensive strategy, whatever it is, would have its best chances of being carried out if we struck first, and that those chances would be brought to a very minimum if the enemy struck first. If we thought only about maximizing our chances of survival, the

---

[2] *Translator's note:* The phrase "strategic armed forces" is a Russian mistranslation of Brodie's phrase "strategic air power." Bernard Brodie, *Strategy in the Missile Age* (Princeton: Princeton University Press, 1959), p. 227.

above circumstances might be considered reason enough for going ahead with preventive war."

American theoreticians are frankly in favor of preventive war and surprise attack. Public officials, even though they always speak of the "incompatibility" of preventive war with the principles of American "democracy" and "morality," in effect fully share these views.

It follows that the threat of unleashing preventive war by American Imperialists against the Soviet Union and the other countries of the Socialist camp is quite real. The slogan ". . . that which [is] inevitable had better come early rather than late, because it would be less devastating that way" is fraught with many temptations, because the beginning of a preventive war is selected by the aggressor to coincide with the most favorable time.

Certain American military ideologists (Kissinger, for example) replace the expression "preventive war" with the expression "surprise (first) attack." The distinction is purely formal, and pointless since the first strike can also herald the beginning of preventive war. No matter what this strike is called, its main aim is the maximum achievement of surprise.

They say that surprise can and must be achieved in striking a preventive blow. Such a blow, in the estimation of American military theoreticians, is allegedly defensive, since it is delivered to an enemy who is preparing for attack (either for the initiation of a preventive war or for the delivery of the first blow). It is considered to be the final and only means of avoiding catastrophe.

This is the evaluation of the surprise factor, which can be achieved by starting preventive war, by striking the first or preemptive blow.

Among other U.S. strategic concepts, the concepts of "guaranteed destruction" and "damage limiting" are of interest and were put forth by the U.S. Secretary of Defense, R. McNamara, in March 1965 in his appearance before the Armed Services Committee of the House of Representatives.

The essence of the concept of "guaranteed destruction," according to McNamara's statement, is that the United States must have the ability of destroying a potential enemy as a viable society even after the U.S. Armed Forces have been subjected to a well-planned and successful attack. In this concept, the forces for "guaranteed destruction" must include part of the intercontinental ballistic missiles, Polaris-type missiles launched from atomic submarines and a fixed part of the manned strategic bombers. It is believed that the primary, vitally important task of the strategic nuclear forces of the United States is their ability to assure the "guaranteed destruction" of the military potential of an enemy, including approximately two thirds of his industrial power. Such damage, according to the plans of the Pentagon, is unacceptable to any industrialized country, and, consequently, will serve as an effective deterrent and vouchsafe the execution of an aggressive policy by the United States. According to the intentions of the military-political leadership of the United States, in the event a war breaks out and "guaranteed destruction" of a potential enemy becomes a reality, he will not be able to regain his status as a powerful state over the course of many years.

The concept of "damage limiting," according to McNamara, means the capacity of the United States to weaken the force of a blow by a probable enemy by using strategic offensive and defensive forces, as well as by taking measures to assure a certain degree of protection of the population from the consequences of the enemy's nuclear strikes.

According to the plans of the political and military leadership of the USA, "damage-limiting" forces must include:

—the remaining strategic offensive means (intercontinental ballistic missiles, Polaris-type missiles on atomic submarines,

387

and strategic bombers), which must contribute to the "damage limiting" by crushing the enemy's nuclear means of attack at the launch sites and bases, if they can intercept them before they are launched against objectives in U.S. territory;

—the defensive forces (surface-to-air missiles and interceptor airplanes, antimissile and air defense means, antisubmarine warfare forces) used to destroy enemy aircraft and rockets on their way to objectives as well as in regions where those objectives are located;

—thoroughly planned measures on a national scale for constructing shelters, assuring a reduction by about three times of the losses among the population from the consequences of the enemy's nuclear strikes.

Thus, the strategic concepts of "guaranteed destruction" and "damage limiting," considered together, suppose the delivery by the strategic strike forces of the United States and their allies of massive nuclear strikes on a whole complex of objectives that make up the military-economic potential of the enemy, and at the same time an active and passive defense of the United States so as to limit to a maximum degree the damage from a decisive retaliatory strike by the enemy. The realization of these strategic concepts, according to the military-political leadership of the United States, requires a balanced combination of strategic offensive forces, defensive forces, and means of passive defense. This fact is characteristically acknowledged in the West, that an all-out nuclear rocket war, no matter how it is unleashed, will be destructive for both sides. In this connection, the U.S. Secretary of Defense, McNamara, already stated in February 1964 in the pages of a journal, *Army Information Digest:* "We could not again create, at whatever price, a situation in which strategic bombings would be a one-sided act. I believe that this factor should be considered one of the decisive factors when determining our policy."

As an alternative to general nuclear war, the imperialist aggressors have promoted the concept of limited wars.

Air Defense and Antimissile Defense Forces. In working out plans for the development of air defense and antimissile defense forces, the U.S. and NATO commands proceed primarily from the fact that the strategic means of a probable enemy can inflict tremendous damage on the United States and her allies in military blocs. Therefore, even a "reliable" defense, against any given type of strategic means, has very limited value. This, according to the U.S. Secretary of Defense, McNamara, is the main reason why the United States, regardless of tremendous expenditures for the development of antiaircraft defenses up to this time, does not have the effective forces and means capable of keeping the damage from an enemy's strike within tolerable limits. To solve this problem it is considered imperative in conjunction with the building up of strategic offensive forces, to develop balanced strategic defense means (antimissile, antiaircraft, and antisubmarine), as well as means of passive defense. This type of organization in the strategic defense forces, according to the U.S. Secretary of Defense, can to a certain degree assure a "deep defense," reducing the effectiveness of the enemy's strikes.

The American command, when working out programs for increasing the means for antiair, antimissile, antisubmarine, and passive defense, proceed on the premise that "with each new increase in defensive forces, the effectiveness of defense increases ever more slowly," and this tendency toward diminishing returns from means expended places a practical limit to the sums spent for the solution of the defense problem.

In evaluating the prospects for development of the Soviet Union's strategic means of attack, and their technical and economic possibilities in this sphere, the American command came

389

to the conclusion that in the next decade the United States will actually be incapable of assuring complete defense of its territory regardless of the forces they will have (offensive and defensive) for the conduct of a nuclear war.

The United States exerts great efforts in the creation of antimissile and antispace defense. This is caused primarily by the fact that according to the views of the military-political leadership of the United States and a number of other NATO countries, the side which first creates an antimissile (antispace) defense, will have a most important strategic advantage which would allow the threatening of war or its unleashing without fear of the enemy's retaliatory strikes. [Emphasis added.]

Nuclear weapons appeared in the Soviet Union at the end of the forties and the beginning of the fifties in the form of atomic, and then hydrogen aviation bombs, and somewhat later in the form of nuclear warheads for rockets of different types and for torpedoes. In the sixties all branches of the Soviet Armed Forces —Strategic Rocket Troops, Ground Troops, Air Forces, the Navy, and National PVO Troops—have been equipped with nuclear weapons. Taking into account the fact that the Soviets created hydrogen weapons before the United States, and, most important of all, that the United States does not possess superpowered thermonuclear charges such as those possessed by the Soviet Union, we consider our superiority over the Western bloc in nuclear weapons to be indisputable. By the admission of competent American specialists, our superiority in total nuclear might of strategic rocket weapons is very considerable.

The supreme catastrophic threat of a world nuclear rocket war is hovering like a specter over mankind. It can break out suddenly, as a result of an initially local military conflict. The alternative to a devastating world nuclear war is the peaceful coexistence of states with different social orders.

390

● Lt. Col. Ye. I. Ribkin, from "The Nature of World Nuclear Rocket War."

All this converts war from a consciously used "weapon of politics" (as a "rapier or sword" as Clausewitz imagined it) into an "enormous historical process," and a peculiar "summation of politics." (See V. I. Lenin, *Works,* Vol. 26, p. 350, and Vol. 30, p. 202.) In this process many opposing forces are at work. From this it is clear that it is absolutely wrong to identify the concepts "continuation of politics" and "weapon (or means) of politics." *War is always the continuation of politics, but it cannot always serve as its weapon.* Besides, war leaves a mass of "side effects" while putting politics under its own sort of examination and test and while exerting on it a reverse, often unseen, influence.

For this reason, the formula "war is a continuation of politics by violent means" can acquire different meanings in connection with one or another interpretation of "politics," "continuation of politics," and "armed violence." While explaining the genuine nature of war, we must confine ourselves strictly to its dialectical-materialistic sense and completely analyze its connections and relationships.

The Nature of the Changes in the Connections of Politics and War. Now let us look at each of the given relationships of politics and war in light of the change caused by the revolution in military affairs, by the rise of nuclear danger, and also by the development of sociopolitical factors.

First Relationship. Thanks to the rise of the socialist system, the sphere of action of the sources of war now are seriously restricted. The presence of nuclear weapons in the Soviet Union serves as an enormous factor deterring the aim of the imperialists to start a world war. However, the contradictions capable of

391

leading to such a war continue to exist and the possibility of its arising remains. And what is more, as a result of the appearance of systems automatically resulting in operation of rocket equipment and in view of the constant adventuristic acts of the imperialists, the danger has grown of an "automatic" beginning of war even as the result of an unimportant international conflict. Therefore, the real possibility of nuclear war, now as before, fashions itself only out of the economics and politics of imperialism. And so, to speak of changes in the nature of war in this relationship cannot be done; if war starts, it will be a result of a continuation of politics.

Clausewitz in his time wrote, "With the all-destroying element of war (a million times weaker than now!—Ribkin) politics turns into only its own simple instrument: the terrible fighting battle-ax, which demands that it be raised with both hands and strains every force for carrying out of one unique blow which, thanks to politics, is converted into an easily maneuverable sword which becomes now and then even a rapier, and they fence with it according to all the rules of the art." (*On War,* Vol. II, Military Publishing House, 1932, p. 99.)

At the time, the inner logic of armed conflict did not demand the *compulsory* concentration of forces of the belligerents in one all-destroying blow of a "battle-ax." Now, in the conditions of the application of nuclear weapons, the demand for such a blow really has become the most important law of the methods of waging world war. Of course, politics under all circumstances will aim at keeping military actions under its control and, in this sense, its role and responsibility has grown colossally, but the possibility of maneuvering, "fencing" with weapons, in the course of a nuclear war has been sharply reduced. Therefore, *the center of gravity of the efforts of politics for the guidance of strategy is carried over into peacetime,* especially in threatened periods. So, the third relationship in conditions of nuclear war undergoes serious modification and limitations.

And what happens with the nature of war in the *fourth and fifth relationships?* Do the armed forces remain the means of clearing the path for politics—to secure for it the possibility of achieving its goal?

In the West many authors of various persuasions have arrived at the idea of the impossibility of victory in nuclear war. "To try to win the war, to set as one's goal victory," writes the British military theoretician Liddell Hart, "is sheer madness because total war with the use of nuclear weapons will be disastrous for both sides." (*Intimidation or Defense?* Military Publishing House, 1962, p. 55.) Encountered also are similar ideas of several Soviet authors. N. Nikolsky, in the book *Today's Basic Question,* writes, "The disappearance of the possibility of victory in world thermonuclear war as a means of achieving political aims of governments, the denial of all military categories of the institution of war in thermonuclear war, testifies to the fact that world thermonuclear war is already in nature, not war, but self-negating war. This is that dialectical limit of the development of phenomena when they stop being phenomena." (*Today's Basic Question,* IMO Publishing House, 1964, p. 381.)

"In our days," writes N. Talensky, "there is no more dangerous illusion than the idea that thermonuclear war can still serve as an instrument of politics, that it is possible to achieve political aims by using nuclear weapons and at the same time survive, that it is possible to find acceptable forms of nuclear war." ("Thoughts on Past Wars," *International Affairs,* No. 5, 1965, p. 23.)

The supporters of such views usually refer to the political results of nuclear war which form spontaneously and get out of control. Such facts actually are inevitable, and they hamper the control over events in significant measure. The destruction of people, the razing of factories and energy systems, the poisoning of topsoil and water, the spontaneous movement of radioactive clouds, the changes in the biosphere of the earth, enormous fires, and so forth—all these threatening forces, of course, can give birth to doubts concerning the real possibility of achieving victory and about the survival of the victors themselves. No one has a right to close his eyes to all the serious results of nuclear war. Exactly therefore, the Communist party and the government of the Soviet Union, all of our people, the peaceloving people of all the planet, propose a maximum effort in order to not permit the unleashing of war, and to curb aggressors. However, to maintain that victory in nuclear war is in general impossible would be not only untrue theoretically but dangerous from a political point of view.

It must be remembered that victory in war depends not only on the character of the weapons but on the *correlation of forces* of the belligerent sides. The achievement of a quick victory over the aggressors that will avert further destruction and calamity might depend on this correlation. There is a possibility of developing and producing new means of waging war which would be able to safely counter the nuclear blows of the enemy.

In addition, other factors and forces which inevitably enter into operation in the event of the unleashing of world war cannot be left out of one's reckoning. These primarily are the decisive antiimperialist actions of the masses of the people, diplomatic and other acts aimed at deterring the aggressors.

The a priori *rejection of the possibility of victory is bad because it leads to moral disarmament, to disbelief in victory, to fatalism and passivity*. It is necessary to carry on a struggle with such views and attitudes of mind. The Soviet people are sure of their victory over the forces of reaction. This sureness

394

is based on the real power of our government and of all of the socialist system, with prepossessing economic, moral, and military-technical opportunities for the rapid, utter defeat of aggressors. [Emphasis added.]

At the same time, it would be a mistake to assert that the presence of potentialities in themselves already predetermines our victory. Such an assertion lowers the role of subjective factors, the role of the activities of the masses and the leaders. The objective advantages of the socialist structure and the strength of its material and moral forces act not by fate but are realized only by the activity of the people.

Recently the party and its Central Committee put to severe criticism worthless methods of management which issued from the idea that the objective advantages of our advanced structure almost automatically assured our rapid successes. Nothing is more dangerous, especially in military affairs, than such ignorant ideas. Any advantages are only potentialities which are turned into reality solely by tenacious labor supported by deep scientific understanding of phenomena and processes. This means that in order for victory to be safely assured, it is necessary to have high daily vigilance of all the personnel of our Armed Forces, further raising of military preparedness, constant development of military science and equipment, and perfection of military art.

Such an understanding of the question of victory in nuclear war promotes the correct training of soldiers and mobilizes their strength on all-round military preparedness, on the further strengthening of discipline and organization in forces, on decisive action in fighting situations, and, at the same time, warns against the danger of "swell-headedness."

So, nuclear war, because of its consequences, leaves the framework of previous ideas about the relationships of politics and war. Remaining as the continuation of politics, such a war

395

now, because of the effect of the consequences of the nuclear means of struggle, is *limited as a weapon of politics.* This fact does not negate either the possibility of our victory in it. The main conclusion from the analysis of this problem consists of the necessity of doing everything for the preclusion of world nuclear war. Along this line, the Program of the Communist party explains to us in this way, *"War should not and must not serve as a means of solving international arguments."* (*Materials of the XXI Congress CPSU,* p. 364.) Together with the Program of the Communist party of the Soviet Union, the decision of the party and government obliges our Armed Forces to be constantly in a condition of full readiness to frustrate with their decisive actions the plans of the aggressors and to carry a shattering retaliatory blow to them.

These are a few of the practical conclusions from a dialectical-material understanding of the nature of nuclear rocket war.

Three basic principles should also be noted, determining the internal logic of the development of the system "man—equipment," and through it, of all military affairs. The first consists of the fact that the means of striking are of primary importance here, since their capabilities determine the level of effectiveness of the entire system.

In terms of the nature and power of the energy used in the means of striking, side arms, firearms, and nuclear weapons are known to history. It is not difficult to notice that the military revolution associated with the appearance of firearms, and the contemporary revolution in military affairs associated with the advent of nuclear weapons proceeded from the appearance of fundamentally new striking means.

The second principle consists of the fact that a redistribution of functions between man and military equipment has been proceeding as development took place within the system. The basis for this redistribution was also the striving for increased overall effectiveness of the system. Man was creating equipment which performed his functions with a constant quantitative increase and with greater efficiency. This process coincided with the process of automation, which is common for any kind of equipment.

The third development principle of the system consists of the fact that the steady power increase of the means of striking brought about the necessity of changing its other elements as well, primarily the means of delivery and the means of guidance.

The contemporary revolution in military affairs is not an exception, and three stages can be conditionally singled out in its development. The first stage was based on the use of nuclear bombs (atomic at first, and thermonuclear later) and strategic bombers as their carriers. The second is involved with the development of rockets as the means of delivery of nuclear weapons. The third is based on the qualitative radical change in the management of troops, expressed in the comprehensive automation of control. (It should be kept in mind that these are the logical stages of the development of the contemporary revolution in military science. They reflect the internal direction of its development. In the historical scale, the indicated stages represent sides, aspects of the development of military science, rather than its stages.)

The basic stages of the contemporary revolution in military affairs cannot be reduced merely to the appearance of qualitatively new equipment, which is the most mobile element of the material basis of internal principles of development and under the influence of economics, science, as well as in accordance with the demands of politics, military equipment also brings about changes in all other elements of military service.

- Marshal V. D. Sokolovsky, from *Military Strategy,* 3d ed., 1968, Harriet Fast Scott translation.

Present means of reconnaissance, detection, and surveillance can opportunely disclose a significant portion of the measures of direct preparation of a nuclear attack by the enemy and in the very first minutes locate a mass launch of missiles and take-off of aircraft of the aggressor . . . thus the *possibilities exist not to allow a surprise attack of an aggressor; to deliver nuclear strikes on him at the right time.*

- Commander in Chief of the Navy Admiral S. G. Gorchov, Introduction to *The Fighting Journey of the Soviet Navy.*

Hence that great attention in the theory of waging contemporary war is now being given to the timely and reliable detection of signs of nuclear attack and one's own combat readiness to seize the strategic initiative.

- Article from *The New York Times,* June 11, 1969, by Bernard Gwertzman.

The Communist party newspaper *Pravda* today underlined Soviet displeasure with the Nixon administration's missile program and its delay in beginning strategic arms-control talks with the Soviet Union.

An article by Boris G. Strelnikov, the newspaper's Washington correspondent, was the latest in a number of Soviet commentaries indicating dissatisfaction with the apparent desire of the United States to proceed with new defensive and offensive missile systems, and with the failure to set a date for the start of arms-control talks.

A commentary in the current issue of *Mezhdunarodnaya Zhizn,* a foreign affairs monthly, said that development of the Safeguard antimissile system and the MIRV offensive system could only complicate future Soviet-American negotiations.

MIRV is the acronym for multiple, independently targetable reentry vehicle.

"The development of these defensive and offensive systems would lead to a qualitative new step in the nuclear arms race and would add billions to the already large and burdensome military expenditures," the commentary said.

"It would open the way to further aggravation of international tensions, first of all in the mutual relations between the two most powerful world powers, the United States and the Soviet Union," it added.

"It would strengthen the mutual distrust between states and would make more complicated the already difficult negotiations on disarmament," the commentary continued. "The destructive force of nuclear rockets would be raised to an unparalleled level."

The *Pravda* article, apparently reflecting current Soviet thinking, said the Nixon administration seems to believe that development of new arms systems would be "a trump card" for future negotiations with the Soviet Union.

"In other words, some in the United States would like to start the dialogue from a position of strength," Mr. Strelnikov said. "If this Pentagon thesis, which is incompatible with improving Soviet-American relations would be approved, it would be a great miscalculation for the United States," he added.

"Practice has shown long ago that any attempts to negotiate with the Soviet Union from a position of strength would doom the talks to failure in advance," Mr. Strelnikov said.

Most Western diplomats here believe that Moscow decided last year to go ahead with arms-control talks with the United States on the assumption that a rough balance of power existed between the two nations.

The Soviet Union now appears to be saying that if the United States begins preparations for large-scale deployment of new weapons systems, this could upset the balance of forces.

So far, the comments in the Soviet press have not ruled out the start of negotiations, but the delay by the United States on deciding on a time for the talks has been criticized.

Pravda said that the United States "has still not taken any practical steps" to begin the talks, which were to have begun last fall. They were postponed in the tense period following the invasion of Czechoslovakia by five Warsaw Pact nations led by the Soviet Union.

"At first it was said in Washington that the United States would be ready to enter into negotiations this spring," said *Pravda*. "Then they began to talk about the summer and now about the fall."

The article took no notice of a statement last week by Secretary of State William P. Rogers that he still believed the talks would start this summer.

There has been an effort among Russians, expressed privately by diplomats and publicly by the press, to disabuse the United States of the thought that Moscow feels itself under pressure to begin arms-control talks.

Some observers have argued that the Soviet Union wants arms reductions to be able to allocate additional resources to its civilian economy. The *Pravda* article rejected this viewpoint.

It said that Washington was making "a miscalculation" if it thought that the Soviet Union was more interested than the United States in starting negotiations. It said that some Americans, believing this "miscalculation," were talking about the forthcoming talks as "a sort of market where the American side will check the price for any agreement."

Pravda criticized Secretary of Defense Melvin R. Laird, saying he was carrying out "anti-Soviet propaganda in the spirit of the worst traditions of the cold war."

Questions and Answers
Concerning Safeguard

Question

What is the Safeguard system?

Answer

The Safeguard defense system involves a phased program closely aligned with the emerging Chinese and Soviet threats. The components of the system consist of (1) radar for long-range detection of any kind of nuclear attack and for accurate

401

guidance of the defense missiles to the incoming weapons, (2) Spartan missiles, for high-altitude interception of attacking weapons, and (3) Sprint missiles, for lower-altitude interception in the atmosphere to provide local protection. It will not be necessary to place missiles and radar sites close to our major cities.

Question

What are the first steps in building Safeguard?

Answer

The initial phase, to be financed in the 1970 budget, will involve the following steps:

1. Continuation of research and development.

2. Beginning of construction at two of our Minuteman fields: Malmstrom Air Force Base, Montana, and Grand Forks Air Force Base, North Dakota. Construction of radars and positioning of missiles at these sites is scheduled to be completed in four years.

3. Acquisition of the remaining sites needed to subsequent phases of Safeguard, but no construction.

Each subsequent phase of the deployment will be reviewed to insure that we are doing as much as necessary but no more than is required at that time. The President announced his intention to review the program annually from the point of view of (1) technical developments, (2) the threat, (3) the diplomatic context, including any talks on arms limitation with the Soviet Union. He asked his Foreign Intelligence Advisory Board—a nonpartisan group of distinguished private citizens—to make a yearly assessment of the threat to supplement regular intelligence assessments. Moreover, maximum advantage will be taken of the information gathered from the initial deployment in designing the later phases of the program. The President noted that this program . . . "is to be closely related to the threat, it is subject to modification as the threat changes, either through negotiations or through unilateral actions by the Soviet Union or Communist China."

Question

What would Safeguard protect against?

Answer

It would:

1. Provide for local defense of selected Minuteman missile sites.

2. Provide an area defense to protect our bomber bases and our command and control authorities.

3. Defend the continental United States against an accidental, unauthorized, or irrational attack.

4. Reduce U.S. fatalities to a minimal level in the event of a Chinese nuclear attack in the 1970s.

Question

What is an "accidental, unauthorized, or irrational attack"?

Answer

A real possibility exists that a nuclear missile might be launched against us by mistake. Or some lower-level official of another country might decide to take policy into his own hands. Or a national leader somewhere, in control of nuclear decisions, might lose control of his powers of reason. Safeguard would permit us to have another choice besides all-out war—we could decide to limit our responses to the destruction of the incoming missile.

Question

What have the Soviets been doing in the missile field?

Answer

The Soviet Union is engaged in a build-up of its strategic forces significantly larger than was foreseen in 1967 when the previous administration decided to go ahead with a different

ABM system, which would have cost twice as much in the first year as the proposed Safeguard system will cost. These are some examples of what the Soviet Union is doing:

1. Continuing the deployment of very large missiles; if these missiles are armed with multiple, independently targetable warheads of high accuracy, the Soviet missile force may be capable of destroying our own land-based missile force.

2. Increasing the size of its submarine-launched ballistic missile force; thus, it is within Soviet power to launch attacks on our bomber bases virtually without warning.

3. Developing a semiorbital nuclear weapon system which also poses a threat to our bombers.

4. Continuing ABM development, after having deployed an ABM system which protects to some degree a wide area around Moscow.

Question

What is the threat from Communist China?

Answer

The potential Chinese threat against the U.S. population cannot be ignored; by the mid-seventies, China will be able to launch nuclear missiles. Nor can we ignore the fact that other countries may in the future acquire the capability to attack the United States with nuclear weapons. We face the possibility that any small country capable of acquiring a nuclear capability would be in a position to blackmail us with only a small and primitive force.

Question

What exactly will Safeguard do for our strategic posture?

Answer

The increasing Soviet land- and sea-based missile force may pose a real threat to the credibility of our ability to deter a nuclear war. To guard against this threat, we must act now to

404

protect our future ability to inflict unacceptable damage on any power which might be tempted to launch a first strike against the United States or our allies. To delay would be dangerous to our security.

Safeguard will guard our retaliatory forces by protecting a significant part of our land-based missile force from a missile attack; by protecting our bomber bases against submarine-launched missiles or semiorbital weapons, and by protecting our national military command centers from crippling destruction. In addition, Safeguard will provide almost complete protection against countries, such as China, which may acquire a primitive nuclear capability and against an accidental or unauthorized attack from any source.

Question

How did the President make this decision?

Answer

The President arrived at his decision after a careful examination of the major alternatives facing him; after obtaining the views and recommendations of the Secretary of State, the Secretary of Defense, the Director of Arms Control and Disarmament, and the Joint Chiefs of Staff; after discussing the alternatives at length with the National Security Council; after considering the advice of numerous experts within and outside government; and after intensive personal study.

Question

Does the Safeguard decision signal a basic change in our defense strategy? Does having a missile defense mean that we are more willing to face the prospect of a nuclear war?

Answer

No. Our program is completely defensive in nature.

Our basic defense strategy has been and will continue to be

the deterrence of both general nuclear war and wars that may lead to general war. In modifying our strategic forces to meet the increasing Soviet threat, Safeguard was selected because it is the most effective way to provide protection for our deterrent forces. The Safeguard missiles have absolutely no offensive capability. Nor can the system prevent large-scale loss of life if a nuclear war occurs with the Soviet Union. The system is designed to protect our deterrent.

Also, Safeguard cannot be interpreted by the Soviets as an aggressive move on our part. Therefore, unless the Soviet Union is in fact determined to threaten the United States, Safeguard will not require Soviet escalation of the arms race.

Question

Will this deployment reduce the chances for successful talks with the Soviet Union leading to a strategic arms limitation agreement?

Answer

The Soviet interest in strategic arms talks has not been lessened by the Safeguard decision. Given our determination to protect fully our second-strike capability, Safeguard was the alternative most compatible with our desire to end the era of confrontation and enter an era of negotiations. The Soviets are well aware of and have openly acknowledged the defensive intent of the Safeguard program.

Question

How would Safeguard affect prospects for arms control?

Answer

The Safeguard program is the least provocative way to insure the survival of our retaliatory forces. As an alternative, we could buy more Polaris-type submarines and land-based missiles and bombers, or we could begin construction of new missile silos in hard rock. Aside from providing only marginal improvements in our deterrent, such programs could be misinterpreted by the Soviets as an attempt to threaten their deterrent. Thus, they would stimulate further the costly competition in strategic armaments that we seek to restrain.

If the Soviet force build-up is designed to strengthen further their own deterrent, our Safeguard program is clearly not a threat to them. If, on the other hand, the Soviets have more aggressive purposes, the Safeguard program demonstrates our determination to maintain at all costs a powerful deterrent to nuclear attacks on the United States and its allies. Thus, Safeguard is designed to encourage the Soviet Union to pursue a responsible strategic weapons policy.

The careful phasing of the Safeguard deployment insures maximum flexibility to adjust the program if arms limitation talks or unilateral actions by the Soviet Union or China result in a reduced threat to our deterrent. If the Soviet Union slows down or stops its deployment of the large payload SS-9 missile or if the likelihood that these missiles will be armed with accurate multiple warheads is materially reduced, we can readily limit that part of the Safeguard program which is designed to defend our land-based missiles. Even more favorable reductions in the Soviet offensive and defensive threat could be matched by further restraints in our ABM deployment. However, those parts of the Safeguard program designed for defense against China, small countries with a strategic delivery capability, or accidental or unauthorized attacks from any source, would not be affected by arms control agreements with the Soviet Union, nor do we expect the Soviet Union to forgo deployments designed for similar purposes.

Question

Why don't we just wait and see if the arms talks succeed before going ahead?

Answer

The risk would be too great to our national security. By beginning now, we should have some missile defense by 1973; if we were to shut down production facilities now and decide later to go ahead, the cost in time would not be months, but years—two or three years. Meanwhile, the Soviet system is operational, and the Chinese are likely to have an intercontinental missile within eighteen months. The advantage of the Safeguard system over previous plans is that it is adjustable; it is designed so it can be slowed down or speeded up in the light of diplomatic considerations, changes in the threat, and technical progress. We are not locked into a series of steps that we cannot modify if there is real progress toward arms limitations and the threat to our security is diminished.

Question

How can we be sure that Safeguard is indeed "adjustable"— that it can be changed if there is progress in arms talks?

Answer

In addition to the continuing review within the government, the President has asked the Foreign Intelligence Advisory Board to make an annual review of the nature of the threat we face. This fresh assessment will be made each year before the Safeguard system moves further forward. In other words, we are not frozen into any rigid schedule.

Question

Will the Safeguard system work?

Answer

We have every reason to believe that the Safeguard system will work for the threats against which it is designed. Moreover, because of the measured pace of the deployment, later phases of the program can benefit from technical progress during the early phases.

We already know, from research and development results, that the missiles and radars in the system will work. Though we have not yet fully tested the system's ability to intercept incoming warheads, a predecessor system, Nike-Zeus has demonstrated this capability. Tests will soon be under way at Kwajalein in the Pacific to check out the performance of the fully integrated system against a missile attack. Meanwhile, the AEC will continue its underground warhead test program.

Question

Does Safeguard protect our cities from nuclear attack?

Answer

It will protect us from the kind of attack Red China would be able to launch in the seventies; it would protect us against accidental attacks. But it would not protect the cities from an all-out sophisticated attack, the kind the Soviets are capable of.

Question

Why not protect our cities against a heavy attack, as well as our ability to strike back?

Answer

There is no way of doing it. Even if we built a "thick defense" around our cities at enormous cost, some attacking missiles would get through—enough to inflict extremely high casualties and damage.

Question

Does that mean there is no way of defending our missiles from a heavy attack?

Answer

Not so—even if a significant number of our missiles were destroyed, we would still have more than enough to destroy the enemy. This means that our deterrent would remain "credible" —the enemy would still believe, and rightly so, that he would doom his own country if he attacked us.

Question

Can penetration aids such as chaff, balloons, nuclear explosions, and depressed trajectories defeat Safeguard?

Answer

Since we are constantly working on penetration aids to strengthen our own retaliatory power, we are familiar with the most advanced techniques of missile attack. We make no pretense of 100 percent effectiveness against a heavy, sophisticated attack on cities. But if even 30 percent of our missiles survive, they will pose an unacceptable risk. The Safeguard system will assist this effort.

Question

How many missile sites will there be?

Answer

Twelve are planned, with none but the site to protect our National Command Center near an urban area. This zone defense is designed to cover the continental United States completely; the first two to be put in operation will be at Malmstrom Air Force Base in Montana and Grand Forks Air Force Base in North Dakota.

Question

How long will the Safeguard system last before becoming obsolete?

Answer

We expect Safeguard to be effective well into the 1980s against the threats it is designed to meet.

410

Question

The decision to use Safeguard must be made in a matter of minutes; can we be sure this decision is made by the President and not by a computer?

Answer

There is absolute assurance that these arrangements will completely reflect the authority of the President. In no case could the human factor be removed and a computer only involved.

Question

Is the Safeguard system dangerous? What are its implications for people living near a Safeguard site?

Answer

Because U.S. nuclear weapons are designed with multiple, serial safety devices, the likelihood of an accidental nuclear explosion or radiation escape is essentially nil. In over twenty years of experience, there has never been such an accident. You will recall that four such weapons fell to the ground after an aircraft collision in Spain, and yet there were no nuclear explosions.

Very detailed safeguards exist to prevent an accidental interceptor launch and firing and to insure that any detonation will occur only in defense against incoming targets. The technical features of Safeguard and the firing doctrine preclude detonation until an altitude is reached which provides safety for people and property on the ground. No Spartan or Sprint can detonate at an altitude low enough to cause severe eye damage.

Question

How much will Safeguard cost?

Answer

For next year, Safeguard will cost $800 million to $900 million, or about one-half the projected 1970 cost of the previous

Sentinel system. The Safeguard decision by itself reduced the defense budget by almost a billion dollars.

The complete Safeguard system over a period of six years will require $6 billion to $7 billion in investment costs—that is, for hardware and construction. A total of $3 billion to $4 billion will be spent for research and development. Even if we had decided against Safeguard, we would have wanted to carry on with an extensive ABM research and development program. On this point there is no disagreement.

Question

Does Safeguard represent simply the down payment on a much larger and more costly system?

Answer

No, definitely not. To go to a thick system would require a new decision, a new deployment, new construction. The Safeguard system is designed for a specific purpose and the completed system will achieve that purpose. This system cannot organically grow.

Question

Wouldn't it be less costly and just as effective to defend our missile sites by "hardening" the sites in which they are hidden?

Answer

Missile hardening would be at least as costly. Also, it would probably be more provocative, because the Soviets would observe us digging new silos and might regard it as the beginning of a major offensive build-up. Hardening cannot defend our ICBMs against the increased accuracy of incoming missiles that is possible in the years ahead. It is our judgment that the best immediate defense will be an antimissile "active" defense. If the Soviet threat should become much larger than we now foresee, a combination of these kinds of defenses might give us the best protection.

412

Question

Wouldn't it be better to use these funds to solve the pressing social and economic problems in the United States?

Answer

The President's first responsibility is to insure the survival of the United States and to meet our commitments to assist in the defense of our allies. Considering the threats we now foresee, the Safeguard system is a strategic necessity. We must survive as well as prosper, and it is within our capacity to do both.